What people

A Left for Itself

This book is essential reading for anyone who is interested in the contemporary state of the left.
Professor Matthew Goodwin, author of National Populism: the Revolt Against Liberal Democracy

In the sometimes febrile environment of contemporary left politics, this book is a measured and evaluative contribution. David Swift cuts through the rhetoric of often violent and divisive exchanges to uncover the roots, motivations, diverse character and strengths and weaknesses of the current phenomenon of so-called 'identity politics'. Ranging from recent work by Fukuyama to the journalistic pages of *The Spectator* and *New Statesman* and beyond, the book is an important addition and contribution to this widespread and multi-form debate over the rise, impact and reaction to a newly-emboldened and assertive 'identity left''
Dr Stephen Meredith FRHistS, FHEA. John Antcliffe Archives By-Fellow, Churchill College Cambridge, 2018-19 and Head of Politics, University of Central Lancashire

David Swift astutely diagnoses the pathological narcissism at the heart of what he calls the 'hobbyist left' - which has captured the Labour Party. With its preoccupation with language and virtue-signalling, and scant interest in the concerns and culture of actual working people, today's middle-class elitist left no longer speaks to the voters who once gave their support to the Labour Party.
Professor Eric Kaufmann, author of *Whiteshift: Populism, Immigration and the Future of White Majorities*

David Swift stakes-out a difficulty but really important political space in this book. He is of the left but launches an assault on a generational cohort of left-wing political activists and their preoccupations and prejudices. His argument is provocative and his style uncompromising. But the underpinning research is careful and his conclusions important.

Professor Andrew Hindmoor, author of *What's Left Now?* and Head of Politics, University of Sheffield

A Left for Itself

Left-wing Hobbyists and Performative
Radicalism

A Left for Itself

Left-wing Hobbyists and Performative
Radicalism

David Swift

Winchester, UK
Washington, USA

JOHN HUNT PUBLISHING

First published by Zero Books, 2019
Zero Books is an imprint of John Hunt Publishing Ltd., No. 3 East St., Alresford,
Hampshire SO24 9EE, UK
office@jhpbooks.com
www.johnhuntpublishing.com
www.zero-books.net

For distributor details and how to order please visit the 'Ordering' section on our website.

Text copyright: David Swift 2018

ISBN: 978 1 78904 073 9
978 1 78904 074 6 (ebook)
Library of Congress Control Number: 2018952689

A CIP catalogue record for this book is available from the British Library.

Design: Stuart Davies

UK: Printed and bound by CPI Group (UK) Ltd, Croydon, CR0 4YY
US: Printed and bound by Thomson-Shore, 7300 West Joy Road, Dexter, MI 48130

We operate a distinctive and ethical publishing philosophy in
all areas of our business, from our global network of authors to
production and worldwide distribution.

Contents

Also by David Swift

For Class and Country: the Patriotic Left and the
First World War

Introduction

Rich in the First Place

A million or two of workingmen's votes for a bona fide *workingmen's party is worth infinitely more than a hundred thousand votes for a doctrinally perfect platform.*
Freidrich Engels, 1886.[1]

The difference between the intellectuals and the trade unions is this: You have no responsibility. You can fly off at a tangent as the wind takes you. We, however, must be consistent and we have a great amount of responsibility.
Ernest Bevin to G.D.H. Cole, 1935.[2]

Can't you see that the problem is you? That politics has nothing to do with being right, that politics is about succeeding...You can wear a T-shirt with the hammer and sickle. You can even carry a huge flag and then go back home with your flag, all while the enemy laughs at you. Because the people, the workers, they prefer the enemy to you.
Pablo Iglesias, founded of Podemeos, 2015.

Around the world, right-wing populists are on the rampage. All too often, voters who traditionally supported the Left fuel their success. In the United States, the 2016 Presidential Election witnessed large levels of white working-class support for the billionaire TV personality Donald Trump. In Israel, Benjamin Netanyahu and the Likud Party alienate many of the original Ashkenazi secular elite, and instead owe their support largely to poorer Mizrahi Israelis and recently arrived immigrants from the former Soviet Union. In Russia and Turkey, reactionary, authoritarian demagogues owe their power to the poor and the poorly educated, while relatively prosperous metropolitan liberals are excluded from government. Understanding this phenomenon is central to the politics of our age: why has the recent crisis of capitalism benefitted not the Left, but the nationalist Right?

Back in 1975, in *The Coming of the Postindustrial Society*, the academic Daniel Bell predicted an increasingly radical middle class and an ever more conservative working class.[3] As deindustrialisation proceeded, argued Bell, traditional economic divisions would decrease in relevance, and social and cultural issues would come to the forefront. While the United Kingdom is some way behind the United States in this process, the same phenomenon is now taking place.

According to Ipsos MORI, the 2017 General Election was simultaneously Labour's best performance among the top three ABC1 social groups, and the Conservatives' best score among C2DEs since 1979, with the two parties improving on their 2015 results among these groups by 12 per cent. Labour gained most ground in seats with the largest concentrations of middle-class professionals and the rich. The Tories, by contrast, made their largest gains in the poorest seats of England and Wales; despite presiding over austerity economics, the increase in the Conservative vote on 2015 was largest in seats where average incomes had fallen most over the past 5 years.[4]

Labour lost Walsall North for the first time since 1976 – the Labour majority there in 1997 was 29.9 per cent. The Conservatives won Mansfield for the first time since its creation in 1885 – back in 1997, the Labour majority was 43.4 per cent. The Tories also gained Middlesbrough South and East Cleveland, and Labour lost East Derbyshire for the first time since 1935.

This trend was also reflected in the education levels of different voters. According to YouGov, 55 per cent of people with GCSEs as their highest qualification voted Conservative, and only 33 per cent for Labour. For those with A Levels the split was more even: 45 per cent for the Tories and 40 per cent for Labour. However, for those with undergraduate degrees and above, fully 49 per cent voted Labour, and only 32 per cent for the Tories.[5]

It is a similar story with newspaper readership. As might be expected, 79 per cent of *Daily Telegraph* readers voted Tory, but *The Times* was the only other broadsheet whose readership substantially backed the Conservatives (58 per cent to Labour's 24 per cent). Surprisingly, the readership of the *Financial Times* was evenly split, with 40 per cent voting Tory and 39 per cent Labour. In contrast, all of the tabloids apart from the *Mirror*, from the *Daily Express* (77 per cent) to *The Sun* (59 per cent) had a readership that was overwhelmingly Conservative.[6]

None of this is necessarily bad for the Labour Party. The party won 40 per cent of the vote in 2017, its highest percentage since Tony Blair's early years. If Labour can win a Parliamentary majority, it doesn't necessarily matter where the votes come from. Nor is there anything new about apparently altruistic politics: throughout the history of the British Left, its ranks have always been swelled by allies acting selflessly; the women's movement had male allies, anti-racist groups had white allies, and gay rights groups had straight allies.

Yet the great radical movements of the twentieth century – from the trade unions and the Labour Party, women's rights activists and feminists, to people of colour and gay people – were always dominated by those who needed to change their own lives. Traditionally, people got involved in radical political movements mostly because they had to, to improve their own lives and communities. Now, very often, left-wing activists are there through choice, sometimes to campaign for abstract issues that don't affect them or anyone they know. The effect of this is that the British Left, once a great mass movement of millions of people and reflective of the mood of Britain, has become increasingly dominated by people motivated more by altruism

3

than need.

In the 1986 film *Platoon* – directed by leading Hollywood leftie Oliver Stone – a privileged young white man drops out of college to enlist and fight in Vietnam. His poor white and black comrades ask what a rich college kid like him is doing there, and he explains that he didn't think it was right that only poor kids should have to fight. He expects that his idealism and selflessness will be met with appreciation, but instead they respond with stunned silence and bemusement. After a pause, one of them exclaims: 'Shit. You gotta be rich in the first place to even think like that.' This idealistic young soldier turned out to be a prototype for a new kind of political subject, first identified by former Labour leader Neil Kinnock: the political hobbyist.

This book is not about how the loss of a fabled 'white working class' and a move to 'metropolitan elites' will spell the end for Labour. Nor is it about the apparent 'hypocrisy' of the relatively privileged helping out other people (an argument that is never extended to the many poor and disadvantaged people who vote Tory).

Instead, this book will highlight how recent years have seen the emergence of a type of left-wing politics that is not primarily motivated by affecting real change, and is better understood as less of a political movement and more as a form of identity or enjoyable past time. The focus of this book is not really on a particular kind of people, but more a particular way of thinking about what it means to be left-wing.

At the same time as traditional class alignments are reversing, there is a growing body of scholarship that suggests political partisanship is an important form of identity, irrespective of effect on governance or policy. Shanto Iyengar, Gurav Sood and Yphtach Lelkes claim that in the United States, even 'race and religion are weaker forms of identity than [political] partisanship'. Another study has suggested that political partisans have a relationship with their political party or cause that is remarkably similar to that of supporters of different sports teams.[7] The political scientist Eitan Hersh argues that Americans, and particularly those on the Left, have taken up 'political hobbyism', and being 'left-wing' as much as a pastime and expression of identity than as a movement for genuine social and economic change.

According to Hersh, signing petitions, online or otherwise, is a common signifier of political hobbyism. He notes that 'individuals from richer neighborhoods are more likely than those from poorer neighborhoods to sign petitions in general', and that further, 'their enthusiasm for petitions appears highest when the issues are unrelated to redistribution'. Hersh explains this by arguing that signing online petitions is 'distinctly low-stakes':

> The only formal barrier to entry is an Internet connection, and yet the policy agenda that forms is dominated by particularistic initiatives and post-materialist preferences. As a class of activists, online petitioners seem to be acting as hobbyists. It is unlikely that civic duty, the common good, or self-interest motivates them to collectively prioritize this way online. As with many other forms of online activity, this is a consumption activity.[8]

In the UK, a comprehensive 2013 investigation into political radicalism found that 'education, political interest, and a sense of political efficacy' were the most important determinants of left-wing activism, while measures such as 'social class and housing tenure' had much less of an effect. In the words of lead researcher Anthony Heath:

> This suggests that the underlying mechanism [for determining political radicalism] is not really about economic resources but about psychological ones. Nor is there any sign of

> protest being a weapon of the weak. Individuals with weaker economic or psychological resources, for example less-educated or working-class individuals, show no sign of being more disposed to engage in protests or boycotts...Grievances do not make as much difference as psychological resources to the probability of being active in a voluntary organization, volunteering, or signing of a petition.[9]

So many comrades on the Left today are either from privileged backgrounds or, if they do have impeccable working-class credentials, usually hail from families with a long history of Labour and trade union activism. They might have gone to bog-standard comps, but often one of their parents is a Labour councillor, the other a trade union official; one of their uncles stood for Parliament, or their grandfather fought in the Spanish Civil War.

This is something they can be justly proud of, but it also insulates people from uncomfortable truths. If, instead of hearing complaints about immigrants from your older relatives every Christmas, as is the experience of millions of Britons, you instead heard tales about marches and demonstrations, this gives you a distorted view of reality. Indeed, I believe that hailing from a family of devoted leftists can be just as insulating from the realities of the world as growing up surrounded by wealth and privilege and attending top public schools.

For example, the Twitter handle of *The Guardian* columnist Owen Jones used to boast that he was a 'fourth generation socialist'; he has spoken about his uncle playing for the Independent Labour Party football team, and of going on marches since before he could walk. It's nice for Owen to have this family history, but exactly how many people in the UK have such experiences, or come from such a background? I'd bet that far fewer people could claim such impeccable left-wing credentials than the five million or so who attended fee-paying schools.

For this proud history of activism is unrepresentative not only of the experiences of the British population in general, but also of the working class specifically. Criticising the inflexible, theoretical Marxists of his time, the legendary socialist historian E.P. Thompson claimed that where they:

> are at their most schematic is in the handling of the concept of class. These classes which are marshalled, sent on manoeuvres, and marched up and down whole centuries bear so little relation to the actual people disclosed in the archives – or, for that matter, in the streets around us...minds which thirst for a tidy [theory] very soon become impatient with actual history.[10]

One argument of this book is that a reimagining of the radical history of Britain is central to left-wing hobbyism. This reimagining distorts the realities of the British Left's history to make it more palatable to modern identitarian leftists.

For example, that the British labour movement owed more to Methodism than Marxism is an old cliché with a real basis in fact: In a survey of the reading material of early twentieth-century Labour leaders, very few claimed to read Marx or Engels, and instead the Bible, William Morris's *News from Nowhere* and John Bunyan's *Pilgrim's Progress* were among the most-cited books. A plurality of early labour leaders – and for that matter, Labour foot soldiers in the workshops and constituencies, came to the movement through religious Nonconformity: from Methodism or through the Baptist or Quaker churches.

But not enough thought has been given to the significance of this in a country were most people are not Methodists. The Nonconformist strongholds of South Wales, West Yorkshire and the Durham coalfield provided a disproportionate number of the men and women of the British Left, and these areas coincided with the skilled, craft industries most prone to labourism: mining, textiles, engineering and shipbuilding. These individuals were often influenced by their faith, their work, but also by the dominant political force in these areas, the Liberal Party. Indeed, although the trade unions founded Labour in 1900, the transference of union loyalty from the Liberals to Labour was not straightforward: the Miners' Federation of Great Britain, for example, only formally affiliated in 1908. Thus, the driving concerns for these people were often Liberal shibboleths: free trade, freedom for Ireland and freedom from publicans.

Despite the pronounced importance of liberalism and the humanitarian and abstemious influence of radical Nonconformists, it was the millions of small 'c' conservative trade unionists, much closer to the average British citizen, who were central to the Left's success, on the rare occasions it was achieved. They ensured it was a truly mass movement, rather than a pressure group for well-meaning eccentrics. That so many socially and culturally conservative people joined and supported the Left, and were dominant within it, reflects the desperate circumstances of the time. Until 1945, most working-class people in Britain lived very difficult, precarious lives, beset by hardship and misfortune. It was therefore imperative to organise, to join a trade union, to become involved in politics, to vote Labour. The trade unions themselves, powerful and influential, but also concerned with practical, pragmatic reforms such as improving hours, pay and conditions, ensured this practical socialism was dominant at conference and in policy.

During my lifetime, however, all this has changed. Margaret Thatcher's ideologically driven crusade against British industry, job security and organised labour has fundamentally altered the British economy, while at the same time the wider effects of globalisation have radically changed British society and culture. The unions themselves, with their membership drawing ever more from the public sector, moving from heavy industry to office workers, have increasingly fallen under the sway of the very hobbyists they used to oppose.

In his office on the top floor of the Holborn headquarters of the Unite union, Len McCluskey recalls 'an old joke about Polly Toynbee', that 'she'd do anything to help the poor...as long as the poor don't do anything for themselves'.[11] The former Home Secretary Charles Clarke concurs with this. When I meet him in a busy Cambridge café, I ask whether he thinks there are many individuals with considerable social and cultural capital involved in left-wing politics as a hobby. Clarke believes there are 'a whole chunk of people' who think like that, and argues that 'they are not playing with their lives, they're playing with other people's lives'.[12]

For McCluskey, trade unions have been the one constant throughout the recent history of the British Left; they are 'almost like a rock' upon which British socialism is built.[13] During the heyday of Labour's successful appeal as a popular party of government, annual conferences were dominated by the Labour Right through the influence of conservative union leaders such as Arthur Deakin of the Transport and General Workers' Union, Tom Williamson of the General and Municipal Workers' Union, and Will Lawther of the National Union of Mineworkers. By the 1970s, however, the unions were moving leftwards under the influence of Hugh Scanlon of the Engineers and Jack Jones of the TGWU. Whereas Clement Attlee had been able to use unions to resist pressure from the constituency parties, leaders from Harold Wilson to Neil Kinnock found this much more difficult.[14]

For Charles Clarke, the victory of 1945 was built upon a successful alliance between the trade unions and the 'Hampstead intellectuals'. This was possible as the differences at the time were never that great; while the unions were generally characterised 'more by conservatism than by socialism', up until the 1960s it was difficult to see a chiasmic distinction. Clarke recalls his own father's Fabian roots, but notes that his parents, despite their positions near the apex of the British establishment, held attitudes not dissimilar to broad working-class sentiment on issues such as law and order and immigration.[15]

Today by contrast, the broad coalition that composed the British Left has been distorted. Increasingly, some supposedly radical figures appear less concerned with aiding the structurally disadvantaged groups than with envying them. As early as 1998, the American philosopher Richard Rorty observed that we 'now have, among many American students and teachers, a spectatorial, disgusted, mocking, Left... [it] is not the only Left we have, but it is the most prominent and vocal one'.[16] He noted that the Left preferred to give 'cultural politics preference over real politics', and undermine the idea that democratic institutions could serve social justice. 'When the Right says that socialism has failed', claimed Rorty, 'and that capitalism is the only alternative, the cultural Left has little to say in reply. For it prefers not to talk about money.'[17] Likewise, the historian Thomas Frank argues that increasingly:

> Liberalism *is* a matter of shallow appearances, of fatuous self-righteousness; it is arrogant and condescending, a politics in which the beautiful and the wellborn tell the unwashed and the beaten-down and the funny-looking how they ought to behave, how they should stop being racist or homophobic, how they should be better people. This is not politics. It's an imitation of politics. It *feels* political, yes: it's highly moralistic, it sets up an easy melodrama of good versus bad, it allows you to make all kinds of judgments about people you disagree with, but ultimately it's a diversion...the virtue-quest is an exciting moral crusade that *seems* to be extremely important but at the conclusion of which you discover you've got little to show for it.[18]

Take this piece from the columnist Laurie Penny in 2011, where she writes that, 'many tens of thousands of protesters and police would rather we all went on a nice civilised saunter to Hyde Park to hear some speeches, but many others are getting their armour ready, digging out their face masks, shining up their riot shields for a rumble in London'.[19] In another column, she writes that she 'is about as close as you can get to the trans rights movement without being trans yourself. I've been associated with trans activism for years, and while I don't know what it's like to be harassed, threatened or abandoned for being transsexual, most of my close friends do.'

If this seems absurd and patronising, try substituting 'black' or 'working class' for trans, and it sounds even worse. Penny continues: 'Right now, I'm watching the rest of the world begin to understand the community that has become my home, and it is incredibly exciting – but it's frightening, too, because the backlash is on', sounding unmistakably like a hipster complaining that their favourite band had achieved mainstream success.[20]

Meanwhile the journalist Afua Hirsch writes of how, although she was 'profoundly shocked by the material deprivation' of her husband's childhood, she thinks that, 'when it comes to identity…he was born with the equivalent of a silver spoon' and of how her 'parents…often joked that I would rather have grown up on a council estate. [This] contained a grain of truth'.[21]

The argument here is not necessarily that hobbyist leftists don't put in the hours, whether through petitions, protests, campaigns and so on, but rather that there is an unmistakable growth of a trend on the Left which sees hardship and deprivation as status symbols to be desired, rather than limitations to be fought against. The crucial point is that being 'left-wing' is becoming an important part of your identity. It is something people think they are, rather than something they believe or even do.

We must not treat the Left as a religion. There is nothing sexy about achieving change and making a difference. It is prolonged, frustrating, tedious work. Not only is it not achieved overnight, it usually takes many long years, and is often only apparent in retrospect, from a distance of time. You cannot achieve real change nor make a difference by retweets, likes, memes or demonstrations alone. First, you need to achieve power. Then the change you wish to execute will involve numerous compromises that the zealous deem a betrayal of the original purpose. People – especially the poorest and those who have the least – are sceptical of grandiose schemes and utopian dreams. The poor and the marginalised are less inclined to fight towards a promised land than young, white, postgraduate students; they know from bitter experience the outcome of such promises.

This book is emphatically not a nostalgic wish to return to an imagined past, nor does it claim that the shift on the Left from economics to issues around ethnicity, gender and sexuality has been a mistake. Firstly, because a person's ethnic, gender and sexual identity can be a crucial determiner of their material situation, and secondly because these arguments around redistribution and representation are tedious and have been well-covered elsewhere.

The focus of this book is the rise of an identity whereby people – overwhelmingly white, middle-class, invariably university educated, usually neither Jewish nor Muslim or gender dysmorphic – obsess with issues around race, gender identity and the Middle East. To understand this jealously guarded and fiercely disciplined identity as a political movement is a mistake: this section of the Left doesn't care about the 'man on the Clapham omnibus' so much as the man on the Shoreditch unicycle.

The point of this book is not to claim that this will be politically damaging to the Labour Party, nor even that it is inherently undesirable. But you cannot understand modern British politics – and that of the developed world more broadly – without appreciating that much of the contemporary Left is driven not by a desire for real change, but rather by a desire for an enjoyable pastime, and a search for an identity. It is a Left for itself.

1. Got Any ID?

The Hobbyist Left and Ethnic Identity Politics

As part of the long-overdue refocus on issues such as race and gender in recent decades, there has been a growth in so-called 'identity politics', particularly in terms of ethnic background. The journalist Laurie Penny, writing in the *New Statesmen* after the election of Donald Trump, criticised the notion that 'if we had all been less precious about gay rights and women's rights and black lives and concentrated on the issues that matter to real people. Real people meaning, of course, people who aren't female, or queer, or brown, or from another country.'[1]

While there can be no doubt that your ethnic identity affects your lived experience and life chances, this form of identity politics is both highly essentialist and reductionist, and holds little appeal for actual ethnic minority voters. It is largely the creation of self-appointed 'community leaders' acting in concert with crank academics and guilty white people. It misses the crucial fact that most of the concerns of women, BME people and gays are the same as those of straight white men. Although certain groups have specific structural and cultural disadvantages, and some issues are of special or unique relevance to certain people, on so many topics – jobs, healthcare, pensions, family values, law and order, immigration, national security – there is a great deal of continuity across different religions and ethnicities, notwithstanding the broad spectrum of opinions and beliefs *within* different groups.

The growth of ethno-religious identity politics on the Left is a result of its emasculation, and both morally and politically wrong-headed. As understood by many on the hobbyist Left, it places the poorest and most vulnerable of white men as fundamentally more exalted than the richest and most privileged women or people of colour.

When Hillary Clinton lost to Donald Trump, it was not because of her stance on gay rights and women's rights and black lives, but rather her substitution of these issues in lieu of a genuine alternative. According to the Vox journalist David Roberts, during Clinton's campaign speeches she mentioned jobs nearly 600 times, but racism, women's rights and abortion only a few dozen times each.[2] But it was not infrequency of soundbites on jobs and the economy that cost Clinton, but rather her lack of vision. She offered marginal improvements to the lives of many disparate groups of Americans, but no substantial change. For many college students, people of colour and lesbian, gay, bisexual and transgender (LGBT) people, the main reason to vote for her (apart from the repulsiveness of her opponent), was her cultural appeal to their specific group, rather than any conviction she would noticeably improve their socio-economic position. For many struggling Americans, of all races and genders, she was offering more of the same. When it comes to the hobbyist Left, the problem is not so much its stance on what might be called 'identity' issues, but rather the precedence it gives these issues in terms of both policy positions and the public image of what it means to be on the Left.

The policies and rhetoric of the Left on feminism and LGBT issues are discussed later in the book; this chapter focuses on the Left's difficulties with appealing to different religious and ethnic groups. Specifically, the problem is that many of the policies and positions devised by the hobbyist Left to appeal to black and Asian Britons have the same alienating effect as they do on the white working class. Furthermore, proponents of essentialist identity politics often use the history of the Left to vindicate their positions and policies, but this is an entirely bogus misrepresentation of labour history in Britain.

There is no such thing as an 'ethnic' political position, nor are there homogenous 'Asian' or 'Afro-Caribbean' beliefs. In the United States, Shanto Iyengar and Sean J. Westwood have tested levels of implicit bias among different ethnic groups, and found that Hispanics and Asians both revealed a slight preference for white people instead of African Americans.[3] Similarly, Jasbir Puar describes the traditional animosity between [South Asians] and blacks due to differential treatment, access to jobs and state resources 'as well as the racist hostility perpetuated by South Asians, for whom racism toward blacks and Latinos has long been a rite of passage into model minority citizenship'. Furthermore, studies conducted since 11 September 2001 suggest that high percentages of African Americans support the racial profiling of Arabs and South Asians by the security services.[4] As one American journalist admitted, the 'ethnic and racist prejudices held by our parents' generation are alive and well in our own, even amongst those of us who left our country of origin and settled in the multicultural United States...what we fail to acknowledge is our own internalized racism'.[5]

In the UK, the experience of Afro-Caribbean Britons and South Asian Britons is emphatically not the same. In a 1994 essay, the sociologist Tariq Modood railed against the sentiment that 'falsely equates racial discrimination with colour-discrimination and thereby obscures the cultural antipathy of Asians and therefore the character of the discrimination they suffer'. He continued: 'White working-class youth are incorporating, indeed emulating, young black men and women, while hardening against groups like South Asians'.[6] Nonetheless, some continue to act as though such blocs exist; they create a dichotomy between rich, white, straight men on the one hand and the poor, women, gays and ethnic minorities on the other.

Speaking in the same year as Modood, a leading National and Local Government Officers union activist claimed:

I've got personal reservations about the policy of self-organization. The rise of self-organization has actually diverted energy to the sidelines...I think the principle of self-organization is not a way forward...I want a broad-based union...I don't want a little gay bit, a little black bit, a little disabled bit, and a little women's bit...The more we have of this separatism...where you say you can't come to this meeting because you're white, the more I find it abhorrent.[7]

Former Home Secretary Charles Clarke was on the front line of politics during the New Labour years, and could be seen to bear some responsibility for the turn away from class and towards 'identity'. He recalls a 1999 investigation into performances in London schools: Back then, notes Clarke, researchers used 'a simple binary characterisation of "white/non-white", and so the turn towards categorisation by specific ethno-religious groups is still fairly recent'. For Clarke, while identity is important, 'there are different ways to handle it, but increasingly the state tries to treat people as individuals, undermining social cohesion. All the mass forms are decaying: trade unions, education, and even television'. Clarke notes that even *The Sun* – not a publication one would associate with 'identity politics' – now thinks in terms of groups, no longing treating its readership as a homogenous white British bloc, and actively trying to court a demographically-varied readership.[8]

For the former New Labour minister John Denham 'the glue' has gone: 'The social democratic Left was based on a particular experience, which has gone.' He argues that in contrast to the common experience which had sustained the mainstream Left since the late nineteenth century, identity politics, based on faith, culture or ethnicity, had undermined that cohesion. This chimes with the comments of current Labour MP Jon Cruddas, who argues that the idea of a 'Common Good' has become seen as conservative and judgemental.[9] Denham concurs with this: 'The Left hasn't done culture since Jenkins and not done faith since...probably since the inter-war period.'[10]

Larry Whitty was General Secretary of the Labour Party during the crucial years of 1985 to 1994. When I meet him in the House of Lord's tea room, he is optimistic, at least for the time being: 'Labour still has a pretty good relationship with Muslim communities, but it is not necessarily healthy. Correspondingly, with Sikhs and Hindus it's not so strong. The Tories had never really *targeted* them before [Zac Goldsmith's 2016 campaign for the London Mayoralty]; it's reminiscent of how the SNP targeted Protestant Tories in Scotland.'[11] Whitty feels that the overt concern of a section of the Labour Party with placating political Islam might allow the Tories room to prise more Sikh and Hindu votes away from the Left.

Ultimately, idea of ethnic 'identity politics' as understood by the hobbyist Left is a chimera. Firstly, because there are too many divisions within and between different religio-ethnic groups, and secondly because most Britons, irrespective of ethnicity, tend to support similar values and policies – and their priorities are often very different to those of the hobbyists.

Communalism and the Left

A particular low point in the recent history of the hobbyist Left's embrace of communal politics is the case of Lutfur Rahman. Having ousted the Labour Mayor of Newham, he was subsequently found guilty of electoral fraud and vote-rigging. The judge condemned Rahman, invalidated the result and reinstated the previous mayor, pending a fresh election. The trial took many weeks, cost a great deal of money and saw a huge amount of compelling evidence presented to the court.

None of this was enough for Andrew Murray. Murray, having worked at the *Morning Star*, became the inaugural chair of the Stop the War Coalition after its formation in 2001. He appeased the Muslim Association of Britain, which had originally refused to affiliate to the Stop the War Coalition, by allowing gender-segregated meetings.[12] In 2011, he was appointed chief of staff for the Unite trade union. Francis Beckett, an expert on the hard-Left, has described Murray as 'more extreme than most of the Stalinists I knew. The Stalinists were known as tankies, but Murray's lot were super-tankies.'[13]

Murray took it upon himself to appear at a rally in support of Rahman, proclaiming the latter the victim of a religiously-motivated witch hunt. He also claimed – erroneously and without permission – that Rahman had the backing of Len McCluskey and Unite. Murray is in many ways a paradigmatic example of the hobbyist Left – white and middle class, he cares little about the boring and prosaic concerns of British workers in terms of the economy, jobs, pensions and the health service. Instead, he fixates on foreign policy, Israel/Palestine and chimerical racial divisions. That such a man holds a key position in the country's largest and greatest trade union is emblematic of the rise of the hobbyist Left.

Before Rahman's conviction, the then *Guardian* journalist Seumus Milne had raged over the decision of Communities Secretary Eric Pickles to send special commissioners to take over Tower Hamlets:

> Pickles claimed that Rahman had dispensed grants like a 'medieval monarch', though neither the police nor the PwC report Pickles commissioned found evidence of wrongdoing – and Rahman's progressive record is widely acknowledged. But the undercurrent of accusations of extremism and corruption was clear – as was the message of the politically driven Charities Commission's decision to put 55 Muslim charities on a watchlist for links to 'radicalisation and extremism'.[14]

Of course, if Milne wants to champion the cause of a convicted election fraudster it is his business. But he has subsequently left

The Guardian and is now chief spin doctor and strategist to the Labour Party.

Meanwhile, for Richard Seymour and Ashok Kumar the Rahman verdict 'was to be expected. There had been a concerted effort by the media and political establishment to smear Rahman...These claims can be seen as part of a wider political attack, intended not just to delegitimise the outcome of this vote, but to stigmatise Rahman's supporters.' Furthermore, 'in recent days, several media outlets have alleged that Rahman's former adviser Kazim Zaidi is threatening street violence unless the outcome of the election is accepted. In fact, Zaidi's actual statement makes no mention of violence, but of a political battle between a grassroots old Labour politics and a machine-driven New Labour spilling "onto the streets"' – reassurance indeed. They concluded: 'The story of Lutfur Rahman is a democratic success story. The fact that it seems dodgy to the political and media classes is indicative of how long they've been insulated from anything resembling real democracy.'[15]

The patronising and Neo-Orientalist reverence in which white middle-class hobbyists hold certain ethnic minorities is not limited to the Muslim community. *The Guardian* journalist Owen Jones strenuously argues that there is no religio-ethnic element to violence and sexual assaults against women. He receives a great deal of pushback on this from people from South Asian communities. For example, one Indian woman on Twitter denounced his comments as a 'Western analysis of Indian women's issues [which is] unhelpful and outdated. Sexism is entrenched in Indian culture.' For Jones, the idea that sexism – or any vice – is more pronounced in a non-Western culture than in the West is entirely unacceptable. He responded claiming he wanted to make 'the undeniable point that VAW [violence against women] is a global issue'. To which the blogger Sunny Hundal insisted that, 'No, it's not THAT simple, especially if you don't understand the situation for Indian women, as [a female

Indian Twitter user] also pointed out.' Jones received multiple comments from various men and women of Indian nationality or heritage, insisting that South Asia had a particular problem with rape and VAW, but he was unrepentant; because these repugnant crimes are universal, to say they are a particular problem in a particular community is racist and irrelevant.

A month later, another privileged white woman, the American journalist Sarah Jones, tweeted that 'it is supremely idiotic to believe the west is some shining beacon of free speech, women's rights, and religious tolerance'. At which point fellow journalist Sohrab Ahmari, who came to the United States as a refugee, sadly replied: 'Only people blessed to have been born in Western societies say things like this – and really man it.'

'Community Leaders'
According to the sociologist Claire Alexander, identity politics has 'encouraged the creation of "closed-down community identities" – and shifted power and money from an openly political, progressive anti-racist politics to older, conservative ethnic politicians – thus the activist gives way to the community leader'.[16] Similarly, Ambalavaner Sivanandan, the late director of the Institute of Race Relations, concluded that:

> The only beneficiaries of the urban unrest [of the 1980s are] the black petit-bourgeoisie, who in a number of social spaces (media, police consultancy, the Labour Party and so on) were able to appropriate the politics of blackness, create self-organized structures to further their own specific class interests, and in the process, wrench apart a more authentic political blackness based on the living, organic connections that had been forged in the course of the struggles of the 1960s and 1970s involving 'ordinary black people'.[17]

Meanwhile Sivanandan claims that 'there is no such thing as

a black-qua-black movement any more. There are middle-class blacks fighting for a place in the (white) middle-class sun and there are the workless and working-class blacks fighting for survival and basic freedoms.'[18] For Sivanandan, so-called community leaders 'do not come out of the struggles of ordinary black people in the inner-cities – and they do not relate to them – but they have attached themselves to black struggles, like limpets, the more readily to gain office'. While he was speaking specifically about people of colour, the same could easily be said of many white people in politics, think tanks, academia and journalism.

In addition to the problems with 'community leaders' based on ethnic/racial identity politics, Meena Patel and Hannana Sidiqui of the Southall Black Sisters have criticised the same process with religion, in that it leads to a 'shrinking of secular spaces' for many women to autonomously struggle for their human rights: 'The rise in power of unelected and unaccountable Muslim (male) community leaders means that those who are able to "shout the loudest" establish a platform and the authority to impose conservative patriarchal religious interpretations which traditionally discriminate against women.'[19]

Similarly, Amina Lone, a Labour councillor in Manchester, has criticised the Labour Party for indulging ethnic separatism and holding meetings where men and women were segregated. Lone claims that Labour has a particular problem with black and minority ethnic women: 'So many black and minority ethnic women in the Labour Party are terrified. The silencing is so acute, the fear is so acute, I'm the only one that's speaking publicly and I've been warned a lot this year.' In nearby Oldham, another councillor, Arooj Shah, claimed she had endured years of harassment from a 'minority of venomous Asian men' after her election in 2012.[20]

As Afua Hirsch writes in *Brit(ish)*, the political multiculturalism of New Labour 'regarded ethnic identities as cartoonish cultural traits...[the] mainly white political class thought ethnic minority people could be lumped into distinct "communities", represented by self-appointed community leaders who could now tap into rich pots of state funding, and follow their own distinct identity-orientated paths to success.' For Hirsch, 'the way multiculturalist policies were implemented amounted to little more than corrupt patronage, through self-styled "community leaders" who extracted funding and favours in return for delivering their community's votes en masse.'[21]

The Positions and Politics of BME Britons

Aside from the erroneous focus on 'community leaders', many of the apparent structural and essential cultural differences between different religio-ethnic groups in Britain – fundamental to the hobbyist worldview – simply do not exist. While certain groups are more likely to suffer from poverty and deprivation, the picture of ethnic minority disadvantage is infinitely complicated. According to the 2001 census, 11 per cent of white people were in professional occupations, but for Indian and Chinese Britons this is 18 per cent and 19 per cent respectively. Indian, African Asian, Chinese and African Britons are all more likely than white Britons to have higher-level qualifications, while British Pakistanis are about as likely as white Britons to have degrees, and Afro-Caribbean people are slightly more likely. Tariq Modood estimates that British Indian children are 2.5 times more likely than whites to be in fee-paying schools and the British Chinese children five times more likely. Even though Pakistanis and Bangladeshis do not have the same representation in fee-paying schools – and despite four out of five of their households being in poverty – these groups still produce a larger population of university entrants than the white population.[22]

The most salient divide in British politics today is not ethnicity, nor even class, but rather education and cultural capital. Hobbyist leftists within the Labour Party, academia and journalism who push radical positions on, say, the Iraq war, security and civil liberties – supposedly to attract BME voters – are themselves contributing to the alienation from Labour of a broad swathe of people of different classes and ethnicities. For many hobbyists, Labour's recent struggles can be attributed to issues such as Iraq, tuition fees, Ed Miliband's immigration mug and attempts to introduce identity cards and 90-day detention. Yet the YouGov pollster Laurence Janta-Lipinski found that none of these factors ranked inside the top five reasons for disapproval of Labour. Instead, people disapproved of Jeremy Corbyn's leadership, economic profligacy in office, too much borrowing, too much immigration and weaknesses on defence and security.[23]

This should not surprise us: after all, if Iraq and other authoritarian measures have resulted in the estrangement of young people, ethnic minorities and the liberal-minded from Labour, why are these groups the most pronounced and reliable supporters of the party today? Research by Nick Pecorelli has found that while support from Settlers (traditional Labour voters with conservative values) has tanked over the past 20 years, support from Pioneers (liberals and metropolitan types) has rocketed.

There is a majoritarian consensus in the UK on many of these issues that you and I might disagree with, but serious political parties cannot afford to ignore. What distinguishes hobbyists, however, is not merely their adherence to unpopular positions, but their insistence that most people are with them – or at least should be – and that their positions protect vulnerable groups. They are right to insist that there is no dichotomy between class-based politics and politics which takes into account the specific experiences and needs of different people. However, the politics that would result from such an approach might not be to their liking.

Most notably, polls have consistently found that there is

a great deal of support for restricting immigration among Commonwealth and other pre-1990 immigrants. Furthermore, according to research conducted by a team led by Anthony Heath, Professor of Sociology at Oxford University, ethnic minorities are generally less supportive of government spending than white Britons. South Asians are more hostile to asylum seekers than the white British, and British Indians are more supportive of the war in Afghanistan than white Britons.

When asked about trust in Parliament, politicians and the police, Heath and his fellow researchers find that: 'Strikingly, on all but one of these indicators of satisfaction and trust, the overall minority level of confidence in British democracy and institutions is either significantly higher than, or no different from, the white British average.' Likewise, Professor Shamit Saggar of the University of Essex concludes that in terms of issues such as criminal sentencing 'there is virtually no potential for constructing an agenda of common interest among ethnic minorities' and that:

Whites, in short have a lot in common with their black and Asian peers. To attempt to build a discrete ethnic minority agenda on this basis would be impossible. That said, there continue to be calls in favour of selective use of this principle in public policy that at least imply a strength of support from among black and Asian potential beneficiaries. Our evidence indicates that there is really very little basis for such a position.[24]

Heath and his colleagues also note that 'class and educational differences' are highly significant: 'The largest cleavages are apparent between graduates and people with low qualifications on the issues of detention without trial and asylum-seekers.' That is to say, the people with the most radical views on these issues are not those who actually suffer, but rather the better-off and better educated. These are the sort of people who dominate the Labour membership: according to Tim Bale's analysis of the Labour membership, as of May 2016 fully 78 per cent were in the ABC1 social categories, 33 per cent were from London and the South, and merely 25 per cent were trade unionists.

In terms of the people most likely to get involved in protests, boycotts or other political activity, Heath's team found that 'Education, political interest, and a sense of political efficacy are pretty consistently important', while 'social class and housing...have much patchier effects'. They concluded that 'the underlying mechanism is not really about economic resources but about psychological ones...protest [is not] a weapon of the weak. Individuals with weaker economic or psychological resources...less-educated or working-class individuals, show no sign of being more disposed to engage in protests or boycotts.' This means that those groups most structurally disadvantaged do not themselves form the front edge of radicalism in the UK, but rather those with the most cultural capital. Those most likely to provide the foot soldiers of movements against austerity, Stop the War and Blacks Lives Matter UK (witness the excruciating episode of the nine white protestors at City Airport in September 2016), are not usually the people on the sharp end of austerity, war or police violence.

Religion and the Left

Religion is a notable issue for dividing the Left – not just the hobbyists, but a broad spectrum of the Left – from various ethnic minorities. This is particularly pronounced when it comes to South Asian and Middle Eastern Britons. Today, over one-third of Brits say they have no religion; yet nearly all South Asian Britons claim to have a religion, and 90 per cent say their religion is important to them (compared with 13 per cent of whites). According to Modood: 'More than a third of Indian and African Asian, and two-thirds of Pakistani and Bangladeshi 16 to 34-year-olds, [say] that religion is very important to how they live their lives, compared to 5% of whites', and just under 20 per cent of Afro-Caribbean people.[25]

This has led for a few on the Left to argue for a renewal of religious sentiment as a means of ensuring greater social cohesion in the UK. The Reverend Giles Fraser appreciates the difference between spirituality – individual, internal, ephemeral – and religion: communal, performative, tradition. He feels that religion is by no means a spent force:

In 1900, the year that Nietzsche died, there were 8 million Christians in Africa. Now there are 335 million...For both Christianity and Islam, the 20th century was numerically the most successful century since Christ was crucified and Muhammad gave his farewell sermon on Mount Arafat. By 2010, there were 2.2 billion Christians in the world and 1.6 billion Muslims, 31% and 23% of the world population respectively. The secularisation hypothesis is a European myth, a piece of myopic parochialism that shows how narrow our worldview continues to be...This is not exactly because atheism is having some hipsterish Hitchens-esque revival, but more because we in the west are less and less a society of joiners. And religion begins not with the metaphysics but with the taking part.

(Indeed, I would imagine that for many young Britons it is easier to imagine a virgin birth and resurrection from the dead than singing along in a Church.)[26]

Meanwhile, for Mehdi Hasan: 'Secular commentators dismiss religion as a malign force in the world. But from Burma's Aung San Suu Kyi to the Arab spring, faith is inspiring the new peaceful protest.' But here he is being too optimistic. We now know how the Arab Spring turned out – and it did little to undermine ideas of religion as a malign force. At the same time, Aung San Suu

Kyi's regime continues to allow the ethnic cleansing of Rohingya Muslims. Having argued that the Arab Spring should not be seen as a secular uprising, Hasan argues that, 'Credit should be given where credit is due. Arab Muslims have been at the forefront of the non-violent protests against the region's tyrants and autocrats - and not just in Syria.'

Even more dubiously, he approvingly quotes the 'ultra-Orthodox Jews from the group Neturei Karta' who joined mass rallies in the West Bank in support of Palestinian statehood, although anyone with the most rudimentary knowledge of Judaism or Israel knows that Neturei Karta are a mad sect of fanatics who couldn't care less about Muslim Palestinians. Hasan ultimately enters an alternate universe when he argues that 'to try to decouple the rise of non-violence in recent decades from religion and religious believers is a hopeless task' – this at a time when the perception of religious violence has never been more emphatic.

To support this thesis he claims that 'the two undisputed icons of non-violent resistance and civil disobedience in the 20th century were both men of faith: Mahatma Gandhi, a devout Hindu, and Martin Luther King, a Christian pastor', despite the fact that Gandhi was murdered by a fervent Hindu nationalist and James Earl Ray was raised in a devoutly Catholic household, which did not stem his fervent racism, and may even have incubated it.[27]

Hasan is on firmer ground when he discusses the motivations for religious terrorism: 'moral outrage, disaffection, peer pressure, the search for a new identity, for a sense of belonging and purpose'. Referring to expert testimony provided to the US Senate in March 2011, he notes that 'what inspires the most lethal terrorists in the world today is not so much the Quran or religious teachings as a thrilling cause and call to action that promises glory and esteem in the eyes of friends, and through friends, eternal respect and remembrance in the wider world'.

For Hasan wannabe jihadists are 'bored, underemployed, overqualified and underwhelmed' young men for whom 'jihad is an egalitarian, equal-opportunity employer...thrilling, glorious and cool':

> Or, as Chris Morris, the writer and director of the 2010 black comedy Four Lions – which satirised the ignorance, incompetence and sheer banality of British Muslim jihadists – once put it: "Terrorism is about ideology, but it's also about berks."...Berks, not martyrs. "Pathetic figures", to quote the former MI6 chief Richard Dearlove, not holy warriors.

But surely what can be said of jihadists can be said of the hobbyist Left? Berks, not socialists. People in need of an identity.[28]

Writing in *The Guardian*, Giles Fraser notes that: 'The most important thing is what you do not who you are "inside". It's a big part of the reason why I prefer the unfashionable idea of religion, with all its practices and public liturgies, to that nebulous language of spirituality that prioritises the inner life and the idea of feeling.'[29] Where the hobbyists accept 'religion' they prefer to see it as a set of lifestyle choices that emphasises their individuality rather than a metaphysical belief system. This won't do. The vast majority of black and Asian Britons are religious, rather than spiritual. If the Left is to come to terms with religion, it must be as 'religion', rather than 'spirituality'.

Religion and the History of the British Left

The sociologist Les Back argues that historically, loyalty to the Labour Party has drawn upon the strengths of different community networks, and particularly those that resisted pressures towards assimilation.[30] These groups could be Pakistani Muslims in Yorkshire in the 1960s and 1970s; Eastern European Jewish immigrants in London in the inter-war period; or the Irish Catholic diaspora across the UK. Very often, where Labour has been successful, it has built on separate religious-ethnic blocs, such as with Jewish and Catholic East Enders in the 1930s.[31] Different variants of Protestant Christianity have also been essential to the Labour Party; in many ways it could be argued that Jesus was the most important figure to the early labour movement, far more so than Marx or Engels.[32] An examination of the reading lists of leading left-wing politicians at the turn of the twentieth century found the Bible and the ubiquitous *Pilgrim's Progress* featured prominently, with tracts relating to socio-economic theory far less so. From the coalfields of South Wales and County Durham to the textile mills of East Lancashire and the West Riding, religious Nonconformity provided a powerful channel towards radical politics, and in many areas, the chapel was as important an incubator for organisation as the trade union lodge.

Writing in *The Guardian*, the journalist Zoe Williams notes:

> People called Anglicans the 'Tory party at prayer' in the 80s, but I thought that was a mistake. It never struck me as Conservative, so much as the constituency of unthinking respectability. So if you wanted to be an actual Christian, you would choose a demonstrable faith – Catholicism, or Methodism, or Baptism – but if you wanted merely to self-identify as a reasonable, pro-social person, with a moral code, an empathetic nature, a sense of decency…the Church of England said it all.[33]

This demonstrates a fundamental misunderstanding of religious differences. Both Anglicanism and Catholicism are 'demonstrable faiths', concerned with ritual and actions and hierarchy. In areas such as Liverpool – initially sceptical of Labour but now solidly left-wing – Catholicism can be seen as more of a form of cultural identity than deeply-held beliefs. (Len McCluskey, General Secretary of the Unite union, remembers that while his parents never went to mass, 'they still considered themselves Catholics. And made sure I went.')[34]

In contrast, Methodists and Baptists believe in *sola fide* – salvation through faith alone.

Its dependence on areas featuring high levels of Nonconformity meant that the pre-First World War Labour Party suffered in areas with high levels of Catholicism, Anglicanism, or both. Liverpool was a case in point. While overwhelmingly working class and featuring some of the most pronounced overcrowding, poverty and deprivation of Edwardian England, Liverpool was a resolutely Tory town. One reason for this was the casualised nature of dock work, a dominant employer in the city, which did not lend itself to robust trade union organisation. Another was the sectarian divisions between the city's Anglican and Catholic communities, although this can be overplayed by some commentators, looking to find a reason why working-class people should not have been on the Left.[35]

In his analysis of Liverpool Labour, the historian Sam Davies notes that, pre-First World War, much of the Catholic population voted for the Irish Nationalists, while Labour was strongest in Protestant wards. After the war, however, as Ireland gained independence and the Irish issue fell into abeyance, 'the political allegiance of the Catholic dockside wards changed significantly'.[36] This resulted in the election of Liverpool's first ever Labour MP at a by-election for the Edge Hill constituency in 1923. Jack Hayes, the victorious candidate, was a former Irish Nationalist and Metropolitan policeman, who had played a role in organising police strikes in London and Liverpool after the war. This multifaceted identity of Hayes – policeman, Irish Nationalist, Labour MP – was no coincidence, and this hybridity was a template for many Labour candidates elsewhere in the country.[37]

Across the UK, the Irish Catholic diaspora was one of the most consistently pro-Labour elements within the working class throughout the inter-war period.[38] Yet at the same time there was a tension between religion and politics that is instructive for the current travails of the Labour Party. As argued by the historian Steven Fielding, there was a mutual distrust between Irish Catholics and their Protestant or atheistic Labour colleagues; in Liverpool they did not even sit next to each other at meetings. The usual source of friction was the issue of denominational schooling and family planning. As early as 1906, Catholic trade unionists in Salford had formed a Catholic Federation due to their objection to TUC and Labour moves to support secular education, while the docker and MP James Sexton strenuously objected to talk of contraception at the TUC.[39] The Labour Left, particularly the Independent Labour Party, was hostile to the Catholic Church, whose priests preached fiercely anti-socialist sermons; for their part, Catholics saw this hostility as an attack on their cultural identity.

While Catholic pressure within the labour movement had some effect as it contributed to the defeat of secularism as official party policy, many Catholics were alienated by the 1918 constitution which seemed to confirm the socialist, anti-clerical nature of the party. According to Fielding, this was especially important as 'Labour was vulnerable' on these issues 'because it had been on the level of culture, rather than explicit ideology, that the party had made its most powerful appeal to Irish Catholic loyalties'.[40]

Labour would discover in the inter-war years that, as far as Irish Catholics were concerned, when ethnicity was employed against class it was the latter which buckled. 'Thus, despite their support for Labour, it is likely that proportionately fewer working-class Catholics became socialists in its strict ideological form than did non-Catholics.'[41] Indeed there is anecdotal evidence from the inter-war period that most of Liverpool's fascists were of Irish extraction. Nonetheless by the 1960s both working- and middle-class Catholics were more likely to vote

Labour than their non-Catholic counterparts. 'This despite the anti-socialism of many priests and their opposition to the Wilson government's permissive reforms.'[42] This capturing of Catholic loyalty, despite travails and many obstacles, can perhaps act as inspiration for Labour's dealing with different communal blocs in the UK today.

Ethnic Minority Conservatism

In addition to the problems with communalism and community leaders, a further issue with ethnic identity politics as understood by performative radicals is the awkward fact that many black and Asian Britons are unashamedly Conservative. Not just small-c conservatives on some cultural issues, but fully-fledged economic neoliberals. None of this is news: the Anglo-Asian Conservative Society – of which Margaret Thatcher was Honorary President – and the Anglo-West Indian Conservative Society, were both established back in 1976.[43] Today, while Labour still enjoys support from the majority of ethnic minorities, much of this can be attributed to perceptions of Tory hostility. If the Tories are able to change their image on issues connected to race and religion, then a Labour Party that practises the identity politics of left-wing hobbyists might find itself losing support from valuable constituencies.

Afua Hirsch describes how when her future husband – a black British man from a working-class background in Tottenham – first met her Oxford friends, he was shocked that they were 'so tentative...so unsure of yourselves'. He assured her that 'if man like me had the opportunities you all had, there would be no stopping me. We'd be up in this country making some serious *money*.' Hirsch notes that where she thinks 'in terms of identity and belonging', 'he thinks in terms of generating wealth and opportunity'. A lot of black people, with their driven, fiercely individual work ethic, have 'right-wing' responses to their own 'left-wing' structural analysis. All about individual struggles.

As Hirsch acknowledges, the Tories speak most to the 'pull-yourself-up-by-the-boot-straps, socially conservative and Republican values that have such resonance in West Africa'. It is a wonder that more black people don't vote Conservative, and I suspect that it is only the inference of racism from the Tories that keeps black support for them so low. If the Tories are able to deal with this, then the coming decades might see increasing numbers of black Britons voting Tory; this might make hobbyist heads explode, given how 'black' and 'Tory' are at the opposite end of the binary they use to make sense of the world.[44]

The identity Left's patronising valorisation of blackness often disintegrates when confronted with a black Tory. Afua Hirsch describes the experiences of her friend 'Femi', who stood as a Tory candidate in a Labour seat. On the doorstep, Tory voters were often surprised to see a black person standing for the Conservatives, but were friendly nonetheless. In contrast, some Labour supporters were furious. According to Femi, their attitude was: 'After everything we've done for you people! This is how you repay us?...It was as if, because I am an immigrant, they own me...I have never experienced that kind of racism from Conservatives.'[45]

The hobbyist Left should probably get used to the sight of black Conservatives canvassing, for both here and in the United States, there is a deep well of black neoliberalism waiting to be tapped. Back in the summer of 2007, the comedian Bill Cosby – back then still seen as 'America's Dad', albeit an increasingly cranky and erratic one, and not an alleged sexual predator – caused some outrage when he gave a speech in Detroit blaming black American men for some of the problems facing African Americans. Nonetheless, as Ta-Nehisi Coates writes:

> Cosby's rhetoric played well in black barbershops, churches, and backyard barbecues, where a unique brand of conservatism still runs strong. Outsiders may have heard

haranguing in Cosby's language and tone. But much of black America heard instead the possibility of changing their communities without having to wait on the consciences and attention spans of policy makers who might not have their interests at heart. Shortly after Cosby took his Pound Cake message on the road, I wrote an article denouncing him as an elitist. When my father, a former Black Panther, read it, he upbraided me for attacking what he saw as a message of black empowerment. Cosby's argument has resonated with the black mainstream for just that reason...They've seen the utter failures of school busing and housing desegregation, as well as the horrors of Katrina. The result is a broad distrust of government as the primary tool for black progress.[46]

This distrust of the government is often combined with a belief in the market, however unwarranted. The American academic Jerry Phillips argues that one of the tragedies of the drug trade for poor black people is that while people are more vulnerable to drugs because of failures of capitalism, this has not led to many people from those neighbourhoods questioning capitalism, but has instead shored up competitive capitalist values.[47]

Paul Gilroy observes in his seminal *Aint no Black in the Union Jack* how: 'Attempts to constitute the poor or the working class as a class across racial lines have been disrupted. This problem will have to be acknowledged directly if socialists are to move beyond puzzling over why black Britons (who as a disproportionately underprivileged group, ought to be their stalwart supporters) remain suspicious and distant from the political institutions of the working-class movement.'[48] Similarly, the sociologist Gargi Bhattacharrya makes the interesting point that 'plenty of those raised in black politics or anti-racist campaigning believe...that we...can do things better than the (racist state)'. Bhattacharrya claims that 'dark-skinned folk of varying hues have embraced the promise of neoliberal subjecthood with enthusiasm' and that 'if anything, there is more vocal enthusiasm for some kinds of markets among black and minority populations' than among whites: 'the compromise of Keynesian-enabled economic and social policy, despite the many gains for ordinary people, did not deliver in an equitable fashion'.[49]

One of the leading black businesswomen in Britain tells me during a phone call that there is a huge contingent of middle-class blacks who vote Conservative; 'people vote with their money'. She lauds the Democratic Party in the US for recognising the shifting socio-economic position of ethnic minorities and acting accordingly: 'The Democrats were good at moving to centre and addressing higher income people of colour, they were able to move with their immigrants, and became more centrist.'[50]

Furthermore, she is acutely aware of divisions within and between different ethnic groups in the UK, and sceptical of universalising attempts to group people together. Discussing the possibility of merging the Asian and Black business awards, she notes that, 'Asians have the wealth; 80 per cent of them are entrepreneurs or business owners...Asians want nothing to do with black people'. She also believes colourism specifically is a major reason for racism and racial inequality around the world, as people with darker skin tones are generally disadvantaged and discriminated against, even within particular ethnic groups. At the same time, we 'have to be careful not to measure our experiences and say this one is worse' and we should not focus on 'who has done better from a terrible system' but rather concentrate on criticising the system itself. Nonetheless she is pessimistic about the abilities of traditional political parties, including Labour, to consistently win black votes going forward, especially when it comes to young people. '[I] don't think political labels apply anymore...[at least they] don't apply to blacks...Labour hasn't evolved' and so people are 'forced to make a stark choice' between the socialism of Corbyn's Labour and the resurgent nationalism of May's Conservatives.

Another prominent black business leader, Gary Elden, has vistas of St Paul's and the Cheesegrater from his City office, but he recalls his childhood in south London, with National Front marches and racist graffiti, notwithstanding friendship across ethnic lines among the kids of his neighbourhood. He recalls that when he was growing up in south London, all of his white friends found jobs through their parents, usually in the trade their family had worked in for years. His black friends, however, often lacked these family connections, and this contributed to an entrepreneurial spirit. As Elden says, 'why would you want to work for someone else?'

He grew up in a *Daily Mirror* household; his dad didn't buy *The Sun* as he didn't like the politics. He remembers Harriet Harman knocking on his door but 'never saw a Tory'. He liked some of Thatcher's ideas, such as the right for council tenants to buy their homes, but was wary of some aspects of her politics. His own kids attend private school in south London and 'live in a bubble..don't understand colour'. In terms of his own politics, he insists that 'Tony Blair was perfect'. Speaking of the Labour leadership, he reckons Corbyn has 'romantic notions' that ultimately 'don't work' although he does admire his values.

For Elden, older West Indian immigrants saw the Royal Family and cartoonish British stereotypes ('like Jacob Rees Mogg and Boris Johnson today') 'as people better than them', people you could trust. Elden himself puts this down largely to the media, but argues that 'young black kids incorporated [this] into their culture and society. Acted like them, dressed like them [but] got separate results.' Ultimately, he believes there's 'no point being at the top if you don't pull other people'.[51]

The American historian Thomas Franks argues that it shouldn't be surprising that attempts to foster identity politics boost neoliberalism, as 'encouraging demographic self-recognition and self-expression through products is...the bread and butter not of leftist ideology but of consumerism'.[52] In the words of Paul Gilroy:

> Many of the younger people in black cultural production haven't had any exposure to radical political movements at all. Their political essentialism often fits neatly with their entrepreneurial aspirations. They are sceptical of the left and may also find the twists and turns of organized sexual politics hard to follow when its insights look to them like good sense. Among those who oppose essentialism, post-modernism has licensed a kind of playfulness that can trivialize the political stakes and minimize the difficulties of actually changing anything institutional.[53]

The African American intellectual William Julius Wilson has argued that there is a notable difference in the experience of the black middle class which encounters prejudice in its competition with whites for a few professional opportunities, and a permanent, workless 'underclass' for whom racism past or present is secondary to the institutionalised effects of multiple economic disadvantage.[54] Nor is this a recent development. Lorraine Hansberry, the playwright and author of *Young, Gifted and Black*, recalls that she was 'the only child in my class who did not come from the Rooseveltian atmosphere of the homes of the Thirties. [Her] father ran for Congress as a Republican [and] believed in American private enterprise.'[55] As early as 1968, Black Panthers founder Huey Newton criticised the Nation of Islam's cultural nationalism as it focused on 'returning to this old African culture and thereby regaining their identity and freedom', while ignoring the political and economic contradictions within the black community.[56]

Today, Keeanga-Yamahtta Taylor argues: 'The most significant transformation in all of Black life over the last fifty years has been the emergence of a Black elite, bolstered by the Black political class, that has been responsible for administering cuts and managing meager budgets on the backs of Black constituents.' Speaking of the response to the killing of Freddie Gray by the Baltimore police force, Taylor writes: 'When a Black mayor, governing a largely Black city, aids in the mobilization of a military unit led by a Black woman to suppress a Black rebellion, we are in a new period of the Black freedom struggle.' As Asad Haider writes, 'the racial integration of the ruling class and political elites has irrevocably changed the field of political action.'[57]

So many on the identity Left assume an easy polarity between white, rich men on the one hand and a rainbow coalition of women, gays and ethnic minorities on the other. However, this takes no account of the variety of political opinions within different groups in the UK. They are in for one hell of a shock when the BME electorate expands and remains steadily indifferent to the claims of the hobbyists. If the Left wants to articulate an ideology and set of policies that appeals to different ethnic groups in the UK, it would do well to eschew divisive fringe issues and concentrate on commonly-held concerns: jobs, pensions, and healthcare; family, education and community.

'The Full Dolezal'

As is readily apparent to anyone who attends one of their meetings, peruses their activity on Twitter, or reviews data pertaining to the current make-up of Labour Party membership, the hobbyist Left is overwhelmingly white, middle-class and well-educated. For many hobbyists, it could be that identity politics functions as a displacement activity that allows them to obviate their own whiteness.

In May 2017, the pop singer Lily Allen tweeted that 'Islamists don't hate women more or less than anyone else. Fear of women is inherent everywhere.' When challenged as to whether she really believed that, she replied 'I know it.' When someone like Allen does this, they get a vicarious thrill from the transgressive, taboo aspect of what they are saying. There is also an element of an ignorant person, who has recently read some postcolonial literature, attempting to broadcast their new-found knowledge. This thrill through transgression can also be seen with Lara Witt. Witt, of Indian and African heritage, wrote on Twitter in March 2017 that 'White people are evil. Whiteness is evil.' Whatever the serious point about the history of white racism, the heavy legacy of that racism in the modern world, and the irrational belief in 'whiteness' itself being a form of racism, it is hard to believe that was Witt's intention. Instead, she did it for the transgressive thrill, and as a way to confront her own obscure identity.

Meanwhile, *New York Times* columnist Johanna Barr wrote her inaugural piece for the paper about how white men talk too much. This prompted the British Nigerian Damian Counsell to warn that 'in the unlikely event Johanna ever finds herself in a room full of black women, it is going to blow her tiny mind'. This neatly encapsulates the motives and problems behind identity politics as practised by the white hobbyist Left. Barr wanted to make a point about white male privilege, in order to make a small contribution to assuaging her own whiteness, but the very act of her doing so reveals her ignorance of black people, and her patronising desire to be seen as 'less white'.

Asad Haider recounts a shambolic debate during an occupation of the University of California a few years ago, where the protestors wrangled for hours over whether or not to stress that university reforms hit students of colour hardest. Haider was against this – after all, he reasoned, it's not as though racial equitable university privatisation would be acceptable – but his biggest complaint about the whole process was that 'a debate that should probably have taken place in a semiotics seminar took up hours at meetings'.[58] This is a prominent feature of ethnic identity politics as understood and practised by the hobbyist Left in the UK. It is usually about middle-class, well-educated white people vocally positioning themselves on the side of the good, and using buzzwords to demarcate their right-on identity. When white British people use terms such as 'global south', 'intersectionality' (as Haider says 'a term originating in legal studies which now has an intellectual function comparable to "abracadabra" or "dialectics"') or even 'people of colour' (a US-specific term which I have yet to hear a black or Asian Briton use) they are doing it to signal their erudition and membership of the community of the good, despite their white skin.[59]

Yet this recourse to self-righteousness reflects the complete lack of influence of these people over the world around them. As Haider writes, 'with the possibility of integrating social equality...destroyed by both political repression and industrial decline, politics is reduced to the anxious performance of authenticity'.[60] This is not necessarily new. In the 1970s, the Weather Underground attacked 'their own privilege by adopting a revolutionary lifestyle. What this amounted to was the self-flagellation...of white radicals, who substituted themselves for the masses and narcissistically centred attention on themselves instead of the black and Third World movements they claimed to be supporting.'[61]

Writing in *Tablet* magazine about the hounding of Bari Weiss, who had added a line from the musical *Hamilton* ('Immigrants: They get the job done') to a picture of (non-immigrant) American Mirai Nagasu completing a complicated figure skating move at the 2018 Winter Olympics, Wesley Yang recounts how:

There were two categories of people attacking Weiss online: those operating with the desperate sincerity that people leading hate-mobs on Twitter bring to positions held in obvious bad faith, and actual bearers of the identity microaggressed-against. Most of the former group were white people (typically women, but a growing number of men) appropriating the resentments of nonwhite people as weapons with which to anathematize and harm other white rivals for power and precedence, at once immunizing themselves (so they believe) from a similar fate, and recasting their own indulgence of malicious personal impulses as politically righteous allyship.

This is the most astute analysis of performative identity politics by white leftists that I have ever read. It precisely nails the intention: to say that I, despite my white skin, can actually obviate my race through the over-the-top hounding of another white person; and to stop a similar thing happening to them one day. Of course, they can't and it won't. Yang continued by noting that Nagasu did not perceive herself to be a victim, and having seen *Hamilton*, got the joke, but that this was entirely beside the point. Nagasu's pleas for her ostensible defenders to stop hounding Weiss counted for nought: 'This is indicative of a rule governing social media mobs: No one has the standing to moderate mob rage at those it deems to be wrongdoers...even the actual "victim" of an ostensible microaggression.'[62]

But this is not only the preserve of white people. Very often people of mixed race, or ethnic minorities who grew up or work in 'white' environments, feel the need to develop a pronounced 'anti-whiteness' as a way of dealing with their own conflicted identity. Haider recalls Philip Roth's review of LeRoi Jones/ Amiri Baraka's novel *The Dutchman*, which Roth claimed was written for a white audience, 'so that they should be moved... to humiliation and self-hatred'. Jones was furious with this implication, but according to Haider, *The Dutchman* was part of an aesthetic insurrection by Jones against his own white Greenwich Village environment, and indeed his own internalisation of its standards of identity.

Since Jones converted to Islam as Ameer Barakat, which he then had Swahilized as Amiri Baraka, it could be said that he was 'mired in identity crisis from the beginning': His childhood was marked by a 'gradient of the black, brown, yellow, and white'. He was not white and middle class, but nor was he black and poor: 'With parents who worked in offices and days spent with white students and the black community in ambivalent, color-coded terms.' When he reached Greenwich Village in 1965, 'the white-out reached its peak'. At an event in the Village in 1964, Jones criticised the two white activists killed in Alabama; in his later autobiography, he admitted that these remarks were hypocritical, and that the white activists 'were out there on the front lines doing more than I was!' The older Baraka wrote that his earlier African cultural nationalism was 'a contrived performance, in essence an attempt at passing for African...an incoherent amalgam of hippie counter-culture and conservative semifeudal traditions'.[63]

The Jamaican-born philosopher Stuart Hall used to tell an anecdote of how, after his move to Britain to study at Oxford, his mother would anxiously enquire: 'I do hope they don't think you're an immigrant over there?' Hall was from one of the finest families on the island, and the thought of white Britons assuming he was just another West Indian migrant worker caused a great deal of upset for Mrs Hall. Her son was experiencing the unnerving identity transition from being a deracinated pillar of the local middle class to being a black man in a racist country. Every September, thousands of students from northern cities descend on elite universities in the South and, surrounded by people from the Home Counties, have a similar experience to Stuart Hall; they've gone from being a bog-standard middle-class 18-year-old, to being 'the Northern one'.

Many of the black students at the same institutions undergo the same phenomenon: although from perfectly ordinary middle-class backgrounds, they are now the 'black' one in an overwhelmingly white environment. The *New Statesman* journalist and Oxford graduate Stephen Bush recounts how he 'became black at university. Not because I experienced any racism worth talking about but simply because for the first time in my life, anyone describing me could mostly get away with "black".'[64] For some this will be a discombobulating and unpleasant experience; for others it is exhilarating.

The former President of the National Union of Students, Malia Bouattia, is clearly one of the latter. Except, unlike Amiri Baraka and Stuart Hall, she's not actually black. Until the age of 7, she had a wonderfully privileged childhood in Algeria, where the Arab majority treats black people disgracefully, before her academic parents moved to the UK.[65] But through adopting the mantle of 'political blackness', by making herself the scourge of the Zionists, she transcends her comfortable middle-class upbringing and the fact she isn't black, and becomes one of the oppressed, an underdog, a new Frantz Fanon (who was himself, not coincidentally, a doctor from one of the most prestigious families in Martinique).

The same is true for so many others on the hobbyist Left. By banging on endlessly about white privilege, Zionism and the global south, they believe they can obviate their whiteness, their blandness and the boring realities of their Home Counties upbringing. Of course, nearly all people say and do stupid things when they're young, and grow up and look back upon their younger selves with embarrassment. A crucial difference for young people on the hobbyist Left today is that they are being encouraged in their embarrassing self-righteousness by academics, journalists and even some politicians.

The apogee of this white guilt and patronising valorisation of blackness is the case of Rachel Dolezal, who hit the headlines in 2015 after it transpired she had been living as a black woman, despite being as white as the Henley Regatta. Now, around the world, there are millions of people on the hobbyist Left who had fairly privileged backgrounds and wish to God that they were born in poverty. There are a great number of people secure in their gender identity who curse their luck that they were not born transgender. And there are millions of white leftists who would give their right arm to have been born black. But none of them go the full Dolezal. Only Rachel Dolezal actually had the guts or lack of shame to actually try and do it. For this white, middle-class, hobbyist leftist, wishing she was black was not enough: she actually pretended to be black.

However, we should not put too much criticism on Dolezal: she only did what plenty of hobbyist leftists would love to do, and what is in some ways the logical outcome of ethnic identity politics. In the words of Haider, 'for intellectuals seeking a way of being political in the absence of such organizations, *passing* is an understandable temptation', and Dolezal 'exemplifies the consequences of reducing politics to identity performances, in which positioning oneself as marginal is the recognized procedure of becoming political'. I would also say that the reverse is true: becoming political might almost suggest you are marginal, despite your privilege. That is to say: if you are a rich white kid, you don't need to actually pretend to be black, you can just shout endlessly about white privilege, and, without making any compromises or sacrifices yourself, you can sort of be black. 'Passing', as Haider concludes, 'is a universal condition. We are all Rachel Dolezal; the infinite regress of "checking your privilege" will eventually unmask everyone as inauthentic.'[66]

Towards an Inclusive Identity Politics

The African American James Boggs wrote in 1993:

> Before the Civil Rights Act...we may have had the money but we couldn't go into most hotels or buy a home outside the ghetto. Today the only reason we can't go to a hotel or buy a decent home is because we don't have the money. But we are still focused on the question of race and it is paralyzing us.[67]

Over a quarter-century later, this problem is even more acute. But as Asad Haider argues, it is much easier to focus on race than on socio-economic change. It is fairly easy to remove discriminatory barriers and allow black and brown people to enter the richest percentiles; it is far harder to reduce differences in income and wealth. It is also no threat to the rich to have black and brown people join their ranks; indeed it makes them more secure, as it appears to legitimise inequality.

Paul Gilroy claims that a failure of the modern Left's appeal to ethnic minorities is from claiming that 'some sort of liberal, redemptive incursion into the capitalist version of democratic political culture is the best thing that [they] can hope for'.[68] It is this attitude that led to one-third of Hispanic Americans voting for Donald Trump, and if British Labour continues down this route, we can expect to see many ethnic minorities deserting the party in the future. Charles Clarke quotes the philosopher Amartya Sen on identity, claiming that we all have multifaceted identities, and choose which to promote at different times. For Sen, no one should be categorised as 'just one thing', and it is 'not realistic to put people in blocs'.[69]

This identitarianism will not do anything to tackle the real-life difficulties of non-white people. Look at Bill Clinton, with his saxophone and his black best friend, hailed as 'the first black President' by no less than Toni Morrison, who massively harmed African American families and communities with his crime and welfare reforms. Meanwhile in 2016, although Hillary Clinton won plaudits for acknowledging the existence of systemic racism, this rhetorical gesture had no effect on black voter turnout nor on her actual policies.

Another revealing case is the Academy of Motion Pictures, with their reluctance to nominate black people for acting awards: in 2015 and 2016, only white people were nominated in acting categories at the Oscars. You would be hard placed to find a more liberal, hand-wringingly anti-racist bunch of (mostly) white people in the whole of the United States than the Academy; yet, within the confines of the secret, anonymous nomination process, with nobody knowing anyone else's vote, they all happened to nominate only white actors, for 2 years in a row. Identitarian, right-on anti-racism is not enough: you need real structural change.

Fortunately, the power relations and racial hierarchies of the eighteenth and nineteenth centuries are not frozen in time for ever. Although it casts a long and grim shadow, continuing to affect the lives of millions – or even billions – of people around the world today, the days of the transatlantic slave trade and European imperialism are a mere blimp in the history of humanity. The resultant power structures are not set in stone. Indeed, they have already begun to shift. Yet so much of ethnic 'identity politics', as understood and practised by the hobbyist Left, acts as if 'white people' are inherently privileged, and 'non-whites' are inherent victims.

The racio-economic power structures established in the eighteenth and nineteenth centuries won't last for ever, and the effects that this history has on the modern world diminishes with each day. Anyone who thinks, for example, that Chinese people see themselves as 'victims' and Westerners as somehow 'superior' has clearly not spoken to many Chinese. Right now, taking the piss out of Chinese people is rightly seen as unacceptable racism, but presumably, as global power shifts over the next few decades, it might become a shorthand for radical satire, as mocking Americans is today. In fact, there is a Chinese word baizuo (or literally, the 'white left'), which is used to refer to people who 'only care about topics such as immigration, minorities, LGBT and the environment', 'have no sense of real problems in the real world'; they are hypocritical humanitarians who advocate for peace and equality only to 'satisfy their own feeling of moral superiority'.[70]

Likewise, Indians see the idea of Britons as powerful and Indians as victims as an absurd anachronism. The BBC reporter Justin Rowlatt wrote on the seventieth anniversary of Indian independence:

> It is sobering to learn what young Indians think of Britain today. When I ask a group of 16 and 17-year-olds at Amity International School in Delhi which of the two countries is most powerful, all but one says India....'It is our economy that is growing at a much faster rate,' says Sarthak Sehgal. Doha Khan draws on history to justify her view, saying: 'Before Britain came to India it gave 22% of GDP to the world and when the British left we were no more than 4%. So I would say that India was much more important to Britain than Britain to India, even then.' Another girl says it is a question of demographics. 'India is the second largest population, so even by numbers India is much greater. We are young and we have great ideas', she says to giggles from her classmates.

As noted by Asad Haider, Ta-Nehisi Coates and others, 'whiteness' was the original ethnic identity, and racism the original identity politics. Now, finally, this sense of whiteness is starting to be undermined, but this long-overdue and much-needed process is being halted by the identity politics of the hobbyist Left, who reinforce the notion of whiteness. As structural change proceeds over the following decades and centuries, whites may more and more come to see themselves as victims, and react to this in violent and unpredictable ways – Trump's election might be the first warning sign of this reaction. In this sense, it is essential to undermine the idea of ethnic separateness, and focus on universal humanity.

Those of us on the Left need to articulate a positive story that embraces all of the different religions, ethnicities and cultures within the UK. But this story must be universal, rather than specific: any attempt to articulate policies and positions specifically to cater to particular groups is wrong-headed and self-defeating. Of course, specific groups and people in certain situations do face injustices that are specific and exclusive to their particular ethnicity, but we need to have clear water between actual structural disadvantages and meaningless identitarianism. For example, yes to reparations for the descendants of enslaved people – this would be a practical, pragmatic response to a real and long-lasting material disadvantage – no to Laurie Penny claiming that they are ashamed to be white or Malia Bouattia claiming a disadvantaged status despite her life of relative privilege. Yes to action to protect women of colour from their enhanced risk of violence and sexual violence, but no to think pieces claiming it's insulting that Harvey Weinstein didn't abuse any black women or complaining about 'brown men falling in love with white women'.[71] Likewise, it is not enough to ensure that privileged black and Asian people can access the highest levels of politics, business, media, law and so on; instead we need to combat privilege itself – including ethnic minority privilege – and work for an equal and just society. Anything else is just integrating the elite.

2. 'Those Fucking Mugs'

Immigration and the Identity Left

A week before the 2010 General Election, then Prime Minister Gordon Brown was campaigning in the Greater Manchester town of Rochdale. He crossed paths with a local woman on her way to the shops, who proceeded to grill him over Labour policy on pensions, the national debt and immigration. A flustered Brown, returning to the presumed safety of his ministerial car, harangued his staff for not keeping the 'terrible, bigoted woman' away from him. Unfortunately for Brown, his lapel microphone was still switched on, the outburst was recorded and instantly relayed across the news networks. Upon hearing of this misfortune, Brown hung his head in despair; if he hadn't already lost the election, he surely had now.

The incident between Brown and Gillian Duffy highlighted the tension between the Labour leadership and much of its voter base on the subject of immigration, and the subsequent years – culminating in the 2016 Brexit vote – have made this division indelibly clear. This friction has been building for a long time, and on no other issue is there so great a divide between the hobbyist Left and the people the Labour Party was formed to represent. Although current Labour leader Jeremy Corbyn has one leg in the old-school Marxist camp, which believes that free movement undercuts wages, he has another with the hobbyists, who feel that the very idea of restricting immigration is inherently wrong, and as late as June 2016 he was restating his long-held position that there should be 'no upper limit' to immigration.[1]

In many ways the EU referendum has temporarily let Labour off the hook over immigration: the electorate decided that Britain should leave the EU, thus ending freedom of movement from within Europe, and tied Labour's hands. Hence its manifesto for the 2017 General Election committed to ending freedom of movement – something one suspects only a Labour leader with the impeccable internationalist and anti-racist credentials of Jeremy Corbyn could have got away with – and this seems to have worked.

In 2017, Labour avoided alienating pro-EU and pro-immigration types, while reassuring many anti-immigration voters that a vote for Labour was a vote to end free movement. The researcher Charlie Cadywould has found that Labour's pre-existing core (who voted Labour anyway and continued to do so in 2017) were the most pro-immigration, but a majority of the late switchers (who decided to vote Labour in 2017 only at the last minute) favoured less immigration. But the 2017 manifesto commitment to end free movement has only postponed the tough decision: how to reconcile the pro-immigration sentiments of the young and well-educated, with the anti-immigration desires of the majority of the population?

For the left-wing hobbyists, there is a different dilemma: many of them believe that immigration is simply not a valid topic of debate. For some, the original sins of slavery and imperialism mean that countries such as Britain do not have a right to a selective immigration policy, and should open their borders to as many people as wish to come.

In a blog post 5 years after Gordon Brown's Rochdale gaffe, in the aftermath of another Labour election loss, Sunny Hundal took aim at the 'boundless outrage about Miliband's immigration policies...I didn't meet a single voter on the doorstep, even in London, who was turned off by the mugs, but plenty who wanted to know of Labour policies on immigration that would stop their wages being undercut. Yet all I heard online was blind outrage about those *fucking* mugs.'[2]

He was referring to a series of mugs produced by Labour highlighting their various election pledges, one of which was to control immigration. For many on the hobbyist Left, the concept of immigration control is intrinsically suspicious. For many young activists and for much of the academic Left, merely *talking* about immigration is enough to upset the stomach and leave an unpleasant taste in the mouth. This despite the fact that immigration is not an ethnic or racial issue: according to a 2014 Ipsos MORI report, an overwhelming majority of pre-1990 immigrants to the UK wish to see the current level of immigration reduced.[3]

In Vron Ware's book on Britishness, she asks various ethnic minority Britons about their thoughts on immigration. For Suja, a Pakistani café owner from north London, 'one of his biggest complaints was his sense that British people were losing their manners'. He told Ware that 'integration shouldn't mean that you should change…you don't compromise with who you are'. Shamser, and a friend of his who had formerly lived in a small town in Yorkshire, reminisced that when he lived there, 'people had time, they queued politely, they didn't get impatient', and he remembered thinking 'that must have been how things were [in Britain] before'. Another man, Tariq from Leeds, said he thought 'the Victorians were more focused, less lazy. Now there is more of a benefit culture' and added that, 'you would be surprised how crazy the imams are who come here…they are from rural areas of Pakistan and would never get a job over there'.[4] Ware began 'to wonder where I was, listening to two young men harking on about the old days', but this sense of conservatism, fear of a rapidly-changing world and a harking back to an imagined past is extremely common. It is important for Labour to realise that many of its voting blocs – young ethnic minorities as much as anyone else – value stability and community over flux.[5]

Immigration is, emphatically, a class issue, and perhaps even an issue of cultural class, rather than material class: according to the 2016 British Social Attitudes survey, those who identified as working class but had middle-class jobs were more likely to have anti-immigrant politics.[6] It is also a generational, geographical and locational issue: the division over immigration is not so much between the fabled 'white working class' and everyone else, but rather between younger people, usually with at least one university degree, and poorer, older people with fewer qualifications.

Academics from different disciplines and political traditions predicted this dilemma. In the 1980s, the Marxist scholar Ambalavaner Sivanandan noted that 'to put it crudely, the economic profit from immigration has gone to capital, [while] the social cost has gone to labour'.[7] In a 2002 article, the sociologist Les Back warned that 'multiculturalism and racism provoke debates about rights and responsibilities that demand explicit resolutions that cannot be confined to the scale of the local and whose resolutions potentially severely compromise New Labour's talent for populist appeal'.[8] In other words, Back predicted that the development of a multicultural UK and the reaction against this – predominantly from the working class, whatever their ethnicity – could spell the end of Labour's ability to appeal to both its traditional heartlands and new-found metropolitan adherents. In 2002 this must have seemed like an implausibly gloomy prediction; from the perspective of today it seems unduly optimistic.

An offensive and inaccurate old canard, often trotted out by hobbyists, talks of Britain's long, proud history of accepting immigrants, from the Huguenots to Eastern Europeans and everyone in between. It fails to mention that every generation of immigrants to Britain has received dog's abuse. For most immigrants over the centuries, the idea that they were welcomed with open arms by the local population would have raised eyebrows, at the very least.

Since the Second World War, British politicians from both of the main parties have been constrained by two inalienable and awkward facts: the economy needs immigration, and yet there has been continuous hostility towards immigration. Since

Ipsos MORI began asking the question in 1989, the percentage of people agreeing that there are 'too many immigrants' has never fallen below 50 per cent, and averages out at around 65 per cent, peaking at nearly 80 per cent in early 2008. In contrast, the percentage of people who felt immigration was the most or one of the most important issues facing Britain remained pretty constant throughout the late 1980s and 1990s, at under 10 per cent, before climbing to over 40 per cent in early 2008. This suggests that anti-immigration sentiment is pretty steady, but people only think it is an important issue at specific times. Nor is this particularly an English issue: according to figures by NatCen, 63 per cent of Scottish people want the same immigration policy as the rest of the UK, and 59 per cent want an end to free movement.[9]

While very few would attempt to deny that Britain needs immigrants, many hobbyists feel compelled to deny the existence of anti-immigration sentiment. Writing in *The Guardian*, and full of confidence about impending victory in the 2015 election, Owen Jones argued that 'Labour has enjoyed a lead for so long because it swept up progressive voters who opted for the Lib Dems... They know the EU is not a salient issue for most voters.'[10] Barely a year later, the salience of the EU – largely but not exclusively because of immigration – would be made all too apparent.

As Zoe Williams rightly observes, 'the left is terrified of [immigration], because it wants to see itself championing the rights of the "white working class" while at the same time dealing with foreigners in an open and fair-minded way'. Because of their ideology, and as so few of them hail from the class they seek to represent, hobbyists cannot help but valorise 'the working class' – at the same time, any objection to immigration is seen as beyond the pale, and indicative of crypto-fascism. In their attempts to reconcile these two positions, there is no amount of sophistry to which they will not stoop. A central message of Owen Jones' bestselling-book *Chavs* was that working-class people are not particularly hostile to immigration, while in November 2013, Terry Christian – a professional Mancunian who was briefly famous in the early nineties – tweeted: 'More middle class people are racist, more upper class people are racist – that's a fact.'

It took the Marxist Richard Seymour to admit that 'most Britons have been hostile to immigration for decades, long before the waves of EU migration in the last decade...We cannot treat racism as the result of elite or rightwing misdirection exploiting people's real concerns.'[11] Giles Fraser concurs that the far Right have been able to channel anger:

> against poor immigrants precisely because those who should have been listening were too busy worrying about their children's next trip to Paris or what their friends at Glastonbury would think if they challenged the liberal consensus. Precisely the same people who are now saying, incredulously, 'but I have never met a [Leave voter]', as if that were a good thing.[12]

Thus, two men hailing from very different parts of British radical tradition are able to articulate the presence of wood among the trees, but many of their fellow travellers on the Left refuse to do so.

The Left and Immigration: What Went Wrong?

In her recent book *Brit(ish)*, despite repeating the tired trope that anti-immigration sentiment has 'little to do with immigration', Afua Hirsch makes some convincing arguments about Labour's immigration record in the period 1997 to 2010. For Hirsch, 'this top-down, social engineering approach to immigration' did plenty of damage to perceptions of migration.[13] Under New Labour, Britons were told that immigration was good for them, and if they didn't like it: tough. As the historian Jon Lawrence argues, both the Attlee and Thatcher governments, for different ends, 'used a combination of public policy and political rhetoric to remake the public's "common sense" [but on immigration] New Labour spectacularly failed to do this – it didn't even try'.[14]

There is a remarkable passage from Nick Cohen's book *Pretty Straight Guys* where he describes the life and career of one Charles Leadbeater. Leadbeater, who claimed to have had several 'mini-careers' before he was 40, described himself as a 'knowledge worker', and one of the people who 'live on their wits'. According to Cohen: 'He "sometimes marvels" at the risks he is taking until he realises that surviving on contacts and creating and selling knowledge is all he, and we, can do... Secure careers...are vanishing. Soon the world will be filled with programmers "providing service, judgement, and analysis", manipulating information – and each other.' For some people, the idea of a Leadbeater-style career would be intriguing and appealing. For many others – I would hazard most people – the idea sounds absolutely terrifying. Yet in some ways, it was this understanding of the future economy, and future ideas of belonging and community, that underpinned New Labour thinking on immigration. In the future, people would be atomised economic units, hiring themselves out hither and thither as freelancers in the knowledge economy. The terrifying insecurity this would entail would be mitigated by the fact that people could just move to wherever the jobs were.[15]

John Denham suggests one problem with recent immigration is that the rate of change to communities has accelerated in comparison to immigration in the past.[16] Whereas Southampton Catholics of Irish descent might be proud of their immigrant roots, they feel their ancestors did not impact on local cohesion as the newcomers are doing. This feeling of being unable to have any agency over the pace of change is common to many people around the world: dislocation and atomisation are responsible for many modern ills. Yet many on the hobbyist Left are, by and large, intensely relaxed about this aspect of globalisation. For many of them, the very idea of community is rather *passé*. They enjoy the McWorld aspect of modernity; indeed, they may thrive on it.

For the former immigration minister Phil Woolas, the problem is more intractable than just the rate of change: he feels there is a large section of the UK population fundamentally hostile to immigration, including many from black and minority ethnic backgrounds. Woolas notes that Commonwealth immigrants are notably hostile to the European Union; Ghanaians in particular.[17] His views are borne out by polling: Ipsos MORI has found that of those who came to the UK before 1970, fully 48 per cent want immigration reduced a lot, and 22 per cent a little; for 1971-1990 immigrants the numbers are 32 and 31 per cent.[18]

Former Home Secretary Charles Clarke disavows Woolas's interpretation, and feels there need not be any great tension for Labour in this respect. For Clarke, people 'didn't see Poles as a challenge, they were motivated more by the newspapers, not by the experience of their own lives...People aren't fundamentally racist; they just want to know that the system is under control. If immigrants have moved in over the street, people want to know that they're there fairly.' Clarke claims Labour 'lost confidence around 2007. We lost faith in our ability to put across a positive message about immigration' hence the 'unworkable slogan, "British jobs for British workers"'. This loss of confidence continued through the Gordon Brown premiership and has not been resolved since: 'Ed [Miliband] and Jeremy [Corbyn] are in the same category. They're not ready to talk about it.' Instead of making a coherent attempt to convince wary voters of the benefits of immigration, Labour has put across a more abstract message: 'It's good for the country as a whole – so if you don't like it it's your problem.'[19]

The Inglorious History of Immigration and the Working Class

Historically, there can be little doubt about the reaction of most of the British working class towards immigration after the Second World War, despite attempted revisionism from the disingenuous. In her warts-and-all history of the working class in the twentieth century, the historian Selina Todd – very much a woman of the Left – does not try to gloss over the experience of mixed-race couples who fell in love:

> Ellen Halliburton, a white twenty-five-year-old, fled with her black boyfriend Alf when her father discovered they were courting and threw his daughter out. After fruitlessly confronting several hostile landlords, they were offered a handful of suburban council flats, but turned them down in favour of a "slummy flat" near the city centre because of the hostility that prospective neighbours showed them. Their experience was far from unusual: a study of London showed that mixed-race couples encountered hostility from their neighbours and landlords.[20]

Perhaps the most telling incident of working-class hostility towards black and Asian migrants is the reaction to Enoch Powell's infamous Wolverhampton speech. After 'Rivers of Blood', around one-third of the registered workforce of the London docks – between 6000 and 7000 men – went out on strike in support of Powell. A much smaller number marched on Parliament – around 500 to 800 assembled at the start of the march, and about 300 to 400 arrived at Westminster – where they abused Ian Mikardo, the left-wing Labour MP for Poplar, and cheered the right-wing shire Tory Gerald Nabarro, who had supported Powell.[21]

This hostility was not limited to right-wing or politically apathetic workers. As early as 1882, the Marxist Social

Democratic Federation passed a resolution claiming that the Chinese 'always remained a distinct race wherever they went. They could swamp us industrially and crowd us out of almost every occupation.' Fifty years later, the Asian Communist MP Shapurji Saklatvala had continuous cause to complain about adverse comments made about 'Negroes and Asians' from fellow British Community Party members.

Many in the Fabian Society had similar views, with George Bernard Shaw writing in his *Fabianism and Empire* that 'states with a higher civilization had a right to take over backward states'. Even the Independent Labour Party (ILP), powered more by Nonconformist moralism than rigid Marxism or bureaucratic statism, still failed to offer a coherent opposition to racism. In the words of the sociologist Satnam Virdee: 'The ILP's success lay in its ability to reflect faithfully the dominant cultural and political outlook of the working class at the time...When confronted with an opportunity to challenge working-class racism, the ILP instead chose to accommodate it.'[22]

The historian E.P. Thompson argued that 'if we are to begin to comprehend the British Left since 1880 we must take very much more seriously the international and imperialist context. One of the grand facts of the twentieth century which the orthodox Marxist model finds it difficult to accommodate is the resurgent nationalism of the imperialist climax.'[23] Lest one think this should be as a result of a deliberate system of state-led indoctrination, the American historian of nationalism and education E.H. Reisner, after his tour of Britain in the 1910s, noted his surprise at the relative lack of patriotic indoctrination in schools, compared to his experiences in North America and continental Europe.[24] Thompson further claimed that 'imperialism penetrated deeply into the labour movement and into socialist groups'.[25] Even the Marxist Perry Anderson, not necessarily known for his acute observation of reality, acknowledged: 'All political groups, Conservatives, Liberals, and Fabians, were militantly imperialist in aims...The nascent socialist movement shared in the general jingoism, Webb, Hyndman, and Blatchford; Fabian, "Marxist" and ILP-supporter respectively, the most "advanced" and the most popular spokesmen of the Left, were all in their different ways vocal imperialists.'[26]

Not merely supportive of colonialism abroad, the labour movement in the first half of the twentieth century was horrified at the prospect of non-white immigration to the UK. A letter to then Labour leader Arthur Henderson in 1916 conveyed a resolution unanimously adopted by the War Emergency: Workers' National Committee, an umbrella organisation representing left-wing groups: 'Having regard to the serious *moral*, social, industrial, and economic considerations in any introduction of coloured labour into this country, supports the Labour Party in its emphatic protest against such introduction.'[27] If the Parliamentary Labour Party had an ambiguous attitude towards racism and an uneasy relationship with immigration, for the trade unions it was usually far more straightforward. In Liverpool in 1919, over 100 black factory workers lost their jobs, as demobilised white men refused to work alongside them.[28] And in 1920 the National Union of Seamen successfully campaigned to restrict the employment of 'non-white' labour in the industry.[29]

A labour organisation, the Movement for Colonial Freedom, tried to promote friendship and co-operation with colonial trade unions, but they were notably unsuccessful. Apparently in the 1930s 'the mere mention of India would empty the smallest hall'.[30] Even when calls for wholesale decolonisation were made, they were mainly based on 'Little England' arguments invoking metropolitan self-interest, not on universalist principles or on the rights or political claims of the colonised.[31] The Marxist Tom Quelch of the British Socialist Party argued that: 'The average English worker would consider it treason to render assistance to the dependent countries against the English authorities.' A number of hard-left Labour figures, including George Lansbury, the Jeremy Corbyn of his day, were won over to Empire Socialism, while the Attlee administration, despite overseeing independence for India and Pakistan, was adamant that Britain should remain an imperial power.[32]

After Labour's landslide win in the 1945 election, 11 Labour MPs wrote to new Prime Minister Clement Attlee calling for the restriction of black immigration on the grounds that 'an influx of coloured people domiciled here is likely to impair the harmony, strength and cohesion of our public and social life and to cause discord and unhappiness among all concerned'.[33] At the same time, the Attlee government – despite Britain facing the most acute Labour crisis in its industrial history – actively encouraged white British emigration to Australia and New Zealand in order to preserve 'British stock'.[34]

Frank McLeavy, Member of Parliament for Bradford East, felt compelled to claim in 1963 that 'we cannot afford to be the welfare state for the whole of the Commonwealth. We have a responsibility to our own people from a trade-union point of view.'[35] Despite the protestations of individual MPs, Labour's general position on immigration in the post-war decades was to avoid the issue. Shelia Wright, a member of Birmingham District Labour Party from 1952 and the MP for Handsworth from 1979 to 1983, claimed that 'we make it worse by bringing it into the open', and that the party was 'sick with fright about the effect on the electorate'.[36]

In the post-Second World War period, the official policy of the Amalgamated Union of Foundry Workers was to refuse membership to Polish workers. Grassroots membership defied the leadership, which eventually caved and allowed them to join, although to a certain extent this was a means of ensuring that the Poles did not join another union.[37] Nye Bevan reported to the cabinet in 1946 that unions objected to Italians in foundries and Poles in mines because 'they were unconvinced of its necessity'.

Bevan tried to reassure them that there was no need to fear, as the foreigners would return once the labour shortage ended, but the unions were not convinced.[38]

Members of the Transport and General Workers' Union were resolute in their opposition to black workers on the buses in the 1950s. In areas that had high levels of unionisation, they were usually able to keep black employment to a minimum. According to labour historian Kenneth Lunn: 'The concentration of Indian workers in the Midlands iron foundries, which can be traced from the end of the Second World War, was the result not only of a labour shortage, but also of the low-level of absence of trade union organization' in those foundries.[39] The colour bar in Bristol was actively supported by Transport and General Workers' Union members, while Smethwick Labour Club itself had a colour bar.[40] Recalling his time in the General Municipal and Boilermakers' Union, Larry Whitty recalls that they accepted a degree of positive discrimination for women, 'but refused to work under black or minority ethnic people...to this day, Unite, GMB, and so on, are unrepresentative in terms of BME people'.[41]

Perhaps the most shameful episode in the history of the Labour Party and immigration came with the passage of the 1968 Commonwealth Immigration Act. This piece of legislation came about as a result of the expulsion of Asians from Kenya by Jomo Kenyatta's government. Left-wing papers such as the *Daily Mirror* warned of an uncontrolled flood of migrants, and a nervous Labour government implemented emergency legislation to remove their right of settlement in the UK.[42] The act took merely 2 days to pass through both houses of Parliament and receive Royal Assent.[43] The Canadian historian Randall Hansen argues that:

The Kenyan Asians' crisis represented both a shift, in the two parties, away from previous commitments to the Commonwealth and, in the Labour party, the triumph of

James Callaghan's strand of Labour ideology – nationalist, anti-intellectual, indifferent to arguments about international law and obligation, and firmly in touch with the social conservatism of middle- and working-class England.[44]

On 1 March 1968 the aeroplanes bringing the refugees were turned away. For Hansen, this signified that Labour was 'at last in touch with the working- and lower-middle-class voters to whom the government owed its office'. The Commonwealth Immigrants Act of that year was the 'culmination of this process'.[45]

Forty years after 'Rivers of Blood', the historian Amy Whipple poured through the vast correspondence Powell received in response to his speech – almost all of it positive - and made many depressing findings. An oft-recurring theme was that Powell, unlike the Labour representatives, was standing up for the working classes, and saying what the Labour MPs would not. 'Someone becomes an MP, gets a head full of liberal ideas, and is no longer "one of us"' read one. Powell, a hard-right Tory MP, whose entire record in public service had been to the detriment of the workers, was able to secure an outpouring of working-class support because of his racist articulations. The overall theme was clear: the correspondents believed Labour had betrayed its traditional supporters by protecting immigrants at the expense of the working class. 'You have the working man behind you,' as many of the letters averred.[46] It is to the enormous credit of Edward Heath and the Conservative opposition that they did not attempt to play the immigration issue to their advantage.

It was not only the East End of London where trade unionists and Labour voters continued to harbour racist sentiments. By the 1980s, the once solidly-Tory city Liverpool had finally been captured for Labour, and today contains some of the party's safest seats. Yet, as the journalist Dave Hill points out in his biography of John Barnes, as of the late 1980s it remained one of the most overtly racist cities in the UK. While most First Division clubs had fielded black players, they were noticeably absent from the squads of Liverpool and Everton. After Liverpool signed Barnes, due to his brilliance on the pitch, racist hostility melted away from the terraces of Anfield, but not at Goodison. Hill made the point, however, that the Evertonians would not have chanted 'N***erpool' and 'Everton is white' if they could not be sure that those taunts would hit their mark, and wound the pride of the Liverpool fans.[47]

Don't Mention Immigration!

A favourite motif of many on the hobbyist Left is that there is greatest hostility towards immigration in areas with the fewest immigrants, and they therefore conclude that anti-immigration rhetoric actually has little to do with immigration: 'Here is a failure of the Left. People want answers to their unaddressed everyday concerns, fears and insecurities: a vacuum has to be filled.' Or at least that it is all to do with hard currency: 'Concerns over immigration could be addressed through an "immigration dividend": extra public money for services going to communities with higher levels of migrants.'[48]

The following quotation neatly encapsulates the painful hotchpotch: 'Nearly 4 million people voted for Ukip at the last election. If they are dismissed as racists rather than working-class people who often have unanswered fears over jobs, housing, public services and the future of their children and grandchildren, they will be lost forever.' Here Owen Jones concedes that we cannot describe the millions of UK citizens who wish to see immigration reduced as racist (not least because many hundreds and thousands of them are not white). Yet he cannot quite bring himself to admit that they are actually concerned about immigration in and of itself; instead it is 'jobs, housing, public services' and 'the future of their children and grandchildren'.[49]

Witness this masterful attempt to describe anti-immigration

sentiment without mentioning immigration:

> A general fragmentation in society and the triumph of individualism; the disappearance of industries that once sustained cohesive communities; the smothering of local government and unions; a political convergence that has left parties quibbling over nuances...here was the expenses scandal, the Iraq war, the Lib Dems' decision to trash what little faith young people had in democracy – all have helped fuel disillusionment with political elites who were never, after all, loved. But for a generation, politicians have surrendered democratic power to the market.[50]

Yet this begs the question: why were Ukip able to pose as anti-elite? Why are the likes of Nigel Farage, Boris Johnson and Donald Trump able to pose as friends of the workers? If it's just about housing and the NHS, then why do people object to immigrants in particular, and not their fellow Brits who also need state resources? And why is the Left unable to articulate a radical response to dislocation? It is because it is hamstrung by the cultural neuroses of the hobbyist Left, the foremost of which is immigration.

Many left-wing hobbyists argue that it is a mistake for Labour to try and outflank the Tories on immigration. They reason that since Labour will never be as trusted on the issue as the Tories, why should it try to outdo them? Yet this way of thinking is electoral self-harm of the highest magnitude. Imagine if the Tories decided: 'People will never trust us on the NHS as much as Labour, so let's just leave it'? On the contrary, they spend a great deal of time and money trying to convince the electorate they can be trusted on the NHS, so that, having mitigated this weakness, they can concentrate on vote-winning policies. Certainly, Labour should not try to *outflank* the Tories on immigration, but it is essential that Labour espouses a position on immigration broadly in step with public sentiment, so it can then concentrate on vote-winning policies. This is especially the case given the hostility of many traditional Labour voters and key ethnic demographics to immigration.

Since the Brexit referendum, there has been a notable shift in the number of people desiring to see immigration reduced. According to Ipsos Public Affairs, in February 2015, 40 per cent wanted to see the number of immigrants coming to the UK reduced by a lot and 22 per cent by a little. Just before the Brexit vote those numbers were 42 per cent and 20 per cent respectively. Immediately after the vote the figures shifted to 37 per cent and 23 per cent. By March 2018, only 30 per cent wanted to see immigration reduced a lot, and 24 per cent a little; the number who wanted things to remain the same was the highest in March 2018 – at 30 per cent – than on the previous three occasions. (The percentage of people who wanted immigration to increase either a little or a lot never rose above 10 per cent.) This supports the theory that the Brexit vote has reduced the potency of anti-immigration sentiment, as voters assume the issue has been dealt with. But after Brexit, the UK will still need immigrants: it is essential that, by that point, Labour has worked out a coherent, plausible and popular position on immigration. To do this it must avoid the knee-jerk open borderism of the hobbyist Left.

How Not to Talk about Immigration

Writing in *The Guardian* before the 2010 election, Mehdi Hasan fumed: 'From David Blunkett's remarks about the children of asylum-seekers "swamping" British schools to Brown's populist pledge of "British jobs for British workers", Labour has spent 13 long years kowtowing to the petty nationalism and undisguised xenophobia of both the Conservative opposition and its echo chamber in the rightwing press.' According to Hasan, 'the truth is that Labour has failed on the issue of immigration...because [Labour] failed, time and again, to tell a positive, hopeful story about immigration and the myriad ways in which it has benefited Britain.'[51]

There is certainly an argument that Labour could and should have done more to stress the interconnectedness of the world and persuade reluctant voters of the benefits of immigration. Nonetheless we can safely say that Hasan's approach is not particularly effective. In the 2010 article he goes on to stress the economic benefits of historical migration into the UK: 'Migrants boost the economy, provide vital services, raise academic standards and enrich our food...the British high street has been transformed by foreign-born entrepreneurs...Tesco, Marks & Spencer, easyJet and countless other leading companies were founded by immigrants or the children of immigrants.' That Hasan feels stressing how many migrants became extremely rich is a winning formula – fully 60 per cent of CEOs of FTSE 100 companies don't hold British passports – gives you an insight into his understanding of beliefs concerning immigration. Yet we cannot promote immigration by talking about the economy, the contribution to the NHS, or other materialistic factors, because this misses the point entirely. As could be inferred from the Brexit vote, some people are willing to make themselves poorer if it means controlled borders. Plus 'the economy needs them' is a very superficial argument for immigration.

Further, Hasan notes that 'in Ed Miliband and Nick Clegg, two of our three major political parties were led by sons of immigrants' – again, I'm not sure that this reflects well on immigration – and that 'nearly a quarter of Britain's Nobel prize winners were born abroad'.[52] He mentioned this presumably because black and Asian Britons in London struggling to find a primary school for their child will be reassured to hear it. Finally, he notes the influence of immigration on sport. Here he is on surer ground, but relying on sport, food or music to praise immigration raises old racist tropes. In Blackburn in the 1960s, people turned out to applaud the West Indian cricket team through the streets; but not soon after attacked Pakistani mill workers with machetes. It is perfectly possible to be virulently anti-immigration while still enjoying a good curry and a bit of Bob Marley, and if we have to fall back on food and sport we have failed to articulate a positive case for immigration.

We cannot do it by talking about ephemeral issues such as food and sport and music, because it is perfectly possible to admire *some* successful immigrants but despise those you live and work alongside. We need a coherent, believable and persuasive argument for immigration. Many of the towns where anti-immigrant sentiment is strongest owed their (now long gone) industries to British imperialism, and we need to stress their interconnectedness with nations and peoples all around the world. It is a mistake to teach a history of immigration to Britain that begins in 1948. Instead it should begin many centuries earlier with the development of the transatlantic slave trade and the first English colonies. We cannot reel off random lists of 'rather pathetic bits of cultural ephemera'[53] or indulge in 'the kind of wishy-washy liberalism that harps on about the cultural and economic contributions of migrants'.[54]

Biting the Bullet on Immigration

Immigration, more than any of the other topics raised in this book, is a zero-sum game: there is no way that Labour can compromise on this issue as it can with other problems, and a painful choice has to be made. But first the issue of immigration needs to be rehabilitated among left-wing academics, journalists and activists. Calling for restrictions to immigration needs to become culturally acceptable on the Left, and at the same time, the mythologisation of the working class needs to stop. Only by accepting the reality of hostility to immigration among its base, and by allowing criticism of its base, can Labour escape this position.

Although the strength of anti-EU sentiment among well to do people in the Home Counties was an overlooked contributor to Brexit, the importance of anti-immigrant sentiment among working-class Britons – obvious for the past 15 years at least to anyone apart from the blind, deaf or wilfully disingenuous – needs to be acknowledged and tackled head on. The reasons behind the Brexit result are many and complex; according to Ipsos MORI, Britain's ability to make its own laws was the most important factor for Brexiteers, cited by 74 per cent. However, the next three most important factors were the number of immigrants coming to Britain and the cost of EU immigration on Britain's welfare system – both cited by 68 per cent of Leavers – and the number of refugees coming to claim asylum, cited by 57 per cent.

Anecdotally, I know people in northern England who voted Leave so that there would be 'fewer Muslims' in the UK. Of course, plenty of working-class people love immigration and immigrants. At the same time, plenty of rich people are racist – but to offer these two qualifiers in response to a call to be honest about working-class anti-immigrant sentiment is an absurd and cowardly cop-out.

Writing of the fatwa issued against Salman Rushdie, the anthropologist Pnina Werbner argues the Western liberal response was flawed as instead of challenging the offensiveness of *The Satanic Verses*, they essentially told Muslims: 'It might be offensive, but it's only religion so you shouldn't care.'[55] There are some parallels here with the response of the Left to anti-immigration sentiment. Instead of trying to persuade people of the benefits of immigration, many on the Left gave in to the easy temptation to ignore them and hope that people didn't care enough for it to influence their vote. The correct response would have been to persuade them that they were wrong about immigration, not to loudly insist that their concerns weren't real or important. As Twitter user Dafydd Foster Evans notes, it is possible to 'believe that much of what passes for the debate on immigration is fact-free scaremongering and demagoguery, whilst also believing that immigration supporters need to seriously improve the way they talk about the issue'.

Responding to heart-breaking scenes of thousands of innocents drowning in the Mediterranean; young men risking their lives jumping onto moving trains; and helpless children living in squalid camps, some wonder whether Britain has lost its moral compass. Where, they ask, is the country that took in the Huguenots, and Jews fleeing pogroms and Nazi Germany? Where is the community-minded nation that stood up to fascism and created the welfare state? Yet the moral community that believes in offering a home to the vulnerable and supporting the weakest can only be sustained by a basic sense of fairness. As Professor Andrew Hindmoor argues, harsh attitudes towards immigration are often underpinned by a 'collectivist ethos in which notions of fairness loom large. People are not simply worried that immigrants will take *their* jobs or their children's jobs. They are worried that immigrants are going to take the jobs of people in their communities.'[56] If this sense of fairness is undermined, then people are more inclined to turn their backs and shut their doors.

If this sense of fairness and community cohesion is not sustained, then public altruism is affected. I sincerely believe that the British public would be far readier to welcome refugees if it had not been for such heavy and unregulated immigration in the early years of the twenty-first century, coupled with a cultural embargo on questioning the morality of this process.

In October 2016, after the arrival of dozens of child refugees from the bulldozed 'Jungle' camp in Calais, right-wing newspapers, notably the *Daily Mail*, printed photographs of some older-looking migrants, and claimed that many adults were brought in with the so-called children. The response of the Twitter Left was predictable and revealing: it posted childhood pictures of prominent sportsmen, arguing that some people simply mature early. This was wrong on two levels: firstly, because it is to be expected that elite sportsmen look older than their peers in early adolescence: a 12-year-old Romalu Lukaku was already over 6 feet, and a 13-year-old Diego Costa already looked as though he'd spent a couple of decades working in a copper mine.

But it was also wrong through shifting the focus from the many children who were prevented from coming to the UK because an adult took their place, and on to how bigoted and terrible the *Daily Mail* was. For it turns out that for months before the closure of the camp, government ministers had ignored offers of help to identify child refugees from social services, who were familiar with underage migrants in the camp. Local councils had offered to send social workers to Calais to carry out age checks, and a delegation from the Local Government Association met with Home Office ministers and officials, requesting they send experts in age identification to France. The chairman of the LGA's asylum, refugee and migration task group, David Simmons, said the Home Office refused to accept their offers of help. Thus many children were denied entry to Britain as grown men were able to take their places. Staff of charities and NGOs who had been working in the camp for months, and were well aware of vulnerable children who most needed resettlement, wrote on social media of their anger at the British government's refusal to consult with them. This was a scandal which demonstrated the government's incompetence and cruelty, and did not become less so just because the *Daily Mail* noticed it.[57]

In the future, the Left needs to take a clear-eyed, unsentimental approach to immigration which accepts the reality of hostility towards migration within its own base and focuses on challenging this, rather than reflexively reacting to the excesses of the tabloids. Hopefully in the future, in the inspiring words of Afua Hirsch, 'the debate around immigration could conceivably be a rational one, based on economic needs, public resources, historical facts and geopolitical realities'.[58]

3. The 'P' Word

The Left and Patriotism in Modern Britain

The very worst thing the Socialist movement could do is convince
the great mass of the people, who must be converted to Socialism if
Socialism is to be realised, that Socialism entails anti-patriotism.
Victor Fisher, early socialist activist.

We have seen a far left driven half-mad by the death of socialism
produce apologetics for the totalitarian movements of the far right.
Nick Cohen, What's Left, 2007.[1]

For most people, patriotism is axiomatic. Nations may well be
'imagined communities', but this is not apparent to the citizens
that constitute these communities. Around the world, whether
based on language, territory, religion or ethnicity, nationalism
is a powerful force. People believe that their nations are tangible
and significant, with real claims on their labour and even their
lives. This is as true in the developing world as in the developed
world, and among the former victims of colonialism as much
as former imperial powers. As Anatol Lieven writes in *Prospect*
magazine:

> Outside Europe, all the most powerful countries possess
> very strong nationalisms. This is true of not just China, India
> and Russia, but the US, where the major party presidential
> candidates of this election were both passionate nationalists,
> albeit of radically different kinds. A belief in American
> national sovereignty rooted in the popular will is an obsession
> in the Republican party, and is also held by most Democrats,
> in a quieter way...Powerful nationalism is also behind other
> smaller but successful states across Asia, from Malaysia to

Iran. Its enduring importance is shown by a negative: most of the deeply troubled, failing or failed states are those where nationalism has proved too weak to overcome the conflicting claims of religion, ethnicity or tribe.[2]

The American philosopher Richard Rorty has warned against the dangers of a world dominated by 'a cosmopolitan upper class' which has no 'sense of community with any workers anywhere' and argued that 'national pride is to countries what self-respect is to individuals: a necessary condition for self-improvement'.[3] Within the United Kingdom today, patriotism cuts across class, generation, ethnicity and religion. In Vron Ware's 2007 book, *Who Cares About Britishness*, she interviews several young Britons from BME backgrounds, and finds that for all of them, some sense of British identity is important, from a British passport to cups of tea, and in some cases her interviewees lament a 'lost' Britishness in a style reminiscent of Peter Hitchens.[4] Furthermore, according to a 2009 study, Muslims in Britain are the most patriotic in Europe, with an average of 78 per cent of UK Muslims identifying as British, compared with 49 per cent in France and just 23 per cent in Germany. The report also found that the strength of religious belief made no difference to how patriotic British Muslims feel.[5]

There is one notable exception to this. All too often it can be tempting for some on the Left to consider patriotism as a gauche anachronism at best and a form of proto-fascism at worst. One of the most prominent characteristics of the hobbyist Left is a deep discomfort with patriotism. That is not just to say they take issue with some of the more reactionary elements traditionally associated with 'British' patriotism – that would be entirely understandable and appropriate – but rather that the whole concept of 'patriotism' makes them squeamish, and they feel that radical patriotism is entirely unnecessary, if not a contradiction in terms. These sentiments – entirely out of step with the patriotism of the labour movement for most of its history – are so damaging not merely because they deny the need to subsume unpopular beliefs for electoral credibility, but because of their delusion that these beliefs are indeed electorally popular.

Some of the identity Left may pay lip-service to wanting to articulate an alternative patriotism built on the British radical patriotic tradition, from the Levellers through the Chartists and William Morris to the Second World War. Yet most of them have no interest in this. They feel any kind of patriotism is inherently reactionary and irredeemably *passé*, and view themselves as citizens of the world. This would be all well and good if their influence was restricted to university campuses, broadsheet columns and social media, but these world citizens have increasing influence within the Labour Party, and increasingly dominate the discourse surrounding what it means to be on the Left. Their positions in relation to patriotism might be practical if we lived in Plato's Republic of philosophers, rather than the exact opposite: the land of *The Sun* and the *Daily Mail*, and one of the most nationalistic and patriotic countries in the developed world. As it is, this strident anti-patriotism is strategically disastrous for a political movement in a modern democracy.

The argument of this chapter is two-fold. Firstly, the Left must reconcile itself to the fact that some of the more reactionary aspects associated with patriotism in the UK are broadly and deeply held. This is true not just for white van men, but also among women, black and Asian people, young people and British Muslims. Rightly or otherwise, the Left is associated with antimonarchism in a country that is overwhelmingly Monarchist, and with weaknesses on defence in a nation deeply fearful of security threats at home and abroad. While it is neither feasible nor desirable for Labour to outflank the Tories on this issue, it is essential to mitigate this debilitating weakness.

Secondly, and more positively, we need to outline an inclusive, radical patriotism. Figures as diverse as the former

Labour MP John Denham and the academic Paul Gilroy argue that, if there is to be any hope for left-wing patriotism, it must be one based on the four nations of England, Scotland, Wales and Northern Ireland. Gilroy criticises the approach that says 'you are either for or against the nation' but claims that 'British' identity is too firmly enmeshed with imperialism to be viable for the multicultural UK. He wants 'to be recognized as being both black and English in addition to everything else that I am... Somewhere between the local and the global there must be a place for [the] nation-state and indeed for the myths and dreams of national or ethnic collectivity.'[6]

Yet I believe that if Labour is to win power, and to return to its recently vacated position as the only political party with broad support in all the constituent nations of Britain, it must be able to articulate a *British* patriotism. Tariq Modood notes that one of the reasons Britain has been remarkably receptive and self-transformative in terms of recent migrants, without parallel in Western Europe, is 'the British imperial connection, felt by many migrants'. Furthermore, he argues that 'English' has so far been treated by the new Britons as a closed ethnicity rather than an open nationality. Hence, while many ethnic minorities have come to think of themselves as hyphenated Brits, they have only recently started to think of themselves as English.[7] I can say from personal experience that this is true of cities such as Liverpool, where many people can find a way to describe themselves as both 'Scouse' and 'British', but might find it difficult to see themselves as 'English'. Furthermore, as Afua Hirsch notes, people who consider themselves to be more English than British tended to vote for Brexit, whereas people who considered themselves 'British' voted to remain: 'It's further evidence that "British" as an identity is more capable of being inclusive than "Englishness", even for people who live in England.'[8]

A common theme of this book is that there is very little difference in cultural values across Britain; despite the fantasies of the hobbyists, there is no 'Celtic fringe solution' where people in Wales, Scotland and certain English cities such as Liverpool share their sentiments about patriotism, defence and security. Jon Lawrence reckons that the:

> Revolution in attitudes to selfhood and personal autonomy since the 1950s means that one cannot hope to resurrect a broad-based politics rooted in supposedly normative moral values, and that worse, the scope for constructing new mutualist alliances in civil society may be more limited than advocates of both the Blue Labour and One Nation projects allow. Yes, they will work in particular places, built around particular causes, and they can help restore a sense of Labour being a 'movement' rather than just an electoral machine, but one must have very grave doubts about the scope for turning such groupings into a coherent *national* movement.[9]

While I think he is right about the impossibility of creating a movement based around national values shared across the UK, there is no reason we cannot create a 'patchwork' identity which takes into account national, regional and civic differences. And I believe that the only framework for a radical patriotism that includes Scots, Welsh and Scousers and the descendants of Irish, Jamaican and Pakistani immigrants has to be based on Britain. But before we can talk more positively about the case for left-wing patriotism, we first need to turn to the dogs' dinner of the hobbyist Left attitude towards national identity.

The 2012 Olympics

The awkwardness of the Left's relationship with patriotism was perfectly encapsulated by left-wing commentary of the run up to the 2012 London Olympics. Even though it goes against the grain of public sentiment, the Left is not allowed to like the Olympic Games: they are based on the idea of national difference, which is inherently wrong; involves sport, with which many lefties have a hostile relationship; distracts from inequality; and consumes funds that could be much better spent elsewhere.

The professional activist Ellie May O'Hagan was one of the most pronounced and prominent misery-guts in the run up to the Olympics: 'For your average left-winger...grandiose patriotic events are usually characterised by post-imperial malaise, myth-peddling and latent racism.'[10] This presumptuous statement calls into question exactly what she means by 'average left-winger'. I very much doubt these are the sentiments of the average Labour voter or average trade unionist, but I suspect they tally well with the opinions of the average hobbyist.

For Seumus Milne, the particular bugbear was the extra security measures taken for the Games:

> The closer you get to the London stadium that will be the centre of the Olympic Games in just over a fortnight's time, the more it's starting to look like a militarised occupation zone. East London has become lockdown London. The Olympics are the focus of Britain's largest security mobilisation since the second world war...Of course, if the state hosting the Olympics is in the habit of invading and occupying other people's countries, the likelihood of terrorist attacks will increase.[11]

From the night of the opening ceremony onwards, as the public pivoted towards an optimistic, feel-good and simple patriotism, the Left was left with nothing to say, and grasping for words, unable to exploit the change in the public mood as they had no credibility. This was repeated 6 years later with the England football team's unexpected progress in the 2018 World Cup, which once again created an upsurge of patriotic sentiment (in England at least) that cut across political, class and racial divides, and confounded the transnationalism of the hobbyist Left.

The Monarchy

Aside from immigration, the British monarchy is the issue with the greatest dichotomy between the hobbyist Left and the people they aspire to speak for. Back in 2005, *Guardian* columnist Zoe Williams wrote of the young members of the Royal Family: 'They have been hailed as the great white hope, this generation... bringing with them a new informality and a new approachability, but it's those very qualities that make them even less viable than their forebears.'[12] It was wishful thinking at the time, and from the perspective of today it appears grossly myopic.

In a similar vein, Laurie Penny penned an article entitled 'The case for disrupting the royal wedding', expounding her trademark belief that real political change is achieved not through the ballot box but through students in V for Vendetta masks making arseholes of themselves:

> Over the next two and a half years, a full calendar of bread and circuses has been scheduled to keep the British public happy and obedient...This year, it's the Wedding of Mass Distraction; next year it's the Diamond Jubilee and after that the Olympics...While everyone gets worked up about a few kids harmlessly tampering with symbols of wartime sacrifice, the greatest war memorial of all – the welfare state – is being ripped to shreds.[13]

A few months later, and apparently without irony, Penny discussed 'The boho wankers of London' and claimed that 'a street party will be held in Shoreditch, in the heart of the capital's trendy art district, to celebrate all things British and bygone – like...the relevance of the house of Windsor'.[14] In May 2018 Ipsos MORI found that 75 per cent of Britons felt the monarchy was 'important to the future of the country' – the highest ever level recorded, which suggests that this prediction was a little naïve.

This deafness to the sentiments of the population is not

restricted to journalists: no sooner had Jeremy Corbyn ascended to the Labour leadership than his pronounced antimonarchism became a liability for the party. At his initiation into the Privy Council, coverage focused on whether or not the ardent republican would kneel before the Queen. This was not the first time in the history of the party that this issue had arisen: with the formation of the first Labour government in 1924, several ministers were loath to invest in the elaborate attire required for the ceremony, much less to pay obeisance to George V. Nevertheless, the party leadership, particularly inaugural Labour Prime Minister Ramsay MacDonald, felt it was essential to convince the general public of Labour's patriotism and compatibility with the constitution and traditions of the United Kingdom. Today, with support for the Royal Family at record levels, Labour would do well to emulate this aspect of the MacDonald ministry.

Labour cannot ignore the overwhelming support for the monarchy in the UK, especially among core Labour voters, and black and minority ethnic Britons.[15] The British national anthem is a tuneless dirge, and there are many convincing arguments for republicanism, yet Labour leaders need to put aside their personal beliefs for the greater good of party unity. Labour has struggled with an image of a lack of patriotism almost since its inception, despite this charge being patently inaccurate for most of its history. From the Zinoviev letter through Michael Foot's 'donkey jacket' to the attacks on Ralph Miliband during the 2015 election, patriotism is one of Labour's Achilles heels, and the first task of any Labour leader is to robustly assert their patriotic credentials. Yet, despite the issue being a clear liability for the party, the current leadership appears determined to stress the difference between itself and the public over the monarchy.

No sooner had the furore regarding the Privy Council initiation ceremony passed, then Corbyn was engulfed in a fresh attack concerning his lack of enthusiasm for the national anthem while at the Cenotaph. This criticism was as manifestly unfair as it was inaccurate: exactly how much gusto should one display at the Cenotaph? Yet the vindictiveness of the criticism, and the fact that Corbyn spent some time meeting ex-service personnel, mattered not a jot: it is the image, the perception, of Corbyn specifically and the Labour Party in general as lacking in patriotism that needs to be vigorously combated at all times.

The Armed Services

As with the more anodyne aspects of patriotism, most people in Britain find support for the armed services unproblematic. Yet this is another area in which the dominant media voices of the Left over the past decade, and now the leadership of the Labour Party itself, are at odds with popular sentiment. Seumus Milne made an explicit attack on the military in February 2014, claiming that they were not 'defending the population against any military threat, but endangering them by feeding terror and racism'.[16] A year later Owen Jones offered a more thoughtful and less voter-repellent take on this issue, when he claimed that as Corbyn 'comes under attack for being "weak on defence" he must take on the government for their betrayal of army personnel – and become the champion of soldiers in Westminster.'[17] Yet this would be impossible for the hobbyist Left, which finds the principle of patriotism absurd and believes that the UK armed forces should not be used under any circumstances.[18]

Back in June 2010, the *New Statesman*'s then political editor Mehdi Hasan tore into a speech by newly-elected Prime Minister David Cameron which had praised the military:

> Put aside the ahistorical (and neoconservative) nonsense about soldiers bringing the 'right to vote' and protecting 'free speech'...and focus instead on the jingoistic and martial final sentence: 'So I want you to help me create a new atmosphere... where we back and revere and support our military.'... Revere? When did the UK become Sparta?...If Cameron (and

Brown before him) really cared about the lives of our military personnel, he would withdraw them from Afghanistan, where they are engaged in a dishonest, counterproductive, immoral and unwinnable war.[19]

It takes a remarkable amount of *chutzpah* for Hasan to talk of historical nonsense, and I deeply resent that he has forced me to side with the likes of Niall Ferguson, but nonetheless it is incontrovertibly true that the First World War brought votes for all men over 21 and most women over 30. It would have been unacceptable for some of the returning troops to be unable to vote; the franchise had to be reformed, and this impetus for reform allowed the pressure for votes for women that had been building for decades to finally tell. It is entirely misleading to think that women's efforts on the home front 'earned' them the right to vote in 1918: most women workers were under 30, and thus excluded from the new franchise.

Like the proverbial stopped clock, Hasan is right that the UK, traditionally, did not revere its armed forces. Reliant on the Navy for foodstuffs, protection and global dominance, the army was held in particularly low esteem, and working-class lads who enlisted prior to 1914 were sometimes disowned by their families. Yet this all changed with the First World War, and today the military clearly holds a play of high esteem in the British consciousness.

There is a quotation – often attributed to George Orwell but in fact coined by the *Washington Post* columnist Richard Grenier channelling Orwell – that those of us on the Left would do well to remember: 'We sleep soundly in our beds because rough men stand ready in the night to visit violence on those who would do us harm.' The point here is that all the hobbyist Left holds dear – the NHS, university education, social media, free speech, a multicultural society, hipster bars in East London, etc, etc – are only made possible because of hard lads from left-behind towns – people who usually didn't have the opportunities most of the hobbyist Left manifestly has had – led largely by honking ' hoorays from the public schools.

It was Clement Attlee and Ernest Bevin who supported the establishment of Nato, and the same people who decided that Britain should acquire nuclear arms in the first place. Furthermore, the Attlee/Bevin partnership set up the Information Research Department, set up to counter Soviet propaganda and infiltration in Britain and the West, particularly among the labour movement. Anyone in doubt of the centrality of patriotism to Attlee's socialism should read his speech introducing the Labour manifesto before the 1951 General Election:

> Peace does not come about through wishful thinking. Peace is not just a negative absence of war; peace means that you get rid as far as you can of the causes of war...when the challenge came in Korea we unhesitatingly went in with other members of the United Nations Organisation representing the democratic forces of the world. We realised that Korea was a test case, we realised that armed aggression had arisen once more in the world and we accepted the logic of the situation, as a matter of responsibility, first of all to our own people and secondly to the whole of the free world...It is common practice of our opponents to try and run down Britain in the eyes of the world and to say that we have lost our influence. It is quite untrue. We hold a unique place. From our geographical position we are a vital link between Europe and the New World. From our position as a leading member of the Commonwealth we bring together nations in all the continents and in particular we unite in one great association the nations of Asia as well as of Europe...Our opponents...regard the economic process primarily as the giving an opportunity to the individual to advance his own interests; community interests, national interests, are regarded as a hypothetical by-product. Their

motto is: 'The world is my oyster; each one for himself.'

As Jon Lawrence writes, 'in 1945 Labour built on radically populist wartime propaganda about a "people's war" to construct a political appeal which was explicitly inclusive and national...They spoke of the eradication of poverty as a patriotic duty.' As late as 1962, Labour leader Hugh Gaitskell opposed British membership of the European Community on the grounds that it would mark the 'end of a thousand years of history'.[20]

Thus the hobbyist Left, with its strident and knee-jerk anti-patriotism, and its deep unease with the British military, is an aberration. Their views are entirely out of step not just with the mass of the British people today – including working-class and ethnic minority Britons – they are out of step with the history of the British Left. Their positions are borne of an ironic contempt for both; safe in their privileged positions, with their hobbyist commitment to politics, they can indulge in their childish anti-patriotism.

The Left and the First World War

Writing in the *New Statesman* in November 2010, Laurie Penny described 'a country that seems to have fundamentally misunderstood the nature of remembrance'. Four years later she claimed: 'This summer marks the centenary of a war that triumphalist historians insist on calling "great".' This is wilful ignorance of the highest degree. You do not need to know anything about the First World War to understand that it is not called 'Great' through some form of triumphalism or aggrandisement any more than are 'Great' Britain or 'Greater' Manchester.[21] She continued 'On the centenary of the First World War, we must remember that millions who died had little idea what they were signing up for – nor how their deaths would be treated 100 years later, in patriotic ceremonies replete with expensive light shows and ceremonial flower-planting, while the international arms trade remains healthy.'

Penny knows as much about the First World War as I know about being a steampunk or a riot grrrl or whatever niche subculture she believes is so important to left-wing politics. Many millions of men *did* fight and died for a belief in their 'country', however bizarre and outré that might seem to her. They did not fight and die to establish everlasting peace any more than the servicemen and women of 1939–1945 fought to combat antisemitism or establish the welfare state.[22]

Meanwhile Seumus Milne moaned: 'It's not just that 40% of men and all women in Britain were denied the vote in 1914 – unlike Germany, which already had full male suffrage – or that the British empire was allied with the brutal autocracy of tsarist Russia.' He continued: 'Celebrate instead the internationalists, socialists and poets who called it right, and remember the suffering of the soldiers – rather than the cowards who sent them to die. Attempts to hijack the commemorations must be contested every step of the way.'[23] This is ahistorical myth-making of the first degree. While it is true to say that Germany had full (male) suffrage, a robust trade union movement many millions strong, and the Social Democratic Party as the largest in the Reichstag, this was all for nought, as the Kaiser picked and dismissed the government at will. In Britain, while all women and many men were disenfranchised, there is no convincing evidence that this harmed the electoral chances of the Left: the primary qualification for the Parliamentary franchise was as a 'householder' – that is someone who was the head of a family. As working-class men tended to leave home, marry and set up families earlier, and as middle-class men were disproportionately likely to be lodgers, this did not *necessarily* undermine the working-class vote.[24]

Robert Blatchford – rightly regarded by labour historians from the Trotskyist Left to the revisionist Right as the most effective proselytiser for socialism in Edwardian England – was convinced that the Left struggled not from institutional disadvantages, but due to the paucity of its message. Specifically, that the Left was seen as unpatriotic, and that some of the most high-profile advocates of socialism were highly-privileged scions of wealth obsessed with niche, abstract issues and entirely divorced from working-class sentiment. *Plus ça change*, eh?

The point Milne makes about Tsarist Russia is entirely valid. In 1914, many socialists admired the Second Reich, due to its statist and corporatist elements as well as the robust labour movement described above. Most socialists despised the Russian regime, regarding it as the most backward and repressive in Europe. Yet this admiration of Germany and hatred of Russia was attacked as hypocritical by those on the Left who supported British involvement in the war, in much the same way as Seumus' views are today. If the war was against Russia, rather than Germany, they averred, there would be no complaint: the anti-war Left were not against war *per se*; they were against this particular war. Similarly, if one can imagine that the 2003 war did not target Saddam Hussein's Iraq, but instead aimed to, say, remove the illegal settlements in the West Bank and forcibly return Israel to its 1967 borders, exactly how many of the same people would have taken to the streets of London in protest? One suspects many would not have been able to march, as they would have been queuing up to enlist.

After the outbreak of the First World War, at a special conference convened to discuss the crisis, a delegate from the London Trades Council argued that if the Left failed to offer support, the British people would say the labour movement 'was against the country'.[25] Future Labour leader Clement Attlee agonised over the war for some days, but finally concluded: 'I attended sundry...conferences where *the self-righteous pacifism* of some of the members rather strengthened my intentions already half formed of joining. I think that I was finally persuaded by the wanton invasion of Belgium and by the German actions therein.'[26] If a Haileybury and Oxford-educated socialist such as Attlee found the exhortations of the peace camp to be self-righteous, then how much harder it must have been for working-class men and women – whether on the Left or Right – to be impressed by the language and manner of middle-class radicals, even if they agreed with the substance of their arguments.

An indication of the extent to which the British working class – and the working-class Left – quickly became staunchly patriotic and anti-German during the First World War is the vilification of supposed pacifists. While their words may have fallen on sympathetic ears in the days leading up to the war, as soon as Britain entered the conflict their viewpoints became treasonable and intolerable. Keir Hardie was 'howled down' at Aberdare on 6 August 1914, and this was in his own constituency of Merthyr Tydfil, emphatically not a working-class Tory stronghold.[27] Further, on 20 October 1914, miners at Lewis Merthyr Lodge walked out and stayed out until Mr Sholback – a German electrician – was dismissed.[28] Up and down the country, trade unionists held strikes against the employment of conscientious objectors.[29]

Left-wing hobbyists are keen to highlight that certain towns and cities formed hotbeds of resistance of conscription and anti-war agitation, but this has been widely overstated. For example, of the 461 young men in the Bradford Independent Labour Party (the ILP was itself considered to be notably pacifistic), by February 1916, 113 were in the trenches, 118 were in training in England, six were in the Navy and 207 had attested their willingness to serve. By 1918 of 442 members eligible for service, 351 were serving while merely 48 were conscientious objectors or doing national war work. This is to say that in one of the most anti-war towns in England, among the members of the most radical political organisation, only 48 men claimed conscientious objection.[30] Similarly, in his discussion of Welsh soldiers in the First World War, Gervase Phillips noted that 272,924 men – or 21.52 per cent of the population – enlisted into the services, and that 145,205 of those – that is to say, over 50 per cent – were volunteers.[31]

At the 1918 General Election, Labour was very careful to select appropriate candidates for each constituency. Along with W.F. Toynbee, prospective Parliamentary candidate for Chelmsford, and J.E. Kneeshaw, former agent in Rushcliffe, Captain Edward Gill, M.C., made up a three-man propaganda team for the 1922 election, and visited over 70 constituencies between them – significantly, Captain Gill was appointed chiefly to the southern and south-western counties.[32] In contrast to the southern English seats contested mainly by former officers, in Scotland, although South Ayrshire was won by the staunchly pro-war James Brown, none of the Labour candidates had a military prefix.[33]

The same was true in 1945. In East Ham, Labour candidate Percy Daines made his patriotism clear in his election material:

> You have before you a man of the PEOPLE; a tough Londoner; a Trade Unionist; Co-operative Committee-man; ex-Councillor; ex-Royal Engineer (this war). A vigorous, forthright Britisher, with an International outlook; a Family Man, son in the Royal Navy. Advocate at Party Conferences of the Soldiers' Charter. *Daines* knows the value of every shilling to a worker's home. DAINES IS ONE OF US.[34]

Incidentally, the anti-war pacifists of 1914–1918 were far from unimpeachable. This was particularly the case with E.D. Morel. Morel, who had previously campaigned against Belgium atrocities in Congo, set up the Union for Democratic Control, to agitate for an end to the First World War, and to prevent a similar catastrophe from occurring in the future. In 1920 he published a pamphlet, 'The Horror on the Rhine', criticising the use of West African troops in the French forces occupying Germany. Morel claimed that France was 'thrusting her black savages...into the heart of Germany' creating 'a terror and horror unimaginable' for 'the barely restrainable bestiality of the black troops'. He continued: 'For well-known physiological reasons, the raping of a white woman by a Negro is nearly always accompanied by serious injury and not infrequently has fatal results', before concluding that 'the militarised African, who has shot and bayoneted white men in Europe, who has had sexual intercourse with white women in Europe' now realises that the white man is 'rather a poor type'.[35]

Parts of the pamphlet were serialised in the Labour newspaper the *Daily Herald,* with the front page headline: 'Black Scourge in Europe: Sexual Horror let loose by France on the Rhine'. Labour leader George Lansbury – one of the few real pacifists and anti-racists on the British Left at the time, and the closest leader Labour has had to Jeremy Corbyn – referring to the 'children of the forests', told the paper: 'We are not amongst those who consider that because a man's skin is black, he should be considered as an inferior human being, but nature has given us all qualities of temperament suitable to the conditions and climate in which we are born.'[36]

This outpouring of racist bile, in many ways uncharacteristic of Morel and Lansbury, is important because it demonstrates how an obsessive fixation on one issue – in this case the inequity of the First World War and the allied occupation of Germany – can lead people to serious lapses of moral judgement. Today, for many on the hobbyist Left, their opposition to the Iraq war, their overriding anti-Americanism and their all-consuming hatred of Israel, can all lead them to support highly dubious regimes and organisations.

The Spanish Civil War

During the 1920s, in step with wider British trends, the Left reacted against the carnage and waste of 1914-1918, and adopted an internationalist, pacifistic stance. Yet the Spanish Civil War, despite its hallowed place in the mythology of the hobbyists, did not result in a great surge of working-class internationalism. Darren Treadwell, archivist at the Labour Party Archive and Study Centre, recalls Jack Jones, legendary leader of the Transport and General Workers Union and veteran of the civil war, reminiscing about the period. According to Jones, despite the image of vast enthusiastic crowds of working-class leftists queuing up to enlist, the event was something of a damp squib that failed to provoke much passion from ordinary workers.[37]

The historian Selina Todd notes that only around 2300 volunteers left Britain for Spain. She quotes one, Gary McCartney from Scotland, who stressed: 'We didn't go to Spain to usher in Communism or anything like that.'[38] Many of the volunteers for the International Brigade, such as Sid Quinn and Sam Wild, had been in the regular army or navy; some, as with George Nathan, had been officers. They had not joined the British military with subversive intentions – although often they were radicalised through their experiences there – but rather for more prosaic reasons of boredom or economic necessity. In this respect, they are entirely different from those who use their name and their sacrifice for their own ends; with the notable exception of the Norwich MP Clive Lewis, it is easier to imagine the end of the world than a member of the hobbyist Left being proud of their service in the British military.

In addition, despite being ostensible Communists who had volunteered to protect a foreign republic, the working-class British men who served in Spain did not have the values of today's left-wing hobbyists, and indeed many would be repelled by some of their views. A great deal of their free time was spent in brothels, and they were all disfigured by the racism of the era, particularly with regards to Chinese labourers and the North African troops used by Franco.[39] Mostly they were not doctrinaire Communists – some were just there because they liked a fight – and nearly all despised the lecturers and meetings forced on them by their superiors; at one open-air meeting on

Marxist theory, 16 men were killed by fascist snipers. They were also no different from men in the first and second world wars in taking inspiration from the gallant and eccentric behaviour of their public school officers; one volunteer recalls Clifford Wattis (brother of a famous actor) cheerfully shaving under an artillery bombardment, which 'cheered us all up'.[40]

From the Falklands to Iraq and Afghanistan

The previous pages have shown how the discomfort of much of the Left with patriotism is a fairly recent phenomenon. One of the chief causes of this distaste is the Falklands War – or more specifically the successful manipulation of that war for political advantage by Margaret Thatcher. Writing of the Falklands in *The Guardian*, Seumus Milne claims that 'British governments only developed a taste for self-determination after they had been forced to abandon the bulk of their empire and saw a way to hold on to colonised enclaves of dependent populations in places like Gibraltar and Northern Ireland.'

This is somewhat disingenuous. Britain 'developed a taste for self-determination' at the same time as it willingly decolonised, and while there may have been a desire to keep hold of strategically important enclaves such as Gibraltar, a united Ireland is prevented largely by the desire of well over half the population of the North to remain within the UK. The Falklands may well have been transferred peaceably to Argentina had not a fascist junta invaded the islands in a bid to maintain itself in power. The real question is why exactly Milne cares so much about the status of these small islands in the South Atlantic; a preoccupation with the sovereignty of the Falklands may well be acceptable for a hard-Left broadsheet columnist, but is yet another ingredient in a politically toxic brew for the leadership of the UK's largest working-class party.[41]

The 2003 Iraq War casts its grim shadow over all discussions of left-wing foreign and security policy; the relationship with the military; and patriotism in general. For many left-wing hobbyists, Iraq is the most totemic security and foreign policy topic, towering over all else, and impacting on their politics more than any other single issue, with the possible exception of the Israel/Palestine conflict.

You do not have to be a crank to believe that Iraq was a monstrous failure that unleashed catastrophe on the region and the wider world. Indeed, it is to the discredit of considered and sensible voices such as David Aaronovitch, Nick Cohen and the late Christopher Hitchens that they cannot couple entirely valid criticism of Saddam Hussein with an acknowledgement of the disaster the invasion became. My intention here is not to praise Iraq but rather to bury it as an issue: for the hobbyist Left Iraq represents not just a foreign policy blunder of the highest magnitude – in this they are surely correct – but rather an epoch-defining blow to the Labour Party. The protracted and seemingly inevitable build-up, the protests surrounding the decision to go to war, and the prolonged horror of its aftermath have all distorted the Left's ability to talk about patriotism. There is also the sense that the war had an impact in disillusioning many people, particularly young voters, from the political process.

In reality, it is mainly hobbyists that still care about Iraq. Most British people – and this includes British Muslims – no longer have their views of Labour tainted by the invasion, and this is true across the UK. Research into the Scottish National Party surge in 2011 has revealed that 'not only was the economy far more salient in 2011 than it had been in 2007 but it gained importance at the expense of all other issues. Some of these, like the environment and Britain's military action in Iraq and Afghanistan, slipped almost completely off the electorate's agenda.'[42] Instead, it is weaknesses on the economy, immigration and security that turn people off Labour. Yet to say this is high heresy for the hobbyists.

Laurie Penny in particular is obsessed with the idea of Iraq symbolising the triumph of a sectional interest over the will of the majority. She describes the invasion proceeding despite a million people marching against it as 'democracy rudely circumvented', despite the fact that it was authorised by a House of Commons elected by tens of millions of Britons, and initiated by a government re-elected with a handsome majority 2 years later. Preposterously, she also claims that for:

> The generation in the west who were children then and are adults now...the sense of betrayal was life-changing. We had thought that millions of people making their voices heard would be enough and we were wrong. What changed in 2003 was that millions of ordinary citizens around the world finally understood that the game was rigged, because only a few weeks after that march the US and its allies went to war anyway. The people had withdrawn their consent, loudly and peacefully and in numbers too big to ignore, and they had been rebuffed with hardly a second thought. Representative democracy had failed to represent...I have no doubt that, a decade from now, people in their mid-twenties will speak of the student riots of 2010–2011 with the same sad sense of lessons learned. At Millbank, when 4,000 students and schoolchildren smashed up the entrance to the Conservative Party headquarters and held an impromptu rave in the lobby, several young people mentioned the Stop the War march of 2003, how all that passive, peaceful shuffling from one rally point to another had failed to achieve anything concrete.[43]

Yet research conducted before and after the conflict demonstrated absolutely no impact on trust in the UK political system, nor on the incidence of voting.[44]

Similarly, Mehdi Hasan argues that 'it is difficult to think of an issue that better illustrates the long-lamented gap between the public and the political class'. Given that this was written back in

2010, one might have thought he was talking about immigration or the neoliberal economic consensus. Yet, incredibly, he was talking about the war in Afghanistan.[45] For this school of thought, what agitates the public most of all is not immigration or the economy or the NHS, but rather small-scale wars against distant Muslim states. Yet an investigation by Professor Anthony Heath revealed that as far as the war in Afghanistan is concerned, 64 per cent of white British respondents and 56 per cent of ethnic minorities favoured the pro-war side of the argument.[46]

Around the same time, the Marxist Richard Seymour expressed his bemusement at public indifference to the invasion of Libya and mooted action over Syria: 'The war on Libya produced a strange effect in British politics. The majority of the public opposed the war, but very little of this opposition was expressed on the streets. Nor is the possibility of intervention in Syria producing sizeable protests as yet.' He simply could not understand why the British people were not taking to the streets at this latest imperial escapade. This highlights the discrepancy between the theories of the hobbyist Left and the actual beliefs of ordinary Britons: for left-wing hobbyists, the rest of the country – and indeed the world – harbours the same beliefs as they do; they are merely confused by the tabloids and consumerism.[47]

'They Can't See Why They Are Hated'

In his 2007 polemic *What's Left*, Nick Cohen argues that the fall of the USSR left the traditional hard-Left without a purpose. However, the outlook:

Wasn't all bleak. Revolutionary socialists could be cheered by the sight of millions of people who hated the United States and 'capitalist' democracy, as they did; who hated globalization, Hollywood and consumerism, as they did. More to the point, among the millions were tens of thousands who – when you got down to the basics – wanted to kill Americans. All the revolutionary socialists had to do was forget about the beliefs of these millions in the literal truth of an early medieval holy book, their elevation of their god over free men and women, their hatred of intellectual freedom, their homophobia, their antisemitism, their supernatural conspiracy theories, their misogyny, their use of state oppression in Taliban Afghanistan, the Sudan and Iran, and their condemnations of godless communism...and they might even be comrades.[48]

Writing in *The Independent* in the aftermath of the Charlie Hebdo attacks, the journalist Robert Fisk claimed that 'long before the identity of the murder suspects was revealed by the French police – even before I heard the names of Cherif and Said Kouachi – I muttered the word "Algeria" to myself.'[49] This sentence perfectly encapsulates the problem with much of the Left: who, upon hearing of a terrorist attack, strokes their chin and thinks 'Ah! Here's years of Western policy coming back to bite them in the arse'?

The argument in this section is that what Shulamit Volkov called the 'cultural code' of antizionism, anti-Americanism and anti-colonialism has spilled over into apparent support for terrorism.[50] These marginal positions, of dubious morality and definite electoral liability, used to be the preserve of broadsheet journalists, but are now enthroned at the apex of the Labour Party. With the naming of the new-look Labour shadow cabinet in the autumn of 2015, an immediate controversy arose over the appointment of veteran left-winger John McDonnell as Shadow Chancellor of the Exchequer. Years earlier, as an outspoken backbencher, McDonnell had spoken in support of the IRA and joked about going back in time to assassinate Margaret Thatcher.

There are compelling reasons to honour the dead of all conflicts, but McDonnell's historical positioning on such matters suggests his gut instincts are deeply out of touch with voters. Similarly, Corbyn's assertion that he would hesitate before authorising police to 'shoot-to-kill' suspected terrorists reveals a naivety in security policy, a deafness to public concerns, a conscientiousness eminently better suited to the backbenches.[51] Two months after his election Corbyn cancelled a planned speech on foreign policy, but released extracts that blamed terrorism on 'a succession of disastrous wars' in the Middle East that had 'increased, not diminished, the threats to our own national security'. He criticised the media for focusing on the Paris atrocity while giving 'hardly any publicity' at all to Isis attacks in Lebanon and Turkey.[52]

Back in 1986, Corbyn was arrested after participating in a protest by IRA sympathisers to demonstrate solidarity with those accused of organising the Brighton bombing, in which five people attending the 1984 Conservative Party Conference were killed. Corbyn had joined a picket outside the Old Bailey to oppose the trial of several people, including Patrick Magee, who was eventually convicted of murder. *Labour Briefing*, the hard-left magazine, had praised the bombing. At the time it released a statement written by the editorial board – of which Corbyn was a member – which read: 'It certainly appears to be the case that the British only sit up and take notice when they are bombed into it.'

Between 1986 and 1992, Corbyn spoke at various republican commemorations to honour dead IRA terrorists, while John McDonnell received a special award from the republican movement for his 'unfailing political and personal support' – it was personally presented to him by Gerry Kelly, who was convicted of bombing the Old Bailey. There is a real possibility that, many decades hence, the IRA's terror campaign will be seen as legitimate, in much the same way as the actions of the military wing of the ANC is today. But this is a purely theoretical point that cannot excuse the actions of elected representatives of the British Parliament. Besides which, what about the peaceful, constitutional efforts of the SDLP, Labour's sister party in the

North, to secure peace? Corbyn and McDonnell were far less interested in that than they were the balaclavas and berets of the IRA. We expect this of student Trots, but not leaders and statesmen.

In addition, there seems to be a racial double standard at play. Imagine if Muslim politicians had this history of supporting Islamic terrorist organisations? Despite their monstering by the right-wing tabloids, it seems Corbyn and McDonnell get away with this in the public eye, both due to the fading memories of the Troubles, their appearance as genial old men, and the whiteness of their skin.

Of all the hobbyist Left, no one is as prominent in their justification of terrorism as the chief strategist and communications director of the Labour Party, Seumus Milne. Some of Milne's most shameful outbursts have come in the immediate aftermath of terrorist attacks in the United States and Europe. The deadliest attack, which served as a curtain opener for this whole bloody and disastrous period, came against the United States on 11 September 2001. Nearly three thousand people from dozens of nations died on that day. After Americans, British nationals constituted the second largest group of victims, with 66 deaths (more fatalities than the London bombings 4 years later), followed by Dominicans and then Indian citizens.

The dead included three toddlers, five adolescents and at least 11 unborn babies. Within 2 days of the attack, Milne released an article titled: 'They can't see why they are hated'. In it he crowed that 'it has become painfully clear that most Americans simply don't get it', arguing the victims lacked 'any glimmer of recognition of why people might have been driven to carry out such atrocities, *sacrificing their own lives in the process* – or why the United States is hated with such bitterness, not only in Arab and Muslim countries, but across the developing world'.[53]

If we can set aside the victim blaming, the motif of anti-Americanism across the developing world – beloved by the hobbyist Left – needs to be qualified. While there may indeed be pockets of political resistance to the US government, there is often an exaggerated reverence for American culture and the idea of America more generally, especially in countries ostensibly at odds with the USA. I visited Venezuela in 2008 at the height of *Chavismo*, and while there was no doubting the dislike of George W. Bush, they were obsessed with American cars, clothes and food; whole families would tune in religiously to watch *Two and a Half Men*, and the plethora of young kids playing baseball in the streets dreamed of following the many Cubans and Venezuelans who had made it in the National Baseball League.

A few months after 9/11 Milne was optimistically wondering: 'Can the US be defeated?'. In a column which discussed Iraq, Iran and North Korea, he noted that 'there is barely even a pretence that any of these three states was in some way connected with the attacks on the World Trade Center. What they do have in common, of course, is that they have all long opposed American power in their regions.' According to this logic, what connects Iraq, Iran and North Korea is not their human rights abuses, widespread use of torture, threats against their neighbours and domination by psychopaths, but rather their principled stand against US hegemony. He also had a warning to the US: 'This is an international order which, as the September 11 attacks demonstrated, will not be tolerated and will generate conflict.'[54] My intention here is not to question the morality of this line of reasoning, but merely to question the probity of having a man with such views as the strategic adviser and communications director of the UK's largest working-class party.

In response to atrocities in Fallujah in 2008, Milne wrote, with apparently no sense of irony: 'To blame the victims for this killing spree defies both morality and sense,' despite his long and established history of blaming victims.[55] Immediately after the terror attacks on London in July 2005, he claimed it was 'an insult to the dead to mislead people about the crucial factors fuelling this deadly rage in Muslim communities across the world'. (An unsympathetic commentator might claim that it is more of an insult to use the murder of 52 people to support your world view). He continued:

> The first piece of disinformation long peddled by champions of the occupations of Iraq and Afghanistan is that al-Qaida and its supporters have no demands that could possibly be met or negotiated over; that they are really motivated by a hatred of western freedoms and way of life; and that their Islamist ideology aims at global domination...The central goal of the al-Qaida-inspired campaign...is the withdrawal of US and other western forces from the Arab and Muslim world, an end to support for Israeli occupation of Palestinian land and a halt to support for oil-lubricated despots throughout the region...Blair has argued that, since the 9/11 attacks predated the Iraq war, outrage at the aggression could not have been the trigger. It's perfectly true that Muslim anger over Palestine, western-backed dictatorships and the aftermath of the 1991 war against Iraq – US troops in Arabia and a murderous sanctions regime against Iraq – was already intense before 2001 and fuelled al-Qaida's campaign in the 1990s.

Content that his predictions had come true, he continued: 'Afghanistan made a terror attack on Britain a likelihood; Iraq made it a certainty,' and threatened that 'the security crackdowns and campaign to uproot an "evil ideology" the government announced yesterday will not extinguish the threat. Only a British commitment to end its role in the bloody occupations of Iraq and Afghanistan is likely to do that.'[56]

So many of the headlines of Seumus Milne – admittedly written by a sub-editor, but accurately conveying the gist of the article – carry a sense of menace. 'There must be a reckoning for this day of infamy', he wrote in 2008, warning that for 'the aggressor states, both at home and abroad, [the impact] has only begun to be felt'. Two years later, he warned again: 'Terror is the price of support for despots and dictators'.[57] He was at it again barely a week after the murder of Lee Rigby: 'Those who send British troops to shed blood in the Muslim world must share the blame for atrocities like Woolwich', ran the headline. (Presumably those who encourage anti-Western violence must share the blame for attacks on civilians in Iraq, Afghanistan and Yemen?)

In the article he blamed British foreign policy and domestic Islamophobia for the murder, noting that 'nearly two-thirds of the population...think there will be a "clash of civilisations" between white Britons and Muslims, up 9 per cent since the Woolwich atrocity' – as if Islamophobia existed in a vacuum and had nothing to do with said atrocities. At the end of that year he wrote:

> Rigby was a British soldier who had taken part in multiple combat operations in Afghanistan. So the attack wasn't terrorism in the normal sense of an indiscriminate attack on civilians...The killing of an unarmed man far from the conflict, however, by self-appointed individuals with non-violent political alternatives, isn't condoned by any significant political or religious tradition... 'Leave our lands and you can live in peace,' the London-born Muslim convert told bystanders. The message couldn't be clearer. It was the same delivered by the 2005 London bomber, Mohammed Siddique Khan, and the Iraqi 2007 Glasgow attacker, Bilal Abdullah, who declared: 'I wanted the public to have a taste' of what its government of 'murderers did to my people'.[58]

He continued in a similar vein after the massacres in France, even though France did not participate in the invasion of Iraq, claiming: 'Paris is a warning: there is no insulation from our wars.' The implication is clear: we have been warned; ignore the warnings of the soldiers of Allah (or comrade Seumus) at our peril.

According to this school of thought, the attacks in France were 'blowback' from Western intervention in the Arab and Muslim world: 'Without the war waged by western powers, including France, to bring to heel and reoccupy the Arab and Muslim world, last week's attacks clearly wouldn't have taken place.' Finally, a trademark warning, should we in 'the West' dare to intervene military in 'the Arab world' again, was proffered: 'What happens there happens here too.'[59] Yet despite his certainty of future attacks on the UK, Seumus is reluctant to fund possible counter-measures against this attack: 'Theresa May says Britain is facing the greatest terrorism threat in its history, and that the security services have foiled 40 plots since 2005. Who would know? Even ministers are in no position to judge the claims securocrats make about themselves. For the intelligence agencies the terror threat is good for business – as Cameron made clear this week when he announced another £130m for their already swollen budgets.'[60] After the terrorist attacks on London and Manchester in 2017, the response of Jeremy Corbyn and Diane Abbott was both morally appropriate and politically astute: by focusing on the devastating impact of police cuts – under Theresa May's tenure as both Home Secretary and Prime Minister – they were able to outflank May on security in the run up to the 2017 election. But imagine if Milne had still been a *Guardian* columnist at that time, able to write whatever he felt? What exactly would he have written as those kids lay dead and dying in Manchester?

Perhaps the most shameful episode of hard-Left foreign policy, which demonstrates the hobbyists' concern for doctrinaire anti-Americanism at the expense of saving lives, came with the Bosnian genocide. During this episode, thousands of Bosnian Muslims were massacred by Serb forces, led by General Radko

Mladic. Three years later, as the British Parliament voted on military action against Serbia, the hobbyist wing of the PLP was steadfast in its opposition, despite the belief from traditional allies in Labour that intervention was justified in this instance. During the crucial vote on the issue, Clare Short – who years later would resign from Tony Blair's Cabinet over the Iraq war – shouted at the group, calling them 'a disgrace to the Labour Party'. On the radio the following day, she drew comparisons between the dissidents and 'those who appeased Hitler'.[61] For Short, ultimately, this righteous interventionism superseded anti-Americanism. For the hobbyists, then and now, nothing does. Even on the day that Mladic was found guilty of genocide, cranks on Twitter were denying that this genocide ever happened: Jason Dunn tweeted that 'Srebrenica was overexaggerated to justify intervention. Corbyn was on the right side of history opposing NATO bombing of Serbia.' Why do these people deny the genocide of thousands of Muslims? Only a consistent mistrust of Britain and America could lead people to such a position.

Russia and Iran

In a hopeful 2002 article entitled: 'Can the US be defeated?', Putin's man in north London lamented that technological advances 'would only increase further what became an overwhelming military advantage a decade ago with the collapse of the Soviet Union'.[62]

Five years later, fellow *Guardian* columnist George Monbiot attacked Gordon Brown's government for allowing parts of a US missile defence system to be located in the UK:

> If, as [then Defence Secretary Des] Browne and Bush maintain, the system is meant to shoot down intercontinental missiles fired by Iran and North Korea (missiles, incidentally, that they do not and might never possess), why are its major components being installed in Poland and the Czech Republic? To bait the

Russian bear for fun? In June, Vladimir Putin called Bush's bluff by offering sites for the missile defence programme in Azerbaijan and southern Russia, which are much closer to Iran. Bush turned him down and restated his decision to build the facilities in eastern Europe, making it clear that their real purpose is to shoot down Russian missiles.[63]

In January 2016 Owen Jones conceded: 'When challenged on the alleged role of Moscow in the murder of journalists, Trump engaged in what is typically known as "whataboutery" (or the "look over there!" approach to debate), responding: "Our country does plenty of killing also."'[64] Yet Milne was having none of this: 'It's not necessary to have any sympathy for Putin's oligarchic authoritarianism to recognise that Nato and the EU, not Russia, sparked this crisis [over Ukraine] – and that it's the western powers that are resisting the negotiated settlement that is the only way out, for fear of appearing weak.'[65]

The hobbyists' advocacy for unpleasant regimes does not stop with Russia. In 2006, Iranian human rights activists asked the Stop the War Coalition demonstration not to march alongside the representatives of the state of Iran. They then manhandled and abused the Iranian activist Reza Moradi, denounced as a 'stooge of America' by a steward. In 2009, Mehdi Hasan wrote that 'Journalistic hypocrisy and cant aside, it is difficult to understand the basic philosophical objection to appearing on Press TV. Is it because the channel is state-funded?...Is it perhaps because of the particular state involved?'[66]

Writing in *The Guardian* 2 years later, Hasan reported:

It isn't just Iran's leaders who are unwilling to back down on the nuclear issue. On Tuesday, around 1,000 Iranian students formed a human chain around the uranium conversion facility in Isfahan, chanting "Death to America" and "Death to Israel". *Their protest may have been organised by the authorities* but even the leaders and members of the opposition Green Movement tend to support Iran's uranium enrichment programme. According to a 2010 University of Maryland survey, 55 per cent of Iranians back their country's pursuit of nuclear power and, remarkably, 38 per cent support the building of a nuclear bomb.

Your eyes did not deceive you – here we have a high-profile columnist and doyenne of the British left (then political editor of the *New Statesman* no less) appearing to regret that students chanting death to Israel may not have been a spontaneous demonstration.[67] If there is to be any progress made in advancing left-wing politics in the UK; if there is to be any hope of a Labour government coming to power, there must be a firewall built between these views and mainstream Labour discourse.

In January 2018, the reactionary theocrats who run Iran faced their most serious popular challenge in years. According to the journalist Oz Katerji, Iranian rebels marched through the Holy City of Qom chanting 'death of Hezbollah'. Yet *The Guardian* ran a column by Simon Tisdall, insisting that the uprising was not challenging the stifling rule of the mullahs, but rather was a reaction to a stalling economy and lack of jobs.[68] During the uprising one Iranian dissident wrote on Twitter of the Western Left:

[They] put the US against poor workers and unemployed who are fighting [the Iranian] armed forces with their hearts in the palm of their hand don't want them to win. It's simple...[w]hen they win, they will not carry hate for the US to the next page of life...They say it's against US domination. No it's against Islamic Regime of Iran. That's a good excuse to once again betray the revolution of those who stand up to the rule of inhumanity and want to be free.

He concluded that Western 'so called' anti-imperialists 'have lived their lives thinking that the US is the enemy, just like Khamenei puts it, the brutal dictator who knows his allies, the so called left that doesn't see love in revolution and formulates everything in their own image: hate'.

Now, let's not be naïve. The US has a long and inglorious history of soft and not so soft imperialism, attempting to topple or undermine governments – democratic or otherwise – around the world. The US State Department, military and intelligence services all have bucket loads of blood on their hands. But to see everything through the prism of anti-Americanism, as the hobbyist Left does, refracts genuine movements for freedom into stooges of the US.

Trident

A totemic aspect of the hobbyists' general distaste for the UK military is the issue of nuclear arms, specifically the Trident missile system. Zoe Williams is on the money when she writes of Corbyn as 'the anti-nuclear campaigner [he] has always been: the throwback; the person whom voters have rejected, modernity has superseded, real life has rendered obsolete'. However, she was on less certain ground by claiming Nicola Sturgeon as 'a walking, talking contradiction of the maxim that Trident is electorally essential'.[69]

During the Scottish referendum campaign, the Scottish National Party made a great deal of its pledge to remove the United Kingdom's nuclear submarine fleet, which carries the Trident missile delivery system, from Faslane naval base. Yet when Lord Ashcroft Polls tested public opinion on the issue they found that 'not only did more Scots want Trident to stay (43 per cent) than go (39 per cent), a majority supported either a like-for-like replacement (20 per cent) or a cheaper nuclear alternative (31 per cent)'.[70]

The recent changes in the Labour Party have seen the spectre of unilateralism – which many had hoped had been permanently banished in the 1980s – return once again to dominate Labour foreign policy debates and damage the party's image with the electorate. Displaying their considerable ignorance of labour history, Emily Thornberry and (former soldier) Clive Lewis claimed in 2016 that 'Labour has always believed fiercely in ridding the world of nuclear weapons'. They may as well have claimed that Labour has always fiercely believed in world peace or the international brotherhood of man. It is a classic example of two individuals attributing their personal beliefs to the historical labour movement, rather than having their own beliefs moulded by the history of the labour movement.[71]

In a similar vein George Monbiot described the desire to possess nuclear weapons as 'a fantasy: a fantasy that the United Kingdom is still a defining world power'. He also claimed: 'The same confusion governs this country's defence policy. The other side of the Channel is forrin. The other side of the Atlantic isn't.' In three sentences Monbiot managed to incorporate a sneer at patriotism, anti-Americanism, and a classist, snide dig at working-class enunciation. Fair play George, that takes some doing![72]

The Reverend Giles Fraser – not particularly known for his embrace of *realpolitik* – notes that 'there's no point in having a deterrent if the PM indicates in advance that she wouldn't use it'. He then claimed that 'Tories voted for Trident out of some backward sense of patriotism, still pretending the UK is a big player in the politics of global power, and New Labour voted for it as an act of non-virtue signalling, still deliberately distancing themselves from the electoral kryptonite of those pacifist hippies of the 1970s'.[73] While there is no little truth in this assessment, one has to wonder what the electoral consequences would be for a party that openly avowed that the UK was no longer a 'big player in the politics of global power'.

In the summer of 2016, Owen Jones perceptively argued

that 'if Trident becomes [a] defining issue...that will further complicate Labour's already imperilled chance of winning popular support'. The party 'must instead focus on the issues that millions of people actually care about, and on policies they are sympathetic towards. If unilateral nuclear disarmament becomes the one clear policy where the electorate are actually clear where Labour stands – the one key issue that cuts through – then the party's electoral prospects are bleak indeed.'[74] But earlier that year he had written that 'our independent deterrent has become virtually irrelevant, except in the context of domestic politics'. In this, of course, he is quite right.

This is not the place to discuss the probity or morality of nuclear weapons or to debate the advisability or feasibility of unilateralism, but the unpopularity of the policy is impossible to deny.[75] Within the labour movement it is itself controversial, with the trade unions – as representatives of ordinary workers who depend on the defence industry for their livelihood, and hence usually of a different opinion to the hobbyists – differing from Corbyn on this issue early in his leadership.[76] Once again, the key issue is one of style rather than substance: the debate over nuclear weapons is highly serious, and needs to be conducted without partisanship. Yet if Labour began to advance unilateralism, if it continues to associate itself with knee-jerk anti-nuclearism, if its leader continues to make ridiculous statements regarding nuclear free submarines, then Labour will remain outside of government and unable to lead these discussions.

True, there is no conceivable situation when Britain might use the Trident missile system independent of American approval, and in many ways it is the world's most expensive cod piece. Nonetheless it is a cod piece that many Britons, especially traditional Labour voters, are proud of, and helps them maintain an image of Britain as a great power. If Labour is in the business of winning elections, it is essential that the party continues to burnish the image of Britain as a great power, and Trident is a vital component of this.[77]

Radical British Patriotism

For much of the hobbyist Left, the domination of the United States since 1945 is a tragedy. These individuals do not merely wish to see radical socio-economic reform; they wish to see the whole international settlement torn up and the geopolitical map re-drawn. To say this does not chime with the wishes of the British people – particularly traditional Labour voters – would be something of an understatement. These people should be free to agitate for their schemes on the side lines, but cannot be allowed anywhere near the reins of power.

If the Left is ever again to win power, it needs to reconcile itself to patriotism. This does not mean embracing the more reactionary elements of 'British' or 'English' patriotism, but it does involve subsuming our naturally anti-Monarchist instincts and revulsion at Britain's imperial past. We also need to move on from the wars in Iraq and Afghanistan; while the former's long shadow impacts on foreign policy and security concerns today, it is not a key issue for most voters. Despite the hobbyists' obsession with Iraq, this is as true for young voters, ethnic minorities and those in Scotland and Wales, as it is for the rest of the electorate.

We also urgently need to articulate a proud, radical patriotism. While some on the Left feel this can only have meaning if it is based on English, Scottish and Welsh identities, these are too restrictive; in order to encompass the broad variety of national and ethnic traditions within the UK, this radical patriotism has to be based on a British identity.

According to a poll conducted before the 2017 election, of those who said they felt 'English not British', over 40 per cent said they would vote Conservative and fewer than 30 per cent would be voting Labour; for those who said they felt 'More English than British', it was again 40 per cent for the Tories and under 20 per cent for Labour. Contrastingly, for those who felt 'More British than English', fewer than 25 per cent said they would be voting Tory, and over 45 per cent Labour; and for those who felt 'British not English', those figures were almost 50 per cent for Labour and 25 per cent for the Tories. Of those who opted for 'Other' (which would have included responses such as 'European', 'no nation' or 'world citizen'), over 50 per cent said they would be voting Labour; for the Tories it was just over 10 per cent.

In Vron Ware's book on Britishness, she observes a group of Indian students in a roleplaying exercise, in which one young woman gave a satirical impression of a well-educated, young English woman, putting on a deliberate 'warm and jolly manner', and claiming, 'I would like to talk to you about ways in which we can help you. We feel so terribly sorry for what happened in the days of the British Empire. We want to be your partners in this new era instead of dominating you.' This patronising, self-abasing attitude does no good to anyone. It does not make any attempt to reverse the material consequences of imperialism. The best that can be said for it is that it is therapeutic for a certain type of white British person; Slavoj Zizek describes it as a 'process of self-blame which is the inverted form of clinging to one's superiority' through the idea that the complex problems of the world today are 'merely reactions to our crimes'.[78]

It is not enough, either to deal with the legacy of imperialism, to combat racism or to help the Left in creating a radical patriotism. Ware wrote of the students she observed in India, 'Their perspective was not developed from an "us and them" mentality. In a sense, they were saying: "This is how the past has shaped our countries in this part of the world. We understand that it is up to us to determine how we tackle the enormous problems."'[79] This is the framework through which we should understand radical British patriotism in the twenty-first century.

4. The Anti-Imperialism of Fools

Israel, Palestine and Identity Leftism

Every night in the West Bank, a team of Israeli soldiers roll up to a randomly-chosen Palestinian house. They enter, search the place and draw an improvised map of the rooms. They then collect the personal details of all family members and sometimes line them up against a wall to take a photograph.

This 'mapping' ('mipuim') procedure is not designed to garner information: the hand-sketched maps and other details are not logged or recorded, and are thrown away afterwards. Instead the purpose is to maintain a constant, low-level of threat and intimidation. According to the evidence of one soldier, 'we have to make sure they know that we can go in any time. All the time. That we can appear at any moment. 3 o'clock in the morning, 6 o'clock in the evening during the Ramadan fast…In order to make it effective, it has to take place when everyone's home, so it has to be at night.'[1]

Another soldier describes a 'mapping' that was deliberately scheduled for during the breaking of the Ramadan fast:

They were after a whole day of fasting, at some point they asked: "Can we have something to drink, the food that grandmother's preparing is burning", this and that. So we sent the grandmother to watch over the oven. I have no idea what they thought she'd do with those carrots and yams, but one of the soldiers sat with the grandmother and watched over her.[2]

A third soldier recalls another night:

They were gathered in one room and we did the mapping and

the children of course wept as people with weapons entered their house waking them up in the middle of the night. Two soldiers stayed by them to guard them. This irrational and unnatural picture of the woman with three small children sitting on the floor next to soldiers with full equipment and loaded weapons.[3]

This relatively unknown procedure is just one example of the continuous low-level of harassment that forms a small part of the brutal practices of Israel's 50-year occupation of the West Bank and other areas. Thousands of Palestinians, and indeed Lebanese and Syrians, have been killed by Israel over the past decades. There is no doubt that the country is in violation of international law and human morality. Furthermore, cynical politicians, led by the despicable Binyamin Netanyahu, use the conflict to further the position of themselves and their families, at the expense of the blood of Israeli conscripts and Palestinian civilians.

There are all sorts of reasons to oppose the policies of the current Israeli government, and the illegal military occupation of the West Bank, East Jerusalem and the Golan Heights. The point of this chapter is not to debate the sorry state of Israeli politics. The point is to question why this is such a totemic issue for the British Left. According to a March 2018 poll of Labour members, more think Israel is a force for bad (65 per cent) than think the same of Iran. Nor is this behaviour restricted to non-Jews: a leaflet by the International Jewish Anti-Zionist Network described the Jewish Labour Movement – affiliated to Labour since 1920 – as 'a representative of a foreign power, Israel'.

But why is opposition to Israel, more than another nation, such a key shibboleth for being left-wing in Britain today, when there are so many more abhorrent regimes? Why are so many – by and large, not Muslim nor Jewish – white Christians and atheists so obsessed with this particular small corner of the world? Supporters of the 2003 Iraq War such as Nick Cohen, Christopher Hitchens and David Aaronovitch did a disservice with their decrying of 'whatabouttery' in relation to the invasion of Iraq. Firstly, because it was a perfectly valid question – why Iraq, and not, say North Korea or Libya – but also because it makes it difficult to ask the same question of the hobbyist Left: why Israel, and not North Korea or Syria? From 2011 to the 2018, President Assad of Syria was directly or indirectly responsible for the deaths of around half a million people. In the period 1920 to 2018, Israel has killed around 90,000 Palestinians and Arabs.

Left-wing antizionists might argue that it is because they have some influence over Israel; that it is in some sense within their power to change things, and at the very least, since their governments support Israel, the actions of the Likud regime are carried out in their name. In reality, the opposite is true: left-wingers in Britain, the US and elsewhere have no influence at all over Israel. Firstly, they are politically isolated within their own country, and exert minimal influence at the highest levels of diplomacy; Donald Trump and Theresa May are not going to take a harder line with Israel because of the protestations of a few thousand activists.

But more significantly than that, Israel ultimately does not care what the British Prime Minister thinks, and, increasingly, what the American President thinks; in fact, some hardliners in Israeli advocate the end of US military aid, claiming that they don't really need it, and doing so would give the country even greater latitude to do whatever it pleases.

In contrast, the United States and the UK do have influence over regimes such as North Korea, Iran and – as demonstrated by the 2003 invasion – Iraq. It is for precisely this reason that the hobbyist Left cares so little about the abuses within these countries: according to the power hierarchy essential to hobbyist leftism, these countries are perceived as weak and as victims of Western colonialism; therefore, their abuses can be understood and possibly even excused. In contrast, Israel is perceived as strong, and as an example *of* Western colonialism, and therefore must be opposed at all costs.

This hostility is entirely counter-productive. It has no bearing on Israeli policy, and serves only to shift the mass of the Israeli population ever further to the Right. Netanyahu and the Likud play the British and American Left like an antique Stradivarius. They use the hatred displayed by the thinking classes of North America and Western Europe to say: 'Look, you can't trust these people. You can only find safety with us, and with ever more oppressive measures against the Arabs.' The more virulent the hostility of the Western Left, the more reactionary Israel becomes.

The key question remains: given its counter-productive nature, why is antizionism so central to the modern Left? Some writers have suggested this is an example of latent antisemitism on the Left, but I'm not sure that this is convincing. To be sure, there is plenty of antisemitism in British society, and this appears on the Left as much as anywhere else, but I think the hobbyist Left's preoccupation with Israel/Palestine stems more from their view of 'brown' people in general and Muslims in particular as perennial victims, through whose cause they can redeem themselves of their own whiteness and relative privilege. It is not so much that they hate Jews; it's more that they 'love' Muslims. But this patronising White Knight syndrome does nothing to improve the lives of Palestinians; it serves only to provide a psychological boost to white radicals in the West. Over a hundred years ago, German Marxists used to describe antisemitism as 'the socialism of fools'; today, the identitarian antizionism of the hobbyist Left is the anti-imperialism of fools.

Contemporary Left Antisemitism

When I first started writing this book, there was relatively little material on left-wing antisemitism. There was the work of the late David Cesarani and Steve Cohen's 1984 polemic, *That's*

Funny You Don't Look Anti-Semitic, but apart from that, little else. Unfortunately, this is no longer the case. I say unfortunately not because of the quality of the scholarship produced by the likes of David Hirsh, Dave Rich, Philip Spencer, Robert Fine and others, but rather because recent events have prompted and necessitated this increased scholarly interest in Left antisemitism. This is because the vehemence of left-wing opposition to Israel often carries sinister overtones and implications, and sometimes spills over into outright antisemitism. This identitarian antisemitism will be discussed below, but first we need to look at some recent examples of hobbyist antizionism.

The recent flurry of robust opposition to Israel has not come from nowhere. Back in September 1983, then leader of the Greater London Council Ken Livingstone had to apologise after claiming on the radio that British policy in Northern Ireland had been 'worse than what Hitler had done to the Jews'. This outburst displayed two of the hallmarks of left-wing hobbyism: a willingness to invoke the Third Reich and the Holocaust at any moment, usually for an egregious and hyperbolic comparison which undermines the significance of the latter; and an instinctive anti-Britishness.[4]

Three years later, at a fringe event at the Labour Party conference, Clare Short – an outspoken advocate of Palestinian liberation – warned how there was a growing danger of supporters of the Palestinian cause 'slipping into the language of conspiracy'. According to a contemporary report from that conference, 'far more vitriolic', than the event Short addressed, was a 'meeting of the Labour Movement Campaign for Palestine, chaired by Mr Jeremy Corbyn, MP'. Speakers included Mr Tony Greenstein, Mr Harry Cohen, MP and Mr Ken Livingstone, 'who was less extreme'.[5]

In 2002, then *Guardian* columnist Seumus Milne wrote that a refusal to acknowledge the 'brute facts of power and injustice' evident in the Israeli-Palestinian conflict was 'a reflection of anti-

Arab racism and Islamophobia, both currently more... acceptable in its polite society than anti-semitism'. In reality, the exact opposite is true: in Britain and much of the developed world, anti-Muslim sentiment is most likely to be found among poorer people with fewer qualifications. In contrast, antisemitism is most pronounced at the highest levels of society, among both braying, drinking society oafs and snide left-wing intellectuals.[6]

During the period of Israel's attack on Gaza in 2009, Seumus Milne continued with his long tradition of threatening articles, warning that 'Israel and the West will pay a price for Gaza's bloodbath'. There is a distinct sound of crowing in the boast that 'after its most pulverising assault ever on the blockaded territory, Hamas remains standing, its administration intact, its rockets reaching ever further into Israel proper'. And he ended with the warning: 'In reality, the naivety lies in imagining that the west can continue to underwrite the injustice and bloodshed inflicted with no respite on the Palestinian people, without paying a price for it.'[7] At the end of that year Milne was prophesising a grim future for Israel and its allies should they continue on their current path: 'The impunity of Israel and its allies will carry a price', warned the headline.[8]

At the same time, Mehdi Hasan reported that 'the Community Security Trust, which monitors anti-Semitism, says that anti-Semitic attacks in the UK doubled in the first half of this year compared with the same period in 2008' from 276 in the period January to June 2008, to 609 in the same period in 2009, a 'record rise'. After citing these sad statistics, Hasan wrote: 'Hmm, I wonder what provoked this rise in anti-Semitic attacks?' There is a clear suggestion here that British Jews somehow deserved to be attacked given Israeli atrocities in Gaza.

Hasan continued that he found it 'ironic that the state of Israel – created ostensibly to protect Jews from across the world from hatred, prejudice and violence' provokes antisemitic attacks against diaspora Jews.[9] If you were to substitute Tell Mama and

Islamophobia for Community Security Trust and antisemitism, these words could come from the pen of a right-wing columnist, although I doubt even the most reactionary voice in *The Sun* or *Mail* stable would go so far as to depict racist attacks upon British Muslims as somehow being the fault of the Iranian or Pakistani regimes.

In 2013 a Labour peer, Lord Ahmed, was sentenced to 13 weeks in prison for his involvement in a fatal car crash, which occurred due to him using his phone while driving. Footage then emerged of Ahmed blaming 'Jewish friends who own newspapers and TV channels'. This prompted Mehdi Hasan to admit that there were 'thousands of Lord Ahmeds out there: mild-mannered and well-integrated British Muslims who nevertheless harbour deeply anti-Semitic views':

> It pains me to have to admit this but anti-Semitism isn't just tolerated in some sections of the British Muslim community; it's routine and commonplace. Any Muslims reading this article – if they are honest with themselves – will know instantly what I am referring to. It's our dirty little secret. You could call it the banality of Muslim anti-Semitism. I can't keep count of the number of Muslims I have come across – from close friends and relatives to perfect strangers – for whom weird and wacky anti-Semitic conspiracy theories are the default explanation for a range of national and international events. Who killed Diana and Dodi? The Mossad, say many Muslims. They didn't want the British heir to the throne having an Arab stepfather. What about 9/11? Definitely those damn Yehudis. I mean, why else were 4,000 Jews in New York told to stay home from work on the morning of 11 September 2001? How about the financial crisis? Er, Jewish bankers. Obviously. Oh, and the Holocaust? Don't be silly. Never happened.

This latent and banal antisemitism is wrong in itself, of course, but it has taken on an extra potency due to the assumption by the hobbyist Left that Muslims are inherently victims, while Jews are powerful and privileged, and thus there should be no question about whose side to take in a dispute. Indeed, the Swedish Liberal MP Fredrik Malm is reported to have said that he 'never thought non-white people could be anti-semitic'.[10]

The casual antisemitism of the Lord Ahmeds described by Hasan can now be seen in a different form among many young, left-leaning celebrities. In 2017, grime star Jme retweeted a comment '*ImSweatingMoreThan* a Jew at a cash machine'. After receiving criticism, he defended himself by arguing that 'the retweet, was a series of "sweating more than" hashtags, which played on Jewish [sic] being rich. I still don't get the anti semite [sic] part???' Likewise, the BBC presenter Reggie Yates had to apologise after trumpeting how current music artists, who 'aint signing to majors', are independent, 'not managed by some random fat Jewish guy from north west London'. This again reveals a belief in a binary opposition: Muslim or black people are poor and oppressed; Jewish people are rich and oppressors.

In August 2016, the Court of Appeal ruled that up to 130,000 of the Labour members who joined the party after 12 January of that year would not be able to vote in the leadership contest. At which point, Steve Bird of the National Union of Journalists questioned why one member of the tribunal, Judge Sales, failed to recuse himself, given 'his connections with one of the factions involved'. Now, Judge Sales has never been a member of the Labour Party, but it was assumed by Bird that since he is Jewish, he would naturally be with the 'Blairites' against Corbyn. At the same time, Steve Brookstein – the lounge-singing, housewives' favourite whom some may remember as the first winner of the *X Factor* – promised his Twitter followers that 'this Jewish thing will stop after the election. It's desperate propaganda from the Owen Smith team to keep media on side.'

These attitudes are not just confined to disgruntled union leaders and Z-list celebrities. According to one poll, only 8 per cent of Labour members who voted for Corbyn in 2016 think that antisemitism is a 'serious and genuine' issue for the party, in comparison to 46 per cent of Owen Smith voters. Only 19 per cent of Labour members, upon being asked to choose which of three statements more closely matched their views, said that antisemitism is 'a serious and genuine problem that the party leadership needs to take urgent action to address'. A total of 47 per cent opted for 'it is a genuine problem, but its extent is being deliberately exaggerated to damage Labour and Jeremy Corbyn, or to stifle criticism of Israel'. Meanwhile fully 30 per cent of Labour members think 'it is not a serious problem at all, and is being hyped up to undermine Labour and Jeremy Corbyn, or to stifle legitimate criticism of Israel'. At the Annual General Meeting of London Young Labour in March 2018, one delegate, Omar Raii, tweeted that it was shameful to 'hear audible sighs when a question on anti-Semitism was asked'.

Those poll results, and that audible sigh, are indicative of the priorities of much of the hobbyist Left. Some may say that I'm being naïve, and failing to appreciate the way right-wing figures – who don't particularly care about antisemitism themselves – are just using the issue as a way to attack Jeremy Corbyn. But the two are not mutually exclusive: let's assume (and you don't need a Tolkienian imagination for this) that a tiny minority of Tory activists are hardened racists; attempts by the Left to expose this would be motivated by a desire to discredit the Conservative Party, but they would still be right to expose them. Yes, it is only on the fringes of the Left where Zionist cabals are believed to run the world, but these extremists still feel they have a home in the modern labour movement. Certainly, this antisemitism is used to attack the Labour Party in general and Corbyn in particular, but then the same can be said about racism and the Tories – it doesn't mean it isn't real.

Jews have been discriminated against, abused, exiled and murdered for thousands of years, culminating in a concerted, multinational, industrialised attempt to get rid of every single last one of them merely 70-odd years ago, still within living memory. Austerity has been around for fewer than 10 years. But for many on the hobbyist Left, any attempt to undermine the current Labour leadership is far more serious than so-called antisemitism, especially since, as David Hirsch says, 'nobody looks like the Nazis' anymore.[11]

Although even that is not quite true – there are still some genuine Nazis around. Recently, a memorandum from neo-fascist group National Alliance claimed that although their group is 'neither pro-Labour nor anti-Labour Party, disagreeing with that party on many but far from all issues' it welcomes 'that party's increasingly critical stance toward Jewish and Zionist power in recent years. We recently republished an essay suggesting that racially conscious Whites in Britain should join the Labour Party.'

Perhaps unsurprisingly, all this has led to a decline in Labour's vote share among the Jewish population. In north London constituencies at the 2017 election, for example, while there was an increase in the Labour vote of between 10 and 17 per cent in constituencies with fewer than 5 per cent Jews, in constituencies with 15–25 per cent Jewish voters, this increase was merely 5 per cent.

The alleged use of antisemitism to undermine the Labour leadership combines with a loathing of Israel to produce a toxic brew for some on the Left. Yet this sad state of affairs is not unprecedented in the history of the British Left and Jewish relations, for there was left antisemitism long before the existence of Israel.

The History of Left Antisemitism
Long before Israel was a gleam in Chaim Weizmann's eye, there

was a deep and virulent current of antisemitism running through the British Left. Very often it was the most radical, Marxist elements of the British labour movement who combined their fierce anti-capitalism with antisemitism, but it was also found among the more anodyne, reformist elements on the Left.

Back in 1884, the Marxist Social Democratic Federation claimed that 'Jewish moneylenders control every Foreign Office in Europe'. By June 1898 they complained that 'it seems to be an open secrecy that the government of France is too much in the grip of the Jews to take active measures against them as a body'.[12] Keir Hardie himself – one of the few genuine internationalists and anti-racists of the early Labour Party – claimed in 1889, when giving evidence before the House of Commons Select Committee on Immigration, that for the Ayrshire Miners Union and Socialist Labour Party: 'As well as opposing Jewish immigration – save for those fleeing persecution – these organisations [are] opposed to Polish Christians being allowed to come and work in the mines, in iron and steel mills and on British ships.'[13] Hardie was also the editor of the *Labour Leader* when, in 1891, it wrote: 'Whenever there is trouble in Europe, wherever rumours of war circulate and men's minds are distraught with fear and change and calamity, you may be sure that a hooked-nose Rothschild is at his games somewhere near the region of these disturbances.'[14] *The Clarion* newspaper, during the height of the Boer War, argued that 'modern imperialism is really run by half a dozen financial houses, many of them Jewish, to whom politics is a counter in the game of buying and selling securities and the people are convenient pawns'.

As Jewish refugees fleeing pogroms in Eastern Europe and the Russian Empire began to arrive in Britain in numbers during the 1880s, the TUC passed several resolutions against these new arrivals. In 1892, the TUC formally committed to a resolution excluding Jews, and in 1895 the issue of immigration was included in a list of questions to be asked of all prospective Parliamentary candidates.[15] Both dockers leader Ben Tillett and the supposed internationalist Tom Mann were in favour of restriction, as were 43 labour organisations, including the trades councils of London, Liverpool and many other cities. J.H. Wilson MP, the Secretary of the Seamans' Union, was one of the first to propose legislation in Parliament, and *The Clarion* eventually came out in favour of total exclusion, describing Jewish people as 'a poison injected into the national veins...unsavoury children of the ghetto...their numbers are "appalling" and they are "unclean"'.

The celebrated children's author and Fabian Beatrice Potter averred that 'the love of profit distinct from other forms of money earning [is] the strongest impelling motive of the Jewish race'. Bruce Glasier, one of the founding members of the ILP – and along with Ben Tillett one of the British representatives on the Second International – wrote in the *Labour Leader*: 'Neither the principle of the brotherhood of man nor the principle of social equality implies that brother nations or brother men may crowd upon us in such numbers as to abuse our hospitality, overturn our institutions or violate our customs.'[16] G.D. Kelley, secretary of the Manchester and Salford Trades Council at this time, both championed the cause of sweated Jewish workers and utilised virulently antisemitic language in his attacks on Jews who did not keep up with their union fees.[17]

After the First World War, Ernest Bevin warned against the dangers of Jewish immigration leading to 'undesirable concentrations of them in the towns'.[18]

Meanwhile, in Germany during the 1930s, the Communist Party often denied that antisemitism was central to the Nazi agenda. The Social Democratic Party produced very little material to challenge the antisemitic arguments of the Nazis and 'the party's attitude appears to have been shaped by fears that it would be over-identified with Jews'. After Hitler took power in 1933, the German resistance against the Nazis refused to prioritise the issue of antisemitism, as it made their job harder, and German Communists 'flirted' with antisemitic discourse.[19]

Perhaps the most romanticised – historian David Cesarani used the word 'manipulated' – event in the history of the British Left's relationship with Jews was the so-called 'Battle of Cable Street' in 1936. This was undoubtedly a hugely significant moment in the history of British Jewry, but to listen to some retellings of the event from left-wing myth-makers, one would have thought that a rainbow coalition, of which Jews were only a small part, stood to block Mosley's fascists, in an act of apparent altruism towards their neighbours.[20]

In reality, the vast majority of those opposing the fascists that day were Jews. If you were a non-Jew at Cable Street, likelihood is you were with the fascists or the police. Even the very location where the key confrontation took place has been shifted in the subsequent mythologisation: as Dave Renton points out, the main clash happened at Gardiner's Corner, but this was a busy junction near the City of London, the heart of British high finance, so over the years it has been moved to the working-class district of Cable Street, to enhance its proletarian credentials.[21] And it was only at the last moment, under pressure from Jewish members, that the Communist Party cancelled its planned demonstration in Trafalgar Square in solidarity with the Spanish Republic and told its members to rally in the East End.[22] The saintly George Lansbury, the Labour leader most reminiscent of Corbyn, refused to endorse a petition calling for the fascist march to be banned, and encouraged other members of the party to stay away from the counter-demonstration.[23]

This has not stopped Cable Street being used as a totemic representation of inter-religious solidarity; Jeremy Corbyn proudly avers that his own mother was there. In fact, Jewish Londoner Clifford Harris claims that at the 2016 event to mark the eightieth anniversary, at which Corbyn spoke, 'the organisers tried to intimidate Jewish attendees by having Palestinian groups parade with banners whilst they tried to rewrite history by minimizing Jewish participation'. Cable Street was entirely unrepresentative of relations between Jews and the British Left, both before and after: it must have come as little consolation to Jews terrorised in the riots of 1947 that 11 years earlier some Irish dockers had stood with Jews against fascism.

Historical Left-wing Support for Israel

Despite – or perhaps because of – the long threat of antisemitism in the history of the British Left, for much of the twentieth century, the labour movement was overwhelmingly positive towards the idea of a Jewish homeland. Furthermore, it was usually those on the hard-Left who were most vociferous in this support, while centrists tended towards pro-Palestinianism.

Josiah Wedgwood – a Labour politician with a long history of anti-imperialist, internationalist activism and a relative of Tony Benn – wrote to Zionist activists in Palestine in July 1938, encouraging resistance against the British authorities there:

> In my experience, especially in times of difficulty, Governments give way only to actions. Demands backed by nothing but a sense of justice play little part in modern history...Arabs, or those who are troublesome, get their way in Palestine because they act instead of petition...You are morally entitled to arm to defend yourselves and your outlying colonies and erect such defences as are possible.[24]

In 1946, Michael Foot and Richard Crossman authored a pamphlet that recommended the partition of Palestine and the establishment of a 'Judean State'. The historian James Vaughan believes that Labour's then Palestinian policy was the result of a profound conviction that the establishment of the national home is an important part of the socialist creed. One of the concepts underpinning the labour movement's sympathetic view of Zionism in the 1940s and 1950s was the notion of Israel as a socialist democracy threatened by Arab authoritarianism and reaction.[25] The position of the Labour Left at this time was that Israel was yet another victim of British imperialism; their Palestinian stance was informed by their internationalism, anti-imperialism and anti-racism. Crossman wrote to David Ben Gurion that while he 'did not think much of "my country right or wrong" as a slogan...the United Nations right or wrong was even worse'.[26] For Crossman, Israel had 'raised the status of the Jew and banished his sense of insecurity which provided for centuries the basis of antisemitism'. Crossman, Tony Benn and Jennie Lee were all members of Labour Friends of Israel. The left-wing Jewish MPs Ian Mikardo and Sidney Silverman had strong links with Zionist organisations. And the left-winger Eric Heffer – later to be a key force in Militant – was one of the most outspoken pro-Israel voices on the Left, as were most of the trade union leaders.

In a 1949 broadside, the editors of the socialist periodical *Tribune* denounced the 'corruption and irresponsibility' of an Arab world united solely by a 'hatred of the Palestine Jews' and 'the social-democracy they were importing into the Middle East'. When Egyptian President Nasser agreed a major arms deal with Czechoslovakia in September 1955, granting the Soviet Union a strategic foothold in the heart of the Middle East, *Tribune* took the 'fumbling' Conservative Government to task for creating 'a situation in which the survival of Israel, our only politically trustworthy and militarily reliable ally in the region, may well be threatened by Arab states armed by the Communist powers'.[27] The magazine then called for Israel 'to have arms to withstand the Arab forces' which were 'encouraged by capitalist greed and Communist betrayal'. It concluded that 'the cause of Israel is the cause of democratic Socialism'.[28]

Historians often point to 1967 as a crucial juncture for left-wing antizionism, but Vaughan notes that when it came to the Six Day War itself, virtually the entire Labour cabinet sided with

Israel, and Prime Minister Harold Wilson felt that Britain and the US should intervene. A pro-Israel Early Day Motion attracted 166 signatures, with 105 of those coming from Labour MPs; a rival, pro-Arab motion garnered only 19 Labour signatures. The Socialist International issued a resolution expressing 'full solidarity with the people of Israel who are defending their existence and their liberty against aggression'.[29] Support for Israel remained steady throughout the war, not only within the PLP, but also in the constituencies and trade unions.[30] A Gallup poll showed that 20 per cent of Britons wanted to intervene on behalf of Israel, and only 1 per cent on behalf of the Arabs.[31]

Fenner Brockway was one of the most consistently internationalist and anti-racist members ever to grace the Labour benches. He was an outspoken voice against the First World War, against imperialism, and became an anti-racist advocate after the Second World War. Nonetheless, towards the end of his life he admitted to being 'more puzzled by the Israeli-Palestinian conflict than by any other issue'. He even wrote a letter to the *Jewish Chronicle* paying tribute to Golda Meir on her death in 1978, calling her 'a real Socialist, with identity with the people'.[32]

The days of left-wing support for Israel are long gone, and – as with so many issues in this book – myth-making and historical amnesia have erased this episode of the labour movement's past. But how exactly did this change come about? How did the Left – and the hard-Left especially – go from full-throated support of Israel to the steadfast, instinctive opposition that sometimes boils over into racism and hate?

From Heroes to Villains

As James Vaughan argues, before 1967 Palestine was not a pressing issue for many in the labour movement. And, while Labour and the unions generally supported Israel during the conflict itself, the subsequent occupation of Palestinian land and the growth of illegal Jewish settlements in the West Bank created a shift in the views of many on the Left. Soon after the war, the Labour Middle East Council was created in 1969, aiming to link the Labour and trade union movements to the Palestinian cause.[33] This was followed 11 years later by the Trade Union Friends of Palestine, which provided a public platform for its General Secretary, George Galloway, to develop a reputation for loquacious and bombastic antizionism.[34]

Support for Israel held up better inside the Parliamentary Labour Party than elsewhere on the Left. As late as 1973, Labour leader Harold Wilson opposed the Tory government's decision to extend an arms embargo to Israel during the Yom Kippur War, although this incident revealed a growing split between the generally pro-Israel MPs, and the increasingly sceptical Labour membership.[35]

In the last decades of the twentieth century, at the same time as increasing numbers of British Jews began to vote Conservative, Labour began to seek the votes of more recent generations of immigrants. In this context, Israel's 1982 invasion of Lebanon, featuring the massacre of Palestinians at the hands of Christian militias at the Shaba and Shatila refugee camps, was met with a hostile reaction on the Left. In response to this, the Trade Union Friends of Israel was established in 1983, but this was unable to stop the steady growth of left-wing antizionism during the 1980s.[36]

An obvious explanation for the shift in attitudes to Israel during this period is the behaviour of successive Israeli governments; the rhetoric of bellicose nationalist leaders; and the lived reality for millions of Palestinians and Israeli Muslims. But the Occupation does not happen in a vacuum, and nor has this change occurred independent of other factors. David Cesarani cited the fall of the Soviet Union as the key stimulus to modern left-wing antizionism: bereft of a *raison d'*être after the defeat of Communism, the hard-Left found a new sense of purpose in opposing Israel and championing the Palestinians.

But neither the reality of the Israel-Palestine conflict nor the need for another great international project after 1991 satisfy the 'whatabout' question: why did opposition to Israel become a shibboleth for some on the Left, when there are regimes infinitely more horrible in word and deed?

Phillip Lopate believes it is because we view both sides in the Israeli-Palestinian conflict as eminently civilised, and 'like us'. Similarly, the Israeli government and its policies are something we're familiar with from Europe and America; Assad, by contrast, wields power in a manner we can't imagine. I think there is a lot to say for this 'Neo-Orientalist' explanation: we somehow think of Syria or North Korea as a barbarous place where these sorts of things happen, whereas Jews are meant to be civilised.

Robert Spencer and Philip Fine argue that this shift cannot just be explained by events on the ground in the Middle East, but also by events in Western Europe and North America: 'the new social and cultural class associated with the New Left', they write, 'was making its presence felt in Labour' during the 1980s.[37] This was catalysed by the decline in private sector unionism – particularly under Thatcher – and the growth of Labour members from the public sector. At the same time, some on the Left 'gave up on the revolutionary potential of the Western working class and looked overseas for radical inspiration'.[38]

In more recent years, the swing between private and public sector unionism and the growth in middle-class Labour members has accompanied the great expansion in university education. As the socio-economic and cultural base of the labour movement has changed, its focus has shifted; less concerned with material class, and with a heightened awareness of other forms of identity. At the same time that power shifted in the Middle East to strengthen Israel over its rivals, much of the political, cultural and intellectual trends on the Left focused on racism, imperialism and post-coloniality. Not only did Israel become more aggressive and expansionist in this period, but as memories of the Holocaust faded and antisemitism gave way to other forms of racism and Islamophobia as cause célèbres for the Left, an intellectual and cultural shift cast Israel as colonialist, racist and inherently wrong. In the words of Hirsh, 'Jews, who could not have been more oppressed in 1944, can be thought of four short years later as the bearers of white European colonialism'.[39]

For Hirsh this was a missed opportunity: as many on the Left felt that anti-racism and anti-fascism were sufficient, they failed to 'understand the complexities of antisemitism': 'Nobody looks like the Nazis', the reasoning goes, 'so how can there be antisemitism?' Likewise, as many thought anti-colonialism and anti-racism by themselves were enough to build consensus on and affect change in the Middle East, hence they failed to 'forge a positive cosmopolitan politics rather than a negative politics of opposition and resentment'.[40]

With the Middle East, because so much of the Western Left has focused exclusively on anti-imperialism as a stance to override all other considerations, they lost the opportunity to work with the Israeli Left, and left-wing supporters of Israel in the West, who nonetheless wanted to see peace in the region. Spencer and Fine concur, criticising the growth in a binary identity over Israel-Palestine that 'blinds us to universal insight that no human being is entirely different from another even where unequal social structures and cultural peculiarities make this hard to see'.[41]

Spencer and Fine have also suggested the increasing repudiation of national identity among some parts of the Left during this period enabled Israel to be depicted as a special example. They write that the substitution of 'peoples' for nation states enables 'the condemnation of "the people" as a "pariah nation"'. This was not a design of post-nationalists, but has created a 'philosophical aperture through which it became possible to reinstate the Jewish question under a postnational or cosmopolitan banner'. Thereby, post-nationalism can itself 'be abused to label others "nationalist" or stigmatise others as enemies'. For Spencer and Fine, Israel is 'the "other" of the postnational'.[42] The very post-nationalism and postcolonialism of the modern Left has allowed for a new kind of intolerance. Since anti-imperialism became an imperative to prevail over all else, Israel is seen as and is powerful, and thus antisemitism can be excused or downplayed as a 'misguided form of resistance'.[43]

Identitarian Antizionism

Some scholars have now begun to consider hostility to Israel as a signifier of identity, connected to opposition to imperialism, neoliberalism and global capitalism, similar to Shulamit Volkov's conception of the New Left's "cultural code" of antizionism, anti-Americanism and anti-colonialism. According to sociologist David Hirsh, Israel/Palestine is a cipher for others to project their identity onto, and there is an 'intense personal payoff' from self-conscious antizionism, which produces a 'feeling of inner cleanliness':

> There are acknowledged and unwritten boundaries which divide 'us', the 'good people', from them, the uncultured, the Tories, the Americans, the Neo-Cons, the Blairites, the Islamophobes, and in particular, the Zionists...In this way one can remain within this community of the good while at the same time enjoying the benefits of middle-class success.[44]

Social media is awash with examples of the most egregious kind of identitarian antizionism. Back in 2016, a young Scottish woman posted on Twitter that she 'went out to dinner with my family tonight wearing a Hezbollah t-shirt', accompanied by a photograph of herself in the said garment. She was quickly contacted by people pointing out that – all opinions on Israel/ Palestine aside – Hezbollah killed innocent people, including children, and were thoroughly antisemitic, misogynist and homophobic. None of these responses impacted on the original tweeter, and it is understandable, for they entirely missed the point. The Hezbollah t-shirt is a cultural, rather than a political statement, and should be understood as such. The punks of the 1970s were not trying to boost the safety pin industry or promote testing for sputum-borne Hepitatis; they were trying to piss off their parents and demarcate their own identity. The same is true for so much of left-wing antizionism, and hobbyist leftism in general.

It is the same as pointing out to people who wear a t-shirt emblazoned with Stalin or Mao's face: they are aware of how many people they killed, but they see that as beside the point. On the day Fidel Castro died, a gay friend of mine texted me to say that he was in an expensive Kings Cross bar, drinking rum and toasting to Fidel. Tedious person that I am I was inclined to text back asking what he felt about Castro's concentration camps for gays, but again this would have been beside the point: young people who ironically venerate tyrants, or who wrap themselves in the colours of Hezbollah and Hamas, aren't oblivious to the crimes committed by the people and organisations; they just don't care. When the young woman put on the Hezbollah t-shirt, she was not making a statement about Israel; she was making a statement about herself. It had nothing to do with the Middle East, and everything to do with the UK.

Similarly, when an online football supporter claims he is 'sick of seeing Celtic fans creaming themselves over Nir Bitton. We are a club open to all...but by all, we mean humans, of different creeds, races and religions. Zionists are sub human, and Nir Bitton is a filthy Zionist rat' this is much less about Palestine than it is about Catholics in the west of Scotland. A friend replied to the post with 'Gas him...pardon the pun,' to which the original poster said that would 'be too good for him'. No doubt these Celtic fans would be horrified by accusations of racism, but they think the power politics of the Middle East means that calling for a Jewish player to be gassed is a legitimate example of anti-imperialism.

Likewise, the use of words such as 'Apartheid' represent a linguistic display of identitarian antizionism. True, it can also be used as a lazy substitute for political debate – in the words of David Hirsh, to invoke Apartheid and treat 'categories of humanitarian law…as trump cards that function to conclude argument' saves people the work of making their own case. Furthermore, it is inaccurate – compare the ANC's Freedom Charter with the Hamas Covenant and Hezbollah Manifesto – and the use of Apartheid allows for Israel to be called by the name of something that was fit only for abolition.[45]

Yet the use of 'Apartheid' carries another, identitarian function. Along with other words and phrases central to the nomenclature of left-wing hobbyism – but often unknown to the actual people whom they are used about – it is a lazy shorthand which demarcates the politics and identity of the speaker. 'Apartheid' is an inappropriate word to describe Israel, but that is not why it is used: like intersectionality, the global south, cisgender, people of colour and so on, the point is to demonstrate the erudition and sophistication of the speaker, and seamlessly and easily position themselves among the community of the good. As David Rich observes, 'for individual anti-Israel activists, imagining themselves to be heroically tearing down a new Israeli apartheid allows them to bask in the reflected glory of their illustrious forebears'.[46] It allows lonely and isolated kids, unwashed students and frustrated academics to pretend that they are Oliver Tambo or Nelson Mandela.

Crucial to identitarian antizionism is a view of 'Israeli' and 'Palestinian' as two homogenous entities in binary opposition. In the words of Spencer and Fine, much left-wing antizionism places 'Palestinians into a single identity script as victims, only as victims and only as victims of Israel'. This process 'subsumes the plural of Palestinian voices to "the Palestinians"' and turns them into 'ciphers of our own resentments'. Thus, Israel is represented not as a complex society with real people but as a 'vessel' into which hobbyist leftists 'project what is most troubling about [themselves]'.[47]

In the same way that many on the Right see faceless stereotypes rather than real people – many can't seem to imagine the day-to-day, mundane lifestyles and ordinary travails that affect say, Muslims or transgender people – the hobbyist Left reduces the complexities of Israeli society and the personalities of individual Israelis to a Manichean binary. As David Hirsh writes:

> In classic antisemitism, 'the Jew' was treated as the symbolic representation of all that is rotten in the modern world. In contemporary antizionism…Israel, Zionism and the Jewish state are treated as symbolic representations of all that is illegitimate in the present-day international community… Certain aspects of what Israel has become…have been converted into the central meaning of what Israel is.[48]

In reality, of course, Israeli society is far more complex than the picture painted by the hobbyist Left. Although militaristic nationalism is widespread, there are all manner of significant ethnic, religious, class and culture-based divisions. For example, the very existence of Mizrahi Jews imperils the simplistic hierarchy of victimhood upon which hobbyist antizionism rests. On the one hand they are Arabs, and therefore victims; on the other hand, they are Israelis, and therefore villains. In fact, Mizrahi Israelis are among the most anti-Palestinian, despite – or quite possibly because of – their shared Arab heritage. I know of a man from a Mizrahi Israeli family who is dating a Palestinian American. At first his mother – despite all her liberal beliefs – was quite sniffy about the match, before she realised that her and the new girl had much more in common – in terms of their taste in food, clothes and interior decoration – than the Ashkenazi women he had brought home before. Likewise, I know of a gay Mizrahi who loved the IDF so much that he stayed on for 15 years. Through this man's multiple identities – Arab, queer, no-nonsense army officer – we can have a glimpse of the myriad complexity of Israeli society, a complexity which hobbyists would reduce to the binary of oppressors and oppressed.

Meanwhile, Palestinian civil society, although equally complex and varied, is painted in the image of the Western Left. Either Palestinians are dirt poor and repressed, or they share the internationalist, secular, liberal concerns of the Left: in the American TV series *Transparent*, the West Bank is portrayed as a sort of hipster Disney Land, but in reality it is a highly conservative society. Similarly, after the Palestinian rapper Tamer Nafar – who attacks the tradition of 'honour killings' in his songs – performed at Colombia University, he was criticised by some antizionist students for highlighting this issue, claiming that honour killings should either be ignored, or blamed on Israeli oppression. The spectre of these privileged Ivy League students attacking an actual Palestinian for telling the truth about his own community exemplifies everything that is wrong with the identity Left.[49]

It is also hard to argue that antisemitism has not become more virulent within the populations of Gaza and the West Bank over recent decades: John Denham recalls how the Palestine Liberation Organization used to be democratic and secular, but 'has become more religious and now sees the *Jewishness* of Israel as the problem'.[50] Nonetheless, despite hostility towards Israel, most Palestinians accept its continued existence as a Jewish state; only 11 per cent of Palestinians support the establishment of a secular state for Muslims and Jews, despite this being the official position of the Boycott, Divestment and Sanctions (BDS) movement – itself a creation of UK academics, and not an authentic Palestinian organisation.[51] As journalist Yair Rosenberg points out, this means that the BDS movement is led by people who claim to represent Palestinians yet push a policy goal Palestinians hate. Similar to the BDS movement itself, one-stateism, although in many ways a desirable aim, did not spring from the Palestinian people; it is done in the name of the Palestinians, but it is not of them.

As we all know, there is a particular pleasure when our prejudices appear to have been proven correct. Likewise, it feels great to be part of an exclusionary community that pours scorn upon 'the Other'. This is true for sports fans, music snobs, real ale drinkers, 4chan hipsters and so on. Traditionally, prejudice played this role – W.E.B. DuBois called it a 'psychological wage' – among poor white men, who might not have much, but at least they weren't black, or gay or a woman. But this sort of pleasure-from-prejudice was and is not restricted to the political Right. Over the past 150 years, social democratic and labour movements across the globe have been buttressed by gender, national or ethnic identity, or very often all three. Today, while most hobbyists would rather die than be thought of as racist, they are not immune from the psychological pleasures of prejudice and exclusion. Some people for whom anti-racism is integral to their identity still look for an 'other' against which to define themselves This is where antizionism comes in. They can rail about Israel and the diaspora Jews that support it until the cows come home, and not only will they not be thought of as racist; they can actually claim to be anti-racist.

Recently, I met an Israeli woman who had been living on the Greek island of Lesbos, working with refugees who had crossed the Mediterranean in perilous conditions and who are now in desperate need of all manner of help and assistance. As I listened to her harrowing tales, I was not only impressed by her selflessness and courage, but I couldn't help thinking that, if she had introduced herself to a group of hobbyist leftists, the first – and perhaps only thing – any of them would have thought is: 'She's Israeli. Urgh.' Her tireless work with the refugees would have counted for nothing against the immutable fact of her nationality.

This absolutely stinks. There is something fundamentally wrong with a worldview that allows even the most privileged, selfish and hypocritical people to lord it over others based only on their nationality. The above-described arrest of Lord Ahmed – which he blamed on 'the Jews' – prompted the journalist and Tory peer Danny Finkelstein to wonder on Twitter exactly what interest the Jews had in staging a car crash in Rochdale. In response to this, *The Guardian* journalist Michael White tweeted: 'Danny, you're a good chap...I agree it's a stinker and typical of double standards. Pity about the illegal settlements though'.[52] What is the connection here? Because, of course, it is not just a 'pity' about the settlements; it's a massive tragedy – the settlements are one of the primary obstacles to peace, have resulted in numerous deaths on all sides, and incalculable deprivations and hardships. But what do they have to do with a car crash involving a British lord? Here we can see how antizionism allows even the most privileged – a 60-something white, male, *Guardian* columnist who uses words such as 'stinker' and 'chap' as though he's Bertie Wooster or Boris Johnson – to glibly assume the role of a victim.

Conclusion

It is not for me to say what should be done in the Middle East. But it is surely crucial that we never lose sight of the real villains: self-serving Israeli politicians with no regard for human lives; hate-filled Hamas leaders and fundamentalist clerics; George Galloway, celebrity antizionists and professional antisemites who drip poison into open young minds as a displacement for their own frustrations.

Ironically, Israel has many attributes of the type of society socialists claim to want, given how important communalism and community is to Israeli citizens. It also raises the troubling question of whether communalism can only be achieved with some sort of exclusionary identity: nearly every society that has aimed to do away with class divisions has been based upon some type of racial, ethnic, religious or national exclusion. This is true of the sinister and evil, such as Mao's China or the *volksgemeinschaft* of the Third Reich, and the affable but nonetheless nationalistic and ethnically homogeneous such as post-1948 Israel and Britain in 1945.

The preoccupations of the British Left will make very little difference to this; if there is to be a solution, it has to be forged in the Middle East and in the United States. Yet to the extent that the British government might have some influence and be able to exert some pressure on Israel, then, as with so much else, it will only happen with a Labour government. And the all-consuming obsession with Israel among some on the Left is one of a myriad of factors that makes a Labour government less likely.

5. Is This What a Feminist Looks Like?

Women's Activism and Left-wing Hobbyism

As with so many other issues, when it comes to feminism, the hobbyist Left displays all its usual hypocrisy, elitism and overriding concern for aesthetics, identity and nomenclature. Very often it appears to have little regard for improving the position of women, and indeed in some instances could be accused of actively working against gender equality. As the proponents of hobbyist feminism are relatively privileged, their concerns are all too often the esoteric issues that only really affect people like them. Furthermore, the abstract, identitarian concerns of hobbyist feminism allow not only ruthless neoliberals to claim the mantle of feminism, but also 'woke misogynists' such as Harvey Weinstein. This chapter will discuss how performative radicalism interacts with feminism. It contains a brief history of the inglorious relationship between the labour movement and women during the twentieth century, before discussing the emergence of 'hobbyist feminism' in recent years. It highlights the overwhelmingly white, middle-class nature of hobbyist feminism, and argues that the development of feminism as an identity has allowed for both male misogynists and various kinds of conservatives to adopt the term for themselves.

Jobs for the Boys

Historically, the Left has had a very poor record on women's rights. During the First World War, the trade unions resisted the introduction of women into male-dominated workplaces, and struck a deal with the government to eject these women as soon as the guns fell silent. As with trade union agitation against immigrants, this was not just about job security and undercutting wages. The historian Gail Braybon claims that 'women were not simply resented because they were unskilled or semi-skilled workers, but because they were *women*, a class apart, who were encroaching upon men's work'. Women in the workplace were still resented even if they were unionised, on equal pay, and with a guarantee that returning soldiers would have their old jobs back. Furthermore, most of the labour movement, despite being 'a relatively radical group of people, concerned with workers' oppression and women's legal and political rights, nevertheless accepted the inevitability of women's domestic role, and did not take the matter of their employment very seriously'.[1]

Intriguingly, in the inter-war era, it was local Labour parties in the coalfield seats, with the fewest women members, who pursued the most progressive policies on issues such as birth control. The UK's first ever birth control clinic was set up in 1925 in the Welsh town of Abertillery after pressure from the local miners' agent. By 1931, the second Labour government decreed it was acceptable for local authorities to give birth control advice, yet the overall consensus is that Labour actually did more for women in the 1920s, and retreated from those issues in the 1930s.[2]

For most of the twentieth century, the majority of British women voted Conservative. In fact, it has been claimed that if women were unable to vote, Labour would have won every general election between 1945 and 1979. This was even the case in areas assumed to be Labour strongholds, such as Wales. According to the historian Sam Blaxland, open-air mass meetings organised exclusively for Welsh women's branches of the Conservative Party in the 1950s and 1960s attracted well over a thousand attendees on each occasion. These women offered not just votes, but also political, financial and social support. In the grassroots organisations and local associations women not only contributed to the day-to-day running of Conservative politics, but were often the driving force behind it. They organised social activities and fundraising events such as 'Bimbo' themed social nights, knit-ins and balloon blowing competitions, as well as the more conventional fayres, bazaars and bingo evenings.[3]

Larry Whitty confirms that the unions were slow to see the coming of feminism as an issue. 'But female employment increased, so they had to. Especially the GMB', given that so many of its potential recruits were women.[4] In Wales, the miners' strike of 1984–1985 saw a large group of miners' wives and other women join – in many cases, for the first time – the political world of picket lines, strikes and nationwide tours, learning about and soaking up the experiences of others in similar situations.

The past few decades have seen an abrupt change in the relationship between feminism and the broader Left. The smoky rooms full of old men that were so central to the labour movement for most of the twentieth century are long gone. Nowadays, the 1945–1979 gender preferences have been reversed, and men are much more likely to vote Conservative than women. Feminism is now, rightly, central to the modern Left. This change was long overdue, but increasingly 'women's rights' are becoming an abstract concept. In the early decades of the twenty-first century, feminism is not exclusively for those who want to improve the structural position of women; increasingly it is an identity, and an identity the cynical and career-minded can adopt for their own advancement.

'Feminism Just Got Interesting'

Despite the haste with which many men and career-minded Tory women – who a few decades ago would have baulked at the idea of describing themselves as feminists – wrap themselves in the flag of feminism, this is not reflective of the wider population. Surveys consistently find that most women – and nearly all men – refuse to identity as feminists. A 2016 poll for the Fawcett Society found that while 67 per cent of people believe in gender equality, only 7 per cent would describe themselves as 'feminists'. Indeed, even some high-profile women who are often held up as examples of popular feminists, such as Sarah Jessica Parker, Demi Moore, Madonna, Marion Cotillard, Katy Perry and Bjork all refuse to describe themselves as such.[5] If you asked people if they believed in certain precepts – equality between genders; full opportunities and equal pay for women; shared parental and domestic duties; and reproductive rights – most people would agree. Why then do most people refuse to describe themselves as 'feminist'?

One reason must be that most people hesitate to describe themselves as an '-ist' of anything. But another is that feminism is often assumed to be something for a certain type of woman: young, white, well-educated and relatively privileged. This is not helped by the hobbyist Left's conception of feminism, which focuses on image, etymology and identity, often at the expense of actions and practicality. In these first decades of the twenty-first century, feminism still has an image problem. And it isn't the crude image of tabloid stereotypes.

The bourgeois nature of contemporary feminism has long roots. Reviewing Betty Friedan back in 2013, professional activist Ellie May O'Hagan notes that Friedan 'only refers to working class women when suggesting they could act as nannies to alleviate the ennui of middle-class housewives'. As the historian Selina Todd concurs, 'the fight for liberation continued to be eased by the labour of less privileged women'.[6] Owen Jones writes that 'progress is not handed down as an act of munificence by the powerful, generously granting, say, women the vote,' but crucially, it was always a small group of committed individuals who forced this change.[7] Historically, despite advances in the liberty and progress of individual women, class continued to matter: working-class women had very little idea about contraception until the 1950s, and right through the 'sexual revolution' of the 1960s, women continued to bear the brunt of childcare and chores.[8]

In *The People,* her book on the British working class, Todd interviewed working-class women involved in women's activism. Most of them, such as Judy Walker of Coventry, refused to describe themselves as feminist, which they associated with 'just talking'. The Warwick University students that Walker met at meetings did not have children, and therefore they could afford the time to sit and discuss sexual and emotional relationships. In contrast Walker, like most of the women she knew, had to 'just get on with looking after my kids'; in fact, she worked as a cleaner for another of the women in the group.[9] Similarly, former Labour Party staffer Ayesha Hazarika recalls:

A women's event in Manchester a while ago where a woman stood up and said she'd never been to an event like this before and she was nervous that it may not be for people like her. She then revealed that she wasn't that Left-wing, she was working class and had voted for Brexit and the whole room went a bit Lord of the Flies...I doubt she'll ever attend another women's event.[10]

This sad state of affairs, where working-class women and women of colour feel that 'feminism' is not for them, persists despite the efforts of the hobbyist Left to 'make feminism fun'.

Although this book is full of predictions that proved less than prescient, this humdinger by Ellie May O'Hagan takes some beating: writing in January 2015, she claimed that 'if 2014 was the year women made their voices heard, 2015 will be the year women take to the streets'. This assertion encapsulates the classic thinking of many on the Left towards 'ordinary people'; O'Hagan loves 'taking to the streets', and she assumes that so too do most women. The article continues: 'I've seen the green shoots of feminism's next phase emerging, because I've taken up invitations to attend the meetings of a new feminist direct action group called Sisters Uncut.' Note the phrasing of this – 'I've taken up invitations' – which puts all of the power and agency into O'Hagan's hands: she has 'taken up' the 'invitations' she receives. It also sounds uncannily like a radio DJ or similar promoting the next big band. This excitement is also revealed when she writes that 'the atmosphere of the meetings is so galvanising, supportive and radical that they're almost addictive' – again, the focus is on how exciting the meetings are; the sensation is intoxicating and 'almost addictive'.

This is particularly ironic given the focus of Sisters Uncut. One of the founders of the group, Frida, said they set it up as 'we were horrified that domestic violence services were being decimated by austerity, and felt it was a result of the fact that women are generally treated as second-class citizens whose needs are relegated'. O'Hagan interpreted this desperate response to an attack on living standards as 'a simple message... feminism just got interesting'. Here we can see the difference between the everyday bread and butter issues of politics and the hobbyists' response to it: domestic violence services were being hit hard by the austerity policies of the government and a group of women decided to resist these cuts. This absolutely does not mean that 'feminism just got interesting'.[11]

The preoccupation with iconography and aesthetics at the expense of actual change is clear in Laurie Penny's description of 'Pussy Riot with their bright balaclavas...the black bloc face-rag, the grinning Guy Fawkes masks on the front lines of riots'. For Penny, 'the iconography of Pussy Riot is infectious' and she instructs readers on 'how you make a balaclava out of old stockings...preferably in day-glo pink or blue or green... Put on your homemade neon balaclava. Now go and start an oppositional art revolution.'[12]

The preoccupation with semantics and etymology that we associate with the hobbyist Left is also the hallmark of middle-class feminism. Writing in the *Buffalo Law Review*, the jurist Lucie White observes that 'the very term for the male sex organ, "testes", is linked etymologically to the root for "testimony" and "testify"'. Which is a very good observation – but so what?[13] Do we honestly think that the aged origins of certain words still control our thinking today? That women and men think that men are more reliable and authoritative because of the etymology of *testify*? Similarly, some researchers argue that the very presence of gender specific pronouns contributes to the continuation of patriarchy. Yet in many languages (such as Spanish), the word for person (*persona*) is feminine, as indeed is the word for 'mankind' (*la humanidad*). Furthermore, gender-neutral languages do not necessarily lead to feminist utopias; see Turkey, Iran and Bangladesh. The writer Martha Nussbaum, speaking of Judith Butler, neatly encapsulates some of the problems with the academicisation of feminism:

> In Butler, resistance is always imagined as personal, more or less private, involving no unironic, organized public action for legal or institutional change...Butlerian feminism is in many ways easier than the old feminism. It tells scores of talented young women that they need not work on changing the law, or feeding the hungry, or assailing power through theory harnessed to material politics. They can do politics in the safety of their campuses, remaining on the symbolic level, making subversive gestures at power through speech and gesture. This, the theory says, is pretty much all that is available to us anyway, by way of political action, and isn't it exciting and sexy?[14]

The case of the Women's Equality Party (WEP) is a particularly apposite example of the solipsism of middle-class feminism. Although founded with good intentions, it was and remains not only irrelevant to most women, but arguably detrimental through splitting progressive votes and helping the Tories. In 2014, Ellie May O'Hagan wrote that 'the Scots shouldn't be the only ones who should have their fun: women of Britain, it's time for us to follow Sweden's example by forming our own party to represent our interests in government'. (Note the use of the word fun – it is not incidental.) She continued: 'Women of colour, and working-class and LGBT women, would be at the centre of the party.' It goes without saying that when this wish materialised as the WEP, it was and continues to be dominated by middle-class white women.[15]

At the 2017 election, WEP leader Sophie Turner stood as a candidate in Shipley, a West Yorkshire constituency home to noted reactionary Philip Davies. This did not go down well with many local women, particularly the grassroots group Shipley Feminist Zealots (SFZ). They called on Walker to withdraw her candidacy, as they did not believe that the WEP would be able to unseat Davies, and would instead split the anti-Tory vote. The SFZ's Jenny Wilson told BuzzFeed that local feminist activists had not been aware of Walker's plan:

> If they genuinely think they can win this seat, then they've gone a silly way about it by rushing in and announcing the candidacy without consulting groups like ours before announcing…Maybe we could have got behind Sophie Walker if there had been some discussions…But they've just leaped in…It's grandstanding, it's putting your own interests before actually considering the needs of the people on the ground.

As Shipley had swung from Labour to Conservative in recent years, it was reasonable to hope that Davies might be unseated – but clearly not by the WEP. Wilson said that while she wouldn't rule out voting for the WEP, she didn't feel the party had done anything to add to the work the SFZ had done to help build unity among local voices who oppose Davies' politics. Another activist, Sue Easterbrook, said that despite having lots of sympathy for the WEP's agenda, she felt 'betrayed' by Walker's decision to run, and that the WEP were 'using Shipley as a publicity stunt': 'They don't have any chance of winning. I think they'll take 1,000 votes, probably from Labour, making it harder for them to unseat [Davies]'. There was also concern that Walker, whose family live in Yorkshire but who is now based in London, did not necessarily understand the concerns of the area. Easterbrook said she had 'never felt as Yorkshire' as when she read Walker's candidacy announcement in *The Observer*: 'I just thought, how dare they!...they're in a complete London bubble...there's all sorts of things that they just don't realise about what it's like living up here'.[16]

In the end Sophie Walker did run, and won 1040 votes – just under half the Liberal Democrat total of 2202. Despite a close race with Labour, Philip Davies was re-elected with 27,417 votes; a majority of just 4681. Even if all of the Lib Dem and WEP voters had transferred to Labour, they would still have fallen 1,439 votes short of unseating Davies; nonetheless, the WEP's deaf ears when it came to the appeals of local women is telling.

The Unbearable Whiteness of Identity Feminism

The feminism of the hobbyist Left is even whiter than it is middle class. Back in 1982, legendary Afro-American feminist bell hooks wrote that:

It is not opposition to feminist ideology that has caused black women to reject involvement in the women's movement. Feminism as a political ideology advocating social equality for all women was and is acceptable to many black women. They rejected the women's movement when it became apparent that middle and upper class college-educated white women who were its majority participants were determined to shape the movement so that it would serve their own opportunistic ends.[17]

Anyone who has seen the look on the face of a woman who's just been told that some 'feminists' criticise anti-female genital mutilation and anti-*sati* campaigns as examples of Western imperialism will understand why so few women of colour identify as feminists. A crank once insisted to me at a party that the defence of FGM by white, middle-class 'feminists' was a straw man; i.e. no one really did it. Yet the very white Canadian feminist academic K.E. Noss argues that 'female circumcision discourse within US feminist contexts and western-based anti-circumcision projects operating in Kenya...perpetuates discursive and material violence against Kenyan Maasai communities'. Rather than see anti-FGM campaigns as an uncomplicated attempt to protect young girls from an abominable procedure, Noss considers them examples of 'neo-colonial violence', and 'part of the white western feminist' (although presumably not white Western feminists such as her) displacing of 'female abjection through the pleasure of whiteness'.[18]

Never mind its lack of concern for BME women – hobbyist feminism is even more unconcerned for BME men. After photographs emerged of US service personnel abusing Iraqi prisoners at the Abu Ghraib jail, some commentators felt the abuse itself was of secondary concern, given that some of the soldiers involved were women. Kelly Cogswell, writing in *The Gully* magazine, worried that the publication of the images would 'inflame misogyny...The image of an American woman holding a prisoner's leash will be used as a potent argument against modernization and the emancipation of women.' Likewise, Barbara Ehrenreich wrote how she had 'hoped that the presence of women would over time change the military, making it more respectful of other people and cultures, more capable of genuine peacekeeping...A certain kind of feminism, or perhaps I should say a certain kind of feminist naiveté, died at Abu Ghraib.'[19]

A good example of the success of neoliberal feminism at the expense of real and meaningful social change is that there are more white women in top roles at FTSE 100 companies than there are minority men. Outside of the UK, Holly Baxter – co-founder and editor of *Vagenda* magazine – observes with pleasure that 'the resemblance of the Al-Wakrah World Cup stadium [in Qatar] to the female genitalia can only be a good thing'. This at a stadium effectively built by slave labour from South Asia and elsewhere, causing the deaths of dozens of workers. According to Baxter, this and the other terrible human rights abuses by the Qatari government should not detract from the more important fact that the stadium looks like a vulva.[20]

None of this stops the hobbyist Left from claiming BME issues as their own; *The Guardian* music critic, a very white man named Ben Beaumont-Thomas, remarks that 'Taylor Swift's groping trial marks her long-awaited political awakening... Attacked for her silence during the 2016 presidential election and over the Black Lives Matter movement, Taylor Swift has, by countersuing a man who groped her, finally made a universal feminist statement.'[21]

The phrase 'intersectionality' is a favourite of the hobbyist Left, almost as well-worn a trope as middle-class white women advising each other to 'check their privilege'. The concept itself makes a lot of sense: the problems of working-class women are different to those faced by middle-class women, and the problems of black women different from both. However, this is not the same as saying that the problems of black women are simply the *sum* of the problems faced by the average black woman and the average woman. And the hobbyist Left wields the concept of intersectionality without a consideration for the specifics of particular situations, thus reducing an important concept to a mere buzzword.

The idea of intersectionality originates in a 1976 case, when a black woman called Emma DeGraffenreid sued her employer, General Motors, for discrimination. At General Motors, women were only considered for certain jobs, mainly administrative roles, while blacks were only considered for another set of jobs, primarily manual factory work. Thus, black women's opportunities for advancement were limited in a unique way that was experienced neither by black men nor white women. According to the researcher Chris Martin, intersectionality started to merge with progressive ideology when Patricia Hill Collins, a black feminist sociologist, moved the theory from 'grounded specificities to ungrounded generalities'.

The assumption here is that discrimination is always worse than the sum of its parts, but intersectional discrimination is dependent not just on identity, but also on specific scenarios. For example, in the United States, in certain educational scenarios, there are examples of pro-black discrimination. Furthermore, studies show that men who are both gay and black are perceived as more likeable than men who are both gay and white. This does not mean it is easy to be a gay black man in America, but does show at least one positive characteristic that gets attributed to gay black men. Therefore, not every intersectional effect is negative: a hiring committee is perhaps more likely to hire a black liberal than a white liberal, but less likely to hire a black conservative than a white conservative.[22]

To give real meaning to the intersectionality, there needs to be a consideration of context, not just identity. To see intersectionality as a means of calculating inherent grievance and discrimination, independent of any particular scenario, does not but buttress the victimhood hierarchy beloved of the hobbyist Left. The academic Jasbir Puar argues that ultimately, 'no matter how intersectional our models of subjectivity, no matter how attuned to locational politics of space, place, and scale, these formulations may still limit us if they presume the automatic primacy and singularity' of an individual's identity. For Puar, this model of intersectionality presumes that 'race, class, gender, sexuality, nation, age [and] religion' are individual components than can be disassembled. Therefore the:

Study of intersectional identities often involves taking imbricated identities apart one by one to see how they influence each other, a process that betrays the founding impulse of intersectionality, that identity cannot so easily be cleaved...As a tool of diversity management and mantra of liberal multiculturalism, intersectionality colludes with the disciplinary apparatus of the state-census, demography, racial profiling, surveillance – in that "difference" is encased within a structural container that simply wishes the messiness of identity into a formulaic grid.[23]

The Rise of the 'Woke Misogynist' and Identity Feminism

As it does to left-wing radicalism more broadly, the hobbyist Left reduces 'feminism' to an identity that can be claimed and performed, rather than a set of political beliefs and moral values. Thus, there are many men ostensibly 'on the Left' who treat women terribly in many different ways. This includes casual misogyny: in September 2017, Steve Topple, a prominent Corbynite on Twitter, lamented that 'apparently [he] can't call a woman a bitch now'. But it also includes harassment – as in the case of Stalinist journalist Sam Kriss – and even sexual assault. The Socialist Workers' Party (SWP) infamously hushed-up the case of 'Comrade Delta', who was accused of raping a subordinate. Instead of reporting these accusations to the police, the SWP tried Delta themselves, and exonerated him. Describing this case, journalist Zoe Williams notes that:

Again, at the time and to this day, when you raise the issue, SWP members will give you a thorough explanation of why this is less important than smashing the system, which is where violence against women, indeed all violence, comes from in the first place. No compromise is possible between these two positions: you either believe equality for women should take second place to equality generally, or you believe equality for women is indivisible from general equality. It cannot cede or defer to a battle over what is more important, because nothing is more important: they are parts of the same whole...This tendency is not so much hard-left as incredibly niche.[24]

Meanwhile, former hero of the hobbyist Left Julian Assange is still, at time of writing, cowering in a broom cupboard in Kensington to avoid rape charges. Of course, Assange remains innocent until proven guilty, but there can be no defence of his refusing to answer charges. This doesn't stop Russell Brand, in his book *Revolution*, talking of visiting Assange in the Ecuadorian embassy, 'where he is forced to live for reasons I've never fully understood'.[25] This is the same Russell Brand who gave a ringing endorsement to *The Game*, the so-called 'Bible' of Pick Up Artists, written by bald-headed lothario Neil Strauss. On the title page, Brand brags that the book 'changed [him] from a desperate wallflower into a wallflower who can talk women into sex'.

If feminism is something anyone can subscribe to and claim for themselves simply through the correct use of language, this allows many men who treat women terribly to describe themselves as feminists without blushing. It may even encourage them in their ways. For example, Hollywood producer and alleged serial abuser Harvey Weinstein donated $100,000 to endorse the Gloria Steinem Chair in Media, Culture, and Feminist Studies at Rutgers University, and was a prominent participant in an anti-Donald Trump women's march in Park City, Utah. The journalist Nona Willis Aronowitz has coined the phrase 'woke misogynist' to describe such people, and they are ten-a-penny, on the internet, on the streets and on university campuses.

The outing of supposedly-feminist men who turn out to be misogynists is seemingly endless. In fact, the American writer Patton Oswalt waspishly notes that 'the "male feminist ally turns out to be a creeper/harasser" is the "family values politician turns out to be gay" for millennials'. Joss Whedon, writer of *Buffy the Vampire Slayer*, is an outspoken feminist and a loud proponent for the portrayal and representation of strong female characters in film and TV. According to the *Huffington Post*, he has been honoured by Equality Now, an organisation that protects and promotes the human rights of women and girls, several times, and sits on their advisory board. Predictably enough. Whedon's ex-wife, Kai Cole, revealed Whedon cheated on her several times, claimed that his treatment of her throughout their marriage made him a 'hypocrite preaching feminist ideals'.[26] Meanwhile the online magazine *Vice*, self-consciously 'radical' and 'transgressive' in the puerile way that appeals to people in their early twenties, has been beset by accusations of sexual harassment in the workplace and failure to create a safe environment for women.[27]

More seriously, Tariq Ramadan, a French academic, is awaiting trial on three counts of rape – allegations which Ramadan adamantly denies; he has filed a defamation lawsuit against one of his accusers – and he is currently being held in custody in France ahead of his trial in 2018. Bernard Godard, a fellow French academic, admitted knowing that Ramadan was 'violent and aggressive' sexually – which presumably he considered acceptable - but insisted that he had 'never heard of rapes' and was 'stunned' to learn of the allegations.[28]

According to a report in the Emirati paper *The National*, Godard said of Ramadan: 'That he had many mistresses, that he consulted sites, that girls were brought to the hotel at the end of his lectures, that he invited them to undress, that some resisted and that he could become violent and aggressive, yes, [I knew].'[29] Ramadan is of course innocent of all charges unless it is proven otherwise, but irrespective of the outcome of the criminal investigation – and again it is worth repeating that Ramadan strenuously denies any wrongdoing – it is worrying that we have two French intellectuals, both of impeccable anti-imperialist, feminist credentials, with one well aware of the misogynist behaviour of the other, but finding nothing untoward about it.

Then there is the infamous case of Lee Salter. Salter, while a lecturer at the University of Sussex, began a sexual relationship with one of his students. One might say this was an inherent abuse of power, irrespective of the maturity and desires of the student. But Salter's work railed against US imperialism, Zionism, and encouraged campus activism at the self-consciously right-on University of Sussex, and the authorities implicitly condoned the relationship. He then became violent, punching her in the face, knocking her out and stamping on her head. He also threw a container of salt in her face, chipping her tooth and causing her nose to bleed; she was left with a black eye and bruises on her side in an ordeal which she said changed her life. Nonetheless, in the 10 months between his arrest and conviction, Salter was allowed to continue to teach at Sussex.

The right-on male academic who rails against imperialism and neoliberalism while seducing his students and who cries about the fate of Palestinian women under occupation and two-times his girlfriends is so wearily ubiquitous as to be almost not worth mentioning. But this hypocrisy has filtered down – now all sorts of ostensibly left-wing men, not just billionaires and academics but professional activists and ordinary Twitter onanists, are proudly averring their feminism while cheerfully continuing in their women-hating ways. Certainly, many would do this without the rise of hobbyist leftism. And there is not necessarily any correlation between radical politics and abuse of women – plenty of right-wing men and the politically apathetic behave terribly towards women. But it does act as a convenient cover, and may well help abusers believe that their behaviour is not that bad. And hobbyist leftism, with its focus on theory, language and identity at the expense of practice, has facilitated this hypocrisy, and created a handy framework for denying and excusing this behaviour.

SWERF That

Sex work is one of the most highly contentious issues among contemporary feminists. As with the division over transgender women discussed in the next chapter, male misogynists are the main beneficiary of this intra-feminist in-fighting. Women (and self-professed male feminists) accusing those who should be their natural allies of being 'whorephobic' is ludicrous, and the passionate defence of sex work by feminists only serves to benefit men who pay women for sex. Nonetheless, there is something unescapably prudist about anti-sex work feminists. All too often, they extrapolate their understanding of sex and intimacy to every woman in the world; since many of them could never imagine treating sex as a commodity to be bought and sold, they find it difficult to believe that any other woman could.

A good example of the 'sex work exclusionary feminist' argument is Zoe Williams, claiming here in *The Guardian* that 'there probably hasn't been a time in history, no pause for breath in the segue from patriarchal considerations of decency to a feminist crusade against objectification, when pornography has been considered as acceptable as it is now'.[30] Williams reckons that this has happened 'because the visual language of stripping has been appropriated by mainstream culture. You'll see a lapdance referenced in a music video.' This is the same sort of language we might expect to read from the pen of a Peter Hitchens or Roger Scruton. Williams continues:

> You might hear a stripper of global renown – Dita von Teese, for instance – talking about how she wasn't objectified because her act is a work of art; women who are light years away from having to strip for cash might do a pole dancing class for a wacky hen night. I'm not getting po-faced about this. I couldn't give a stuff about middle-class women kidding

themselves that pole dancing is a smashing experience. I am simply surprised at what I suspect has happened: that the mainstream cultural usage of stripping as just a way to be a bit saucy has impacted so profoundly on the way we see sexual commerce that the government forgot why it had regulated lapdancing clubs in the first place.[31]

Of course, just because something pleases the johns doesn't mean it is wrong. The political scientist Cas Muddle describes the 'Nordic Model' as 'a return to the darkest periods of left-wing paternalism, in which self-professed progressives fight for middle class utopias at the expense of the socially weak'. Muddle points out that the key sticking point for progressives in opposing the selling of sex, rather than any other product, is 'that sexuality is something "personal," which is intrinsically linked to (strong) emotions' and that 'it is the selling woman who is harmed, not the buying man, reflecting a long-standing gendered notion of sexuality, in which female sexuality is inherently problematized'.[32]

The intra-feminist dispute over sex work shows how dangerous divisions can emerge from the abstracting of feminism to an ideology which can be claimed by all. Since being a feminist is a crucial shibboleth for being on the modern Left, these issues, rather than being debated in good faith with the seriousness they deserve, can often serve as ciphers for ideological battles within 'feminism'. That so many self-professed left-wing men believe that they can call women 'swerf bitches' and the like simply because they disagree over how the state treats sex work, while still claiming to be feminists, makes this all too clear.

Neoliberal Feminism

Zoe Williams posits that contemporary feminism is at a crossroads: 'For every feminist summer school, we have Caitlin Moran's swashbuckling, blokey feminism, which seems to be about making lots of witty observations about sexism, without ever putting them in the context of social oppression.' This suggests a polarity between staid, wholesome feminism on the one hand and a feminism of the everyday on the other. Williams continues: 'For every campaign against objectification, we have the Sex and the City brand of feminism, as personified by a burgeoning movement in America calling itself "sexy feminists", which reassures us that one can believe in gender equality and still pay hefty sums of money to have pubic hair ripped out at the root.' This neatly highlights the emergence of neoliberal, individualistic feminism, or as Williams has called it, 'capitalism with tits'. [33]

This is the subject of investigations by the academics Angela McRobbie and Catherine Rottenberg, the latter of whom has written on the growth of 'neoliberal feminism', as personified by high-flying business executives Ann-Marie Slaughter and Sheryl Sandberg. It is also nicely encapsulated by supposed feminists such as Beyoncé and Katy Perry. Perry collected $25m for her role as a judge on American Idol, making her one of the highest-paid judges on the show, behind high-waistband enthusiast Simon Cowell, who reportedly makes $45m. Not that Perry felt upset: she told a US radio station that she is 'really proud that as a woman, I got paid. I got paid more than any guy that's ever been on the show.'[34]

This does not mean that feminism needs to be staid and boring – far from it. But surely it cannot simply be about the success of individual women. A handy dichotomy is the difference between what you might call 'Beyoncé feminism' and 'Rihanna feminism'. Whereas Beyoncé makes a great deal of noise about women's rights and has self-consciously created a feminist public image, Rihanna has made much less noise. Yet with her pioneering Fenty make-up range she has had a much larger impact on the lives of women of colour than Beyoncé has ever done.

Similarly, senior female Tories have co-opted the terms feminist and feminism. During the premiership of Margaret Thatcher, leading Conservative women explicitly denied that they were feminists, despite arguably supporting some feminist positions. Today, in contrast, politicians as diverse as Theresa May, Amber Rudd and Nadine Dorries proudly aver that they are feminists, and that their possession of values traditionally associated with the political Right – in terms of markets, limited taxation and a reduced state – does not impede their feminism.

Conservative women throughout this period have projected an abstract version of feminism that helped them construct their own identity; both through distancing themselves from it during Thatcher's era, and co-opting it in the time of David Cameron and Theresa May. While several elements of modern Conservative thought are compatible with elements of 'feminism', the adoption of feminism language by women of the Right generally owes more to expediency than conviction.[35] This is why it is not enough, in the words of Zoe Williams, for Westminster to have more women in it: 'It needs more feminists...and the first principle of feminism is that you don't need to be a woman to be one...The sine qua non of feminism is battling for collective rights.'[36]

This chapter has aimed to show how the hobbyist Left interacts with women's rights. The abstraction of 'feminism' to a label and identity, and the necessity of claiming that label for those who wish to consider themselves on the Left, means all types of people can claim to be feminists, irrespective of how they act. This is dangerous for the Left, for women and for humanity in general, as reactionaries can easily adopt the mantle of feminism to justify and enable their policies. To reclaim the word feminism, we should judge people on their actions alone, not by loud and prominent claims to be a feminist.

6. TERF Wars

Gender Identity, Hobbyists and the Feud dividing Feminists

One of the few successes for progressive politics in recent years – and perhaps the most notable social change during the last 3 decades – has been the advance of LGBT people. It is astonishing for someone of my generation to remind themselves of the anti-gay bigotry of the recent past; and it must be yet more astonishing for younger people. One reason for this is that unlike the other issues discussed in this book, there is increasingly little correlation of opinions on homosexuality with class and education: whether you are an arts teacher in Islington or an ex-docker in Bootle, the odds that you, or your son or daughter, are LGBT are exactly the same.

Despite the recent advances in gay rights, many left-wing hobbyists have been able to find fault with this progress, and many of the heroes of the gay rights struggle – as with some of the earlier heroes of feminism – now find themselves abused by those ostensibly on the Left. In the summer of 2017, legendary gay rights' activist Michael Cashman came under attack from *Red Pepper* magazine, prompting Rob Fanshawe – with whom Cashman co-founded the Stonewall organisation – to remind the author that 'Stonewall achieved just a bit of change.' Twitter user Katie Donovan even claimed that 'the gay community did nothing to free itself before we trans came along with your spines in tow'.

This last outburst brings us onto the theme of this chapter. Of all the internal arguments that divide the Left, the most vicious – and bizarre to outsiders – is that surrounding transgenderism, in particular transgender women. Many radical feminists, used to facing opprobrium from the tabloids and the political Right, now find themselves under attack from erstwhile comrades due to their refusal to recognise that transwoman are women in the same sense as biological women.

Branded as TERFs – trans-exclusionary radical feminists – these women have been outflanked by a (usually) younger generation of feminists, who denounce them as bigots. Yet very few of these young feminists are transgender themselves. They are generally young women – or men – at university or recently graduated, from relatively privileged backgrounds. As usual, there is more than a whiff of hobbyism about the obsession of these cis-gendered women with the transgendered.

I don't presume to weigh in on issues such as self-identification or whether transwomen have the same experiences as cis-women – as a man it's not my place to do so. Furthermore, I want to minimise whatever offence I cause trans activists, given their tenacity and organisational capacity, although I fear that this will still not protect me. What I want to do in this chapter is highlight how trans activism has been added to the roster of hobbies for identity leftists, and why it is, in some ways, an emblematic issue of identity leftism.

It is unmistakable that many of the loudest voices in trans activism are not trans themselves, and you do not have to be the most cynical person in the world to suspect that there is a great deal of hobbyism about this. In many ways, the relationship between issues facing trans people and non-trans online activists is the same as that between the notorious and now discontinued President's Club Dinner and its charitable benefactors; yes, it might have raised money, but that wasn't really the point. It was about getting pissed and ogling women, but also about identity and belonging. Likewise, for so many of the hobbyist Left – almost entirely non-trans – their full-throated trans activism owes a great deal to identity and hobbyism. For trans people themselves of course, there is nothing hobbyist about it. It is deadly serious.

Talking about her experiences in Liverpool in the 1970s, the artist Jayne Casey recalls:

We were well prepared to have a fight because we'd all grown up fighting. We weren't soft kids, we came from heavy working class backgrounds and we knew how to fight. Peter Burns was a fantastic fighter. We'd shock them; the scallies would come for us and we'd batter them! We attracted violence, every night, which was good; we hated the world and expected the world to hate us.[1]

For Casey and Burns, pioneering gender fluidity while growing up among rigidly-conformist communities, life was hard. But they were of the communities they came from, so they were hard too. They knew they had to expect ridicule at the least and violence often, and were prepared to dish it out as well as receive. They had to fight to survive.

This stands in stark contrast with many young people today, who look to associate themselves with the victims of violence without actually being persecuted or attacked themselves. They draw parallels between verbal and physical abuse on the one hand and intellectual disagreements on the other. They claim that some kinds of speech can actually entail violence in and of itself. As one trans person writes on Twitter, it is hypocritical of 'middle class American and British trans activists' to 'pretend they face the same dangerous lives as transsexual street prostitutes. It is a shameless fraud.' For many on the hobbyist Left, as they don't take any real risks in their behaviour, they can enjoy the 'transgressive' experience and the thrill that it brings, without committing to their lifestyle the way Casey and Burns did.

This reaches its most egregious and insensitive conclusion in the writing of Laurie Penny on trans issues: 'I'm about as close as you can get to the trans rights movement without being trans yourself. I've been associated with trans activism for years, and while I don't know what it's like to be harassed, threatened or abandoned for being transsexual, most of my close friends do.' Imagine an alternative sentence that ran like this: 'I'm about as close as you can get to being working class without being working class yourself. I've been associated with the working class for years, and while I don't know what it's like to be poor, unemployed or unable to afford the finer things in life, most of my close friends do.' It would seem absurd and patronising. It's even worse if you substitute 'black' instead of 'working class'. In the same article, Penny continues: 'Right now, I'm watching the rest of the world begin to understand the community that has become my home, and it is incredibly exciting – but it's frightening, too, because the backlash is on', sounding unmistakably like a hipster whose favourite band was about to make it mainstream.[2]

One Twitter user, responding to a call for TERF-persecutors to 'go after tenured women's studies professors...not the powerless 20-yr-olds on Tumblr they've brainwashed', argued that 'the women you call TERFs are mainly grown up experienced intelligent resistant women. The fuckwit pink haired tumblrkin are all yours'. This last comment accurately picks up on the interaction of generation, aesthetic and choice of social media important not only to TERF-persecutors but to the hobbyist Left more generally.

The Guardian's Jackie Ashley wonders: 'Again and again I meet people of my generation who are simply baffled by the apparently sudden emergence of transgender, or transitioning, or gender-neutral or even polymorphous queer issues. Where did all these people come from?'[3]

It's estimated that only 0.5 per cent of the world's population are transgender, so why do we talk about this so much? One radical feminist argues on Twitter that if you think 'trans rights went from zero 2 state policy in 3 yrs because of altruism...

Think again. It's capitalism folks. Homophobia, misogyny & capitalism'. There may well be some truth in this: anti-lesbian homophobia and a desire by *some* men to colonise women's bodies and every possible woman-only space. Certainly, the decision by some companies that they can make more money by sponsoring trans rights has something to do with it, as has the laudable albeit cynical embrace of gay rights by multinational corporations over the past 2 decades.

But another reason may be that this is an issue which, since it affects so few people and yet could be seen as the latest battle in a long struggle for women and LGBT people, is the perfect crusade for hobbyists to adopt.

One online trans activist – a non-trans gay man – asked whether cisgender people 'can imagine what it's like leaving your home in constant fear of assault, harassment and ridicule?' To which a female Twitter user gave the deadpan response: 'No idea. Can't imagine it at all. – Said no woman, ever'. This exchange reflects the hobbyist nature of non-trans fixation on trans rights: the original poster is enjoying a new fad, and in the zeal of his emersion into this new hobby, he forgets that these issues have been experienced by half of the population for thousands of years. Never mind that, though, traditional feminism is boring; trans activism is where it's at.

Another trans activist writes that 'people on Twitter ask me "why do you always go on about transphobia when you're cis" and calling me a "white knight", and saying I care too much… and you look at all the transphobia across society, the rising far right, the suicide rates…and I ask, how can you not care?' Rather than making the point he thinks it does, this does the exact opposite; it shows how hobbyists use the all too real inequalities and injustices of the world as justifications for their self-promoting campaigns against people just like them, but not quite radical enough.

In order to show how this issue became such a totemic topic

for the hobbyist Left, we first need an overview of the seismic shift in the position and image of gay people over the past 3 decades.

LGBT and the Left

As mentioned above, gay rights are one of the few areas where the Left has been able to make huge strides in recent years, effecting wholesale changes to both personal attitudes and public policy. When asked about the notable changes over the course of his political life, apart from the emergence of immigration as a key valence issue, John Denham notes the 'huge change in the attitude to gays...this is part of a broader "live and let live" attitude that has developed. The traditional values of British people haven't changed, it's just that they found a way of getting homosexuality to fit with those values.'[4]

Nonetheless, it is important not to equate success in this area with a robust, influential and powerful labour movement more generally. All too often, victories in the LGBT cause can be used to occlude pervasive failures elsewhere. Significantly, we need to avoid thinking that there is some sort of binary, with gay men and women joining hands alongside socialists and anti-racists on the one hand, and homophobic white, Conservatives on the other.

On the contrary, both the gay rights movement and the gay 'community' is itself riven with fissures and divisions. One notable issue is the homophobia – or at least 'camphobia' of many gay men. Writing of his response to a PETA advert featuring the comedian Alan Carr, Owen Jones says he thought to himself: 'Yuck...that'll really help along the stereotype of gay men as a bunch of mincing court jesters' before going on to criticise this tendency in himself and other gay men. Another issue is racial stereotyping. For whatever reason, black men are assumed to be more masculine, and more likely to be 'tops', while Asian men are assumed to be 'bottoms'. This can cause difficulties for gay men whose sexual proclivities don't match up to their ethnic stereotype. When the gay dating app Grindr asked a white man and an Asian man to let each other run their Grindr profile for 24 hours, messaging men and receiving pictures and propositions via the app, the Asian man's profile was on the receiving end of racist remarks and racial stereotypes, while the white man's was soon full of naked photos and suggestions to meet up.[5]

Furthermore, just because someone is gay does not mean they have a keen awareness of the history of the gay rights' movement. During an acceptance speech at the 2016 Oscars, singer Sam Smith wrongly claimed to be the first openly gay man to win an Academy Award. Then, when told that lyricist (and gay man) Howard Ashman was also an Oscar winner, Smith replied: 'I should know him. We should date,' only to find out that Ashman had died of Aids in 1991. Smith received a great deal of criticism, but was this necessarily fair? After all, he's not a chronicler of the gay rights' struggle, just a gay man.

Another way that gay men and women fail to live up to Left-Right polarisation is through attitudes to money and wealth. Owen Jones claims that 'Pride events have increasingly become corporate junkets with politics relegated, and for many younger LGBT people, trawling through Netflix and finding Milk…may be their only flirtation with past sacrifices.'[6] This might be the case, and it is certainly true that the multinationals which so ostentatiously support gay rights do so out of cold calculation, and would probably do the opposite if they thought it would earn them a few more quid. As Jasbir Puar writes, 'the market may not care if individuals are gay…but the appeal to market-niche status as site of gay liberation seriously underestimates the intertwining of the value-free with values and of the market and the state'.[7]

But does it matter if memories of persecution fade for younger gays, and Pride events become dominated by corporate endorsements and straight couples? Writing of the 2018 French film *120 Beats Per Minute*, Caspar Salmon argues that 'the new gay theme is one of acceptance of homosexual people by their straight families. Coupled with the return of the appalling minstrelsy of Queer Eye, we are seeing a more emollient culture, one aimed at happy and accepted gay people who are sick of anguished depictions of suffering victims. But we need to rekindle some of our abrasiveness.' The problem is that while there are plenty of LGBT people who agree with Salmon politically, there are loads of gay people who don't want to be abrasive and instead want boring, conventional lifestyles and politics, and 'heteronormative' relationships and families. Salmon concludes the article with a call for a 'queerness [that is] open and generous – turning outwards rather than in on itself, to other marginalised communities, in empathy, solidarity and riotous communion'. But what about LGBT Tories, and all the gay people who have no idea what a 'riotous communion' might involve but suspect very much that it's not for them? Are they somehow less gay? The insinuation that being LGBT should involve a measure of political radicalism suggests that sexuality is less fact of birth and more a form of identity.[8]

As with so many of the other issues discussed in this book, historically the Left has a very poor record on gay rights. Speaking after he was attacked by the NUS, Peter Tatchell wearily declares he has a 'feeling of déjà vu':

The last time I was attacked by leaders of the NUS was in 1973, when I staged what turned out to be the first-ever gay rights protest in a communist country, East Germany. When I attempted to speak in defence of gay rights, I was stopped. When I attempted to lay a pink triangle wreath at Sachsenhausen concentration camp, in memory of the gay men killed there, I was stopped. When I held up a gay rights placard at the final festival rally, I was stopped. The key stoppers were leading members of the NUS. They opposed gay rights and did not want to offend the communists.

He continues by recalling that 'at this stage, the British left were homophobic. They said that homosexuality was a "bourgeois perversion", a "manifestation of capitalist degeneracy", and it would disappear in a pure Socialist society.'[9]

As Larry Whitty remembers, the issue of sexuality 'disrupted the views of people who were traditionally "on the left"'. For many who were proud of their consistently radical history, there was a great deal of psychological displacement. Whitty recalls Dennis Skinner MP, after attacking section 28, claiming: 'of course, we're not like that in Bolsover', his home constituency. For Whitty, it was only in the late 1990s that the traditional Left came to terms with gay rights, and then 'only reluctantly. The world had changed around them.'[10]

It is important to remember that while the series of private members bills that liberalised Britain during the 1960s happened under a Labour government, Labour itself was acutely concerned about being seen as soft on gays, as well as on abortion, and crime. In the 1960 vote on putting the recommendations by the Wolfenden Committee on homosexuality into law, Enoch Powell, Margaret Thatcher and Keith Joseph all voted in favour of decriminalisation, but only 73 out of 258 Labour MPs joined them.[11] Writing of Labour's attitude towards out-gays such as Tom Driberg and George Brinham, historian Lucy Robinson claims that 'Labour's move into the private sphere through the law reforms in the late 1960s were not the product of a coherent engagement with the politics of sexuality.'[12] In other words, 'Labour as a whole was very uncomfortable associating itself with what it continued to interpret as a bourgeois and dangerous issue.' Harold Wilson himself warned colleagues that Wolfenden's recommendations were so out of line with public opinion that they would cost the party six million votes.[13]

The long-time gay rights campaigner Allan Horsfall, who was

born and brought up in Bolton and spent most of his life in small mining and industrial towns, knew that in places such as those 'the pressures for social and legal conformity, bore most heavily'. The Buggers' Club in Burnley – an example of a genuinely proletarian space for working-class gay men – was closed after pressure from the trade unions.[14] The hard-Left of the 1970s and 1980s were not necessarily better than the Parliamentary Labour Party in the 1960s. At a huge march against the Heath government's proposed Industrial Relations Bill, members of the Gay Liberation Front were attacked, and the International Socialists forced them to march at the back of the procession. Meanwhile the Workers' Revolutionary Party and Militant both suggested that homosexuality would disappear under socialism.[15] When the Local Government Act 1988 (featuring the infamous section 28) came to the crucial stage, Labour's frontbench joined with the Conservatives to allow the passing of the Bill without a vote. The party's Environment spokesman, Jack Cunningham, 'made it clear that the real Labour Party was not in the business of "promoting homosexuality". He said that was confined to the Inner London Education Authority and the London Borough of Haringey'.[16]

'Wackiness' and Identity in the Gay Rights' Struggle

The historical gay rights movement in the UK had its own problems with performative radicalism. The Gay Liberation Front, set up to advocate for gay rights through orchestrated wackiness, 'like the counter-cultural events behind it, was largely dominated by white, middle-class men'. In fact, GLF squatters in North Kensington prevented the rehousing of homeless families, and after their ejection the council was able to house five homeless families in their squat.[17] In her book, Robinson relates the toe-curling antics behind a GLF attempt to disrupt an evangelical Christian meeting in the 1970s, and it reads like an excerpt from the plot of a Wes Anderson film. It is as close to an example of performative politics for performance's sake as you will find. Plenty of gay rights advocates were aware of the self-serving, counter-productive nature of these antics at the time. The actor Michael Cashman – famous for playing the first openly gay character on a major British soap opera, a long-time LGBT campaigner who later became a Labour Lord – blamed Ken Livingstone and the wacky Left for section 28. Speaking in 1999, he said that 'it has taken us years to undo the appalling gesture politics of Livingstone's reign at the GLC. We do not need him again.'[18]

For Robinson, groups like Lesbians and Gays Support the Miners 'offered glimmers of pride and when the strike was over and the mining communities were sunk, these groups were the ones who could salvage their own successes from the experience'. Therefore, the experience of standing in solidarity with the miners did more to help the cause of gay liberation than it did protect jobs and communities. Robinson continues: 'After the miners' strike the fantasy of working-class masculinity was reformed...In the new world, there may be no jobs or communities, but fathers have reconfigured their relationships with their sons, and working-class heterosexuals have had lesbians and gays round for tea.'[19]

This seems to suggest that mass job losses, the devastation of communities and countless lives, and the consigning of generations to worklessness might all have been worth it if it had some intangible effect on working-class masculinity. This is not to say that the experiences of the 1980s changed much by themselves. In 1991, a social attitudes survey conducted by Health Promotion Wales found that over 70 per cent of men and 60 per cent of women felt homosexual relations were wrong.[20]

Trans Activism and the Reassertion of Gender

A common concern among so-called 'TERFs', which I think is warranted, is that after decades of feminist arguments for gender to be understood as a social construct, trans advocacy reasserts 'gender' as a fixed and defined category, and instead casts biological sex as a construct.

Writing on Facebook, one trans activist argues that 'cis woman [sic] should stop acting like their bodies are the epitome of womanhood'. The author continued by complaining that she was 'super tired of having to take a backseat to cis women in feminism' and 'vaginas aren't inherently...female. Not everyone with a vagina is a woman, not every woman has a vagina'. Another claimed that, 'if you think your sexuality can be affected by trauma, you are a transphobe. "Penis aversion due to trauma" is a textbook transmisogynist assault tactic and it is not and will never be valid.' Thus female victims of rape and sexual assault, who might suffer from degrees of trauma and psychological damage due to their experience, can never have a legitimate fear of penises. Meanwhile, model and prominent trans activist Munroe Bergdorf argues that 'centering [sic] reproductive systems at the heart of these demonstrations is reductive and exclusionary.'

Green Party activist Phil Vabulas gives the definition of a 'woman' as someone who is 'self-identifying' as such: 'Not for five minutes to "sneak into changing rooms", but living life as [a woman].' But this begs the question of exactly what 'living life as a woman' constitutes, and it's not hard to suspect that some of the answers – wearing dresses; having long hair; wearing make-up – reinforce the exact kind of gender essentialism that feminism has long fought against. Vabulas's sentiment was echoed by another tweeter, responding to the question 'what is a woman?': 'In short, an adult who generally follows the stereotypes of womanhood (wears dresses, heels, make-up etc).'

Hobbyist trans activists may argue that these are isolated, unrepresentative individuals, but it is these people – not the millions of trans people around the world, many without any access to the internet, graduate school educations and social media – who are at the forefront of trans activism, and they have a tendency towards threats and the demonisation of anyone they disagree with.

In a *Huffington Post* column, Stonewall's Ruth Hunt makes several sensible points, noting that being trans is 'not about dressing like how you would expect a boy or a girl to dress, and frankly it's insulting to suggest it is. In fact, what clothes you wear has nothing to do with your gender identity.'[21] However, many trans activists disagree with this. For example, one transwoman uploaded to Twitter a picture of her feet, clad in a pair of red strappy shoes, and called on the American clothing store Old Navy to, 'let your...employees know not to call a trans woman wearing these shoes "sir"'. Thus sticking two fingers up at decades of feminist arguments that a person's femininity or womanhood is not determined by the clothes she wears. Another uploaded a photo of her legs clad in pink trousers, and noted that 'self acceptance as a trans lady has allowed me to work more pink clothing into my wardrobe'. The trans blogger shon faye tweets that *The Times* writer Janice Turner decided 'in her kitchen, probably' that young people seeking gender healthcare were self-hating women. In this case we see the exact language previously utilised by sexist men against women being deployed by a transwoman against a woman.

In a report in *The Times*, Dr K – anonymous due to the threats made against people perceived to be anti-trans – recalls one patient, who came from a family where older female relatives had been raped. This patient said that she 'can't be female because girls are fragile and weak, and I don't feel like that'.[22] Andrew Fisher, head of Frensham Heights school in Farnham, Surrey, lets a female student sleep in a bedroom in a boys' boarding house wing because she was questioning her gender. Says Fisher: 'We are a progressive school. In the past, girls identifying as boys would simply have been called tomboys, and boys who felt more like girls would have been described as effeminate. The ability to medically transition [using hormones and surgery] has changed the whole conversation.'[23] I can't help but feel that, far from being 'progressive', this is a reactionary assertion of gender binaries: girls who don't conform to gender stereotypes are not girls, they are boys. One Twitter user stated it explicitly: 'Biological sex is the physical look and function of a human, which can be changed. Gender is how that person identifies. Cannot be changed.'

Trans Activism and Free Speech

In March 2016, the potential for irony on the hobbyist Left reached new heights. First, Germaine Greer – pioneering feminist and for decades a leading light of the liberal-left – was denounced as a transphobe for comments made about transwomen, and barred from speaking on a university campus. As if the denouncement of one of the world's most famous feminists as a misogynist was not enough, what followed was even more incredible. Peter Tatchell, rightly revered across the political spectrum for his tireless and selfless campaigning for LGBT rights, was himself 'no platformed'; not for supporting Greer's remarks, but merely for asserting her right to free speech. Now, the parents of these overwhelmingly white, cis-gendered young women and men who barred Greer would barely have been in their teens when *The Female Eunuch* was published; they themselves were mere glints in their parents' eyes when Peter Tatchell was being beaten and abused by homophobic thugs. The question those of us who want to see a sensible, compassionate, compelling Left need to ask is: how did this happen?

Paris Lees wants a world where 'the overwhelmingly white, middle-class, Oxbridge-educated, male-dominated commentariat' takes '"freedom from prejudice" as seriously as it takes "freedom of expression"'. Yet white middle-class university students are among the biggest supporters of trans rights, and there is a clear correlation between socio-economic privilege, education and whiteness and respect for trans rights, with BME and working-class people likely to be more sceptical. In that same article, Lees avers that Stephen Fry only has a platform due to his demographic background, but this displays a tremendous lack of self-awareness; Lees' own media profile owes everything to her being a transwoman; frankly, if you are a transgender journalist who *hasn't* been published in Comment is Free, you must be a pretty crap writer.[24]

As recently as 2013, Zoe Williams could claim that:

> all the prejudice that has been disallowed by modern standards is now concentrated on this one, pretty small group...it is very extreme, these days, to refer to gay people as deviant, but still allowable to make this insinuation about transsexuals. It is apparently permissible, in our mean-spirited age, to talk about how much disabled people cost the state, but I can't imagine it would be OK to laugh at them. Transsexuals are dealing with a prejudice way out of proportion to their number.[25]

Here we can see how much trans rights have progressed in merely 5 years.

By 2015, Williams was arguing that 'the real root of no-platforming [people with contrary views on transgenderism] is this impervious modern absolutism. It was devised for racists and fascists, on the basis that moral legitimacy was conferred upon repellent positions just by allowing them in to debate.'[26] Peter Tatchell was even more strident: 'In the worthy name of defending the weak and marginalised, many student activists are now adopting the unworthy tactic of seeking to close down open debate.' Tatchell himself was denounced as racist and transphobic by student crank Fran Cowling, 'even though I've supported every anti-racist and pro-transgender campaign' in half a century of human rights work.

According to Tatchell, Cowling claimed to be speaking for the NUS, 'suggesting that she was acting on behalf of the NUS membership, who "believe" me to be racist and transphobic'. Unfortunately, I suspect that the majority of NUS members – and certainly the majority of students – do not know who Peter Tatchell is, much less possess opinions on his politics. Tatchell queried the NUS over when and where this decision was taken by the membership: 'They conceded that the membership had never decided against me.' After stressing that he had, over several decades, 'opposed feminists such as Germaine Greer who reject and disparage transgender people and their human rights' he concluded:

This sorry, sad saga is symptomatic of the decline of free and open debate on some university campuses. There is a witch-hunting, accusatory atmosphere. Allegations are made without evidence to back them – or worse, they are made citing false, trumped-up evidence…This looks and feels cowardly. When challenged, they run, hide and denounce from the 'safe space' of their laptops…Anyone who doesn't toe the line politically risks being denounced, even over the tiniest disagreement. The race to be more Left-wing and politically correct than anyone else is resulting in an intimidating, excluding atmosphere on campuses. Universal human rights and enlightenment values…are often shamefully rubbished as the ideas of Western imperialist white privilege.[27]

Unfortunately, this totalitarianism is not limited to the sad case professional activists that constitute the ranks of the NUS leadership. James Caspian is a gender psychologist who has helped many patients transition over 17 years in the field. He proposed to undertake a research degree at Bath Spa University to investigate changing patterns in gender dysmorphia, yet his proposed project was blocked by the ethics committee as 'politically incorrect'.

The question is why constraining speech on this issue is such an important component of identity for elements of the modern Left. Why do those debates on this issue, more than any others, require such stringent policing? Back in 2015 the pop singer Will Young released a music video, *Brave Man*, which featured images of a naked trans man. While there was some applause for this cultural and transrights moment, there was criticism from some quarters that the actor was white, or able-bodied, or had some other kind of privilege.

The gender fluid blogger and chef Jack Monroe had a moment similar to Sunny Hundal with the mugs: 'I logged back onto Twitter in the evening to see friends, activists and campaigners raging, furious...Outrage at the abuse depicted in the film, as though we live in a world of cotton candy and universal acceptance.'[28] Why was the reaction of some people to criticise the video for its apparently 'unrepresentative' nature, especially when so many of them are not trans, never mind black or disabled? One explanation is that this is the perfect issue to express outrage and denounce others without having your own credentials questioned. It is the activity itself that signals you are one of the good guys. This is the essence of the identity Left.

Conclusion

In a 2014 discussion with the trans actor Laverne Cox, bell hooks suggested that 'one of the issues I think that many people have with trans women is the sense of a traditional femininity being called out and revelled in – a femininity that many feminist women feel, "Oh, we've been trying to get away from that."' For many on the Left that would be enough for hooks to be branded a TERF, but Cox herself engaged with hooks' arguments and conceded that she herself might be 'feeding into the patriarchal gaze in my blond wigs'. But, Cox continued:

If I'm embracing a patriarchal gaze with this presentation, it's the way that I've found something that feels empowering. And I think the really honest answer is that I've sort of constructed myself in a way so that I don't want to disappear...I've never been interested in being invisible and erased. So a lot of how I'm negotiating these systems of oppression and trying not to be erased is perhaps by buying into and playing into some of the patriarchal gaze and white supremacy.[29]

This exchange provides an example of how two women – and two feminists – can sit down and hear each other's arguments without hatred or exclusion. Yet the trans activism as practised by many on the identity Left – online and full of hostility – does not allow for this. It also empowers young, male, white cisgendered men to denounce someone like bell hooks – bell hooks! – as some sort of bigot.

The Slovenian philosopher Slavoj Zizek writes that although hobbyists like to stress how they 'reject normativity ("the imposed heterosexual norm" and so on)', their stance is in fact 'one of ruthless normativity, denouncing any minimal deviation from the PC dogma as "transphobia" or "fascism" or whatsoever'. For Zizek, this 'tweet culture' combines an 'official tolerance' with 'extreme intolerance towards actually different views'.[30] This disciplining of speech is not merely morally wrong, ineffective and self-defeating; it isn't really aiming to do what its protagonists hope to do. The activity of millions of online transactivists does nothing to stop actual trans people suffering fear and abuse. Plus, the persecution and exclusion of people with whom they have a political disagreement may well backfire.

One of the most fascinating things about the next few decades will be seeing what cause(s) emerge for the next generation of the hobbyist Left. Whatever it is, it is safe to say that many of the most ardent trans rights warriors will find themselves outflanked; the new cause will be too radical for them, and they will go to great lengths to stress their right-on credentials, but it will not be enough for the next generation. Today's hobbyists will wail about how they denounced Greer and Tatchell, how they abused TERFs online, how they punched radical feminists who challenged them, but it will not be enough. They will stress how truly radical they are, and how they have legitimate misgivings about whatever the new frontier issue is but it will not be enough. The trans rights warriors of today will find themselves outflanked and denounced by the next generation. They too will be confused and abandoned, as the radical frontier moves on and leaves them behind.

7. The New Labour Aristocracy

Cultural Elitism and the Identity Left

We must avoid the elitism of cultural vanguardism that devalues and despises where the ordinary majority of any group or social formation is at.
Tariq Modood, 1994.[1]

If the Labour Party could select a King, he would be a...Temperance crank, a Nonconformist charlatan...an anti-sport, anti-jollity advocate, a teetotaller, as well as a general wet blanket.
Ben Tillett, 1908.

For as long as there has been a British Left, its appeal to those who would benefit most from its success has been limited by the suspicion that many of its adherents are, frankly, a bit odd. For a movement that seeks to represent and mobilise the majority of the population, prominent left-wing leaders and activists have often had niche interests and esoteric concerns. This characteristic has grown more prominent in recent years, as trade union and local government decline has resulted in fewer 'ordinary' people at the apex of the labour movement, while the rise of the identity Left has brought about an ascendancy of hobbyists in high places. 'There used to be a broad spectrum of people in the [Parliamentary Labour Party]', recalls Larry Whitty, 'but no longer. The professionalization of politics hasn't helped. There are plenty of people whose sole intention is to become an MP.'[2] This has led to a host of rather boring careerists, where once there might have been charismatic campaigners, but it has also resulted in a preponderance of people who, while not strictly careerists, have leisure pursuits and personal peccadilloes largely alien to most Britons.

More than 100 years ago, Vladimir Lenin used the term 'labour aristocracy' to denigrate the better-off, better-paid workers who sided with the bourgeoisie against the proletariat, and thus hindered revolution in nations such as Britain. In reality, it was the more secure workers in skilled occupations who were most likely to be in trade unions and most likely to vote Labour, while the unskilled, casual workers had lower rates of unionisation and would often vote Liberal, Tory or not at all. Today, there are new 'Labour aristocrats' on the scene, harming the image of the Left among its natural supporters, and hampering the cause of socialism in the UK. Instead of being composed of miners and engineers, this new aristocracy is filled by the ranks of the hobbyist Left, who proudly assert their elite culture and esoteric concerns, and often look with contempt upon the values and leisure pursuits of the unwashed masses.

Discussing the nation's favourite sport, Laurie Penny claims that 'there is something suspect about a people's sport that violently excludes more than half the people' – making a terribly sexist assumption that women don't enjoy football, similar to Jeremy Corbyn's misguided assumption that women don't like after-work drinking.[3] Meanwhile George Monbiot, recalling an experience with a now-defunct video rental store, sneers: 'When I once made the mistake of stepping into a Blockbuster video shop, I found myself walking past aisle after aisle of Hollywood movies.' An article in *The Guardian* from August 2017 goes further, with various contributors to the newspaper telling readers why their favourite TV shows – from Seinfeld and the Simpsons to Sex and the City – are 'problematic'.[4]

The writer and journalist Afua Hirsch describes the first time her future husband – a working-class black man – met her Oxford friends for the first time. She recalls his shock at seeing them 'sitting crossed-legged', a group of 'misfit Oxford graduates...feasting on vegan food': 'In all his life...he had never seen a scene like this – people talking so earnestly, almost conspiratorially, in low, hushed voices, even eating the way we were eating, an array of strange plant foods being passed around on little plates.' He remarked later how he was struck by her friends 'sitting there with your herbal tea'.[5] The difference here is not about race – Hirsch's maternal family are from Ghana and there were different ethnicities represented among her friends – nor even of education; Hirsch's husband has a law degree and was at the time training to become a barrister.

Instead the difference was one of class-culture, and it is this division that demarcates the hobbyist Left from the majority of their fellow citizens. It is not how much money they earn, or even how they earn it, but rather what they choose to spend it on: take away or vegan food; a holiday in the sun or an eco-friendly hiking trip; a widescreen TV and Sky package or a shelf full of books.[6] Reality is more complicated than those binaries, and many people enjoy all of the above, but these cultural differences are not meaningless. For example, the single biggest predictor of voting to Leave the European Union was not class, but support for the death penalty. Another indicator was their opinion of the television 'comedy' Mrs Brown's Boys.

The focus of this chapter is on four different areas where the cultural values of the hobbyist Left demonstrate their estrangement from the people they believe they represent: music, clothes and fashion, youth culture, and academia. I am not arguing necessarily that this disparity presents problems for the electoral success of the Labour Party. But nevertheless I do not think it is too great a stretch to imagine that the position of the hobbyists towards popular culture – either failing to understand the values and pastimes of their fellow citizens, or affecting a disdainful elitism – undermines the Left and prevents us from reaching out to the very people we are meant to represent.

The History of Working-Class Cultural Conservatism

Cultural conservatism is a notable feature of most people across the world – and this is as true of those in modern industrialised economies as it is of those in developing nations. Whether Maasai herdsmen or Surrey stockbrokers, people tend to be wary of change. This is particularly so when it comes to their traditions and pastimes. The majority of society may well eventually adopt the habits and tastes of the *avant guard*, but in any given generation, cultural elites are isolated, ridiculed and often despised.

This cultural conservatism is particularly pronounced among traditional Labour voters. Over 70 years ago, the veteran trade unionist and Labour politician Jimmy Thomas lamented that 'the workers are more conservative than the Conservatives'.[7] Describing the inter-war growth of the Labour Party, as working men and women switched their allegiance from the Liberals and the Tories, the historian Martin Pugh describes the importance of the sentiments of 'a conservative working class that, in certain circumstances, was prepared to vote Labour'. By the 1960s Richard Hoggart – author of *The Uses of Literacy* and one of the founders of cultural studies – observed that 'the more we try to reach the core of working-class attitudes, the more surely does it appear that that core is a sense of the personal, the concrete, the local; it is embodied in the idea of, first, the family, and, second, the neighbourhood'.[8] Contrastingly, the Marxists of the 'New Left', such as Perry Anderson and Thomas Nairn, attacked the 'bovine' nature of the English working class, with their 'ill-conceived attempt for equality and bottomless philistinism'.[9]

This cultural conservatism was by no means uniform: apart from the long tradition of working-class eccentrics who have determinedly set themselves against the conformity of their communities, there was a deal of cultural variation according to nation, religion and geography. Often specific regions bucked the trend: for example, the coalfields of South Wales and North East England, and the textile districts of West Yorkshire and East Lancashire, were home to a proud radical tradition, often arising from the coincidence of religious Nonconformity with skilled jobs in staple industries. In these areas, workers who were concerned more with the chapel and library than the pub and the music hall might be in step with the priorities of the wider community. Nonetheless, this tradition was generally absent from large areas of Scotland, West Lancashire, London, the Midlands and most towns in southern England.

As the historian Gareth Stedman Jones argues, there was a distinct lack of this tradition among the radical artisans in London. Fellow historian Elizabeth Ross describes a pre-1914 East London where 'church goers often had to face choruses of mockers'; in one incident from 1889, a born-again sinner walking with a missionary in Bethnal Green was actually assaulted by his former drinking companions.[10] The impression conveyed by Charles Booth's survey of the turn-of-the-century London poor was of a working-class culture:

Both impermeable to outsiders, and yet predominantly conservative in character: a culture in which the central focus was not 'trade unions and friendly societies, cooperative effort, temperance propaganda and politics (including socialism)' but 'pleasure, amusement, hospitality and sport'.[11]

According to an 1899 map depicting the 'Distribution of Drunkeness' in England and Wales, the North West and the North East had the highest rates of convictions for drink-related crimes, with over 1000 offences per 100,000 people. In contrast, most of the south of England had fewer than 250 offences per 100,000, apart from London, which featured between 500 and 750 offences per 100,000 people. Port cities featuring high levels of the kind of casualised labour which inhibited left-wing recruitment were particularly well-oiled: in the Addison area of Liverpool in the 1890s, fully one-seventh of shops were licensed properties, while in the Hard district of Portsmouth, 13 out of 27 premises had a licence.[12]

Control of alcohol was traditionally a big concern for some in the labour movement, despite widespread opposition among the workers. In fact, despite its traction on the Left at around the turn of the twentieth century, the movement for restriction of liquor had its roots in the disciplinary priorities of the newly formed industrialist class. Historian John Greenway describes how:

> The new urban elite of iron masters, factory owners and the like had a direct social and economic interest in increasing the efficiency and security of their workmen. These were to form the backbone of the temperance movement. As society became more mobile and fluid, and as the effect of industrialisation and urbanisation was to multiply the opportunities for the fulfilment of individual desire, so the response was to promote new measures for regulating those passions by the governing classes.[13]

The First World War occasioned the first major reform of licensing in decades, and at the time, workers generally accepted these restrictions as a necessary evil to help win the war. After the Armistice, and even though most restrictions on beer were relaxed by mid-1919, there was some anger at continued state interference into alcohol consumption. In early May 1919, the hard-drinking dockers' leader and Salford North MP Ben Tillett complained that it was an unacceptable infringement for his constituents to be unable to obtain liquor on Easter Monday, which had caused 'serious discontent' and was fast 'becoming a scandal [that] interferes with the disciplinary work of the [trade] Union'.[14]

Indignation about government restriction of boozing notwithstanding, the per capita consumption of alcohol continued to decline after the war, and the issue of licensing reform gained more support at the top of the Labour Party. Prime Minister Clement Attlee proposed that the sale of alcohol in the 'New Towns' built after the Second World War should be under state control, but ultimately few Labour MPs saw alcohol as a major legislative priority, and the issue faded into abeyance in the 1950s.[15]

Of course, even within apparently homogenous working-class communities there were always exceptions and nuances. In Salford during the Great Depression, far from being an omnipresent background to daily life, 'people took part in pub culture when they could afford to'; and although football was enormously popular among working-class men, very often people could not afford to attend matches featuring Manchester United or Manchester City, and had to make do with more humble teams.[16] Yet over all, most working-class areas exhibited a culture centred on the pub, the music hall, sport, family and patriotism, which often inhibited their recruitment to socialism, given that many left-wing activists took a dim view of that same culture.

For example, the Social Democratic Federation – the leading socialist society in London – never had more than 3000 members out of a population of more than 6.5 million.[17] Of London, Stedman Jones concludes that the 'republican and international culture which had been such a characteristic feature of artisan tradition in the first three quarters of the century had all but died out by 1900'.

The Tories attempted to exploit this working-class culture, and the evident unease of many on the Left with boozing and sport. According to Jon Lawrence, in late-Victorian and early Edwardian England, local Tory candidates in Wolverhampton obtained a 'stranglehold' over Wolverhampton Wonders Football Club, and appealed to local working-class voters through this connection. Likewise, in Liverpool the President of Everton Football Club, Jon Houlding, also one of the city's leading brewers, used his connections with sport and beer to secure votes.

Many early socialist proselytisers – notably the editor of *The Clarion* newspaper, Robert Blatchford – were well aware of this problem. Ruminating on the issue in an article entitled 'Why Labour and Socialist Papers Do Not Pay', he asked: 'Is it because the working people don't know what's good for them; or is it because the Labour and Socialist journals do not know what the working people want? Men like ourselves...always make the mistake of assuming that the millions of British workers have tastes, interests, habits of minds and concentration of purpose exactly like our own.' After calling for more sports reportage in left-wing newspapers, he concluded:

> I think the chief reasons why Labour and Socialist papers fail are, firstly, that they give the public too much Labourism and Socialism, and, secondly, that in the nature of things they appeal to a small minority of the people. The kind of daily paper that might succeed, if it were backed financially, is, I think, a bright newspaper of broad and comprehensive general interest with an editorial brief for Socialism or Labour.'[18]

This argument was summarised in a leading article from October 1915, which argued, 'it is the fault of those who do not understand *The Clarion* that the very name of Socialism is despised and detested by the great mass of British people'.[19]

While successful recruiters for socialism such as Blatchford blamed cultural differences for the limited appeal of Labour, those with an orthodox Marxist standpoint, such as the Plebs' League, often took a different view. In most cases, they were frustrated and antagonised by the apparently obnoxious and pig-headed nature of much of the working class. In a May 1917 editorial in *Plebs* magazine addressed 'To Our Critics', they claimed that the difficulties of the labour movement could be overcome if only the workers spent more time studying economics, and learned to view the world from a more scientific and logical perspective.[20] A later article in the same publication went further. Attacking the 'contention that the weakness of the Labour Party is that it is not as it should be, the Party of all Workers', it argued that this was 'scarcely a criticism of the Labour Party; since the Constitution of that body makes it abundantly clear that, if it is not the Party of All Workers, then it is the Workers' and not the Party's fault'.[21]

It was this contemptible argument – that workers should naturally move towards the labour movement but were too obtuse to know their own best interests – which the most successful socialist proselytisers fought against. They knew full well that to convert the mass of the working classes to the Left they needed to offer pragmatic and practical means to achieve palpable goals, while rooting their appeals in the local culture and vernacular. In the words of one C. Brown, whose letter appeared in *The Clarion* in March 1916: 'What we shall need to keep before us will not be so much of Marx, or even [NUR President Alfred] Bellamy, but of [William] Morris.'[22]

Railway trade unionist Charlie Cramp wrote a strongly-worded letter to the union paper the *Railway Review* on exactly this subject in May 1916. After asking why the people did not understand the radical-left Independent Labour Party, he argued that it was because the ILP 'does not understand the people':

One of the most important things is…to learn that the world is not a huge cosmopolitan Sunday school, but a planet peopled with men and women who are the heirs of instincts, habits, and frailties accumulated by the race through ages of pain and striving. The Socialism which they will adopt will be as an easy-fitting garment, not a straight-jacket composed of fads intended to restrict their liberties; and all the time that ILP MP's [sic] run after Temperance Bills…and other Liberal nostrums, the people will not understand them.[23]

This point about Temperance Bills was eluding to the common Liberal aspiration – shared by many socialists – to curb alcohol consumption. But this attitude towards drink was largely crafted by religion, region and class. Since in London, 'a bar was a normal fixture in radical workmen's clubs and provincial socialists were often shocked by' the Marxist Social Demoratic Federation's 'tolerant attitude towards beer'.[24] While many socialists with impeccable working-class credentials were temperance reformers, overall they were in a minority, and thus attempts to restrict drinking had the indelible stamp of middle-class interference, something seized on and exploited by the Conservatives. Thus in April 1915 *The Clarion* thundered that, 'Socialism is to the bulk of our people a novel and foreign idea. One is sufficiently handicapped by an open championship of Socialism without having Labourism, Pacifism, Little Bethelism, Teetotalism, Anti-Patriotism, Pro-Germanism, and all the fantastic vagaries and flatulent sentimentalities of the Lib.Lab. rump stuck in one's hair like straws.'[25]

Alongside *The Clarion*'s Blatchford, Ben Tillett was one of the great working-class socialist agitators of the time. He had a long history of struggle for working men and women in Britain, and had suffered blacklisting and violence at the hands of employers and the police.[26] His greatest asset was his ability to speak directly to the ordinary concerns of the working class in a language they understood. Writing in the 1950s of his memories of Tillett, Graham Thompson remembers: 'Ben Tillett had the indefinable gift; in common with the greatest of the old time music hall performers and actors generally of being able to do anything with an audience with a look or a gesture.'[27] Another anecdote from S.F. Whitlock neatly encapsulates the differences between the rambunctious, demagogic Tillett and the sober and abstemious men more typical of the Labour leadership: 'At a Labour Conference the headquarters was in a large hotel. In the lounge sat Ramsay MacDonald, Arthur Henderson, Philip Snowden + other self righteous leaders, when in comes Ben Tillett, with one of the gayest birds in town, + went upstairs with her.'[28]

In the decades before and after the Second World War, some on the Left began to use 'Tory' methods of winning working-class support. Daryl Leeworthy has shown how local Labour parties in Wales used sport to win votes, through clubs such as the Splott Labour Amateurs and the Brynmawr Labourites and assistance to acquire playing fields. The Labour MP David Lewis Davies, who represented Pontypridd between 1930 and 1937, was a former chairman of the parks committee and was responsible for developing a variety of sports in the local area.[29]

Beyond electoral politics, popular culture often played a leading role in the evolving political allegiances of communities. The historian Keith Gildart argues that Liverpool's working-class 'created a popular culture that could be found in the home, street, pub, club, concert hall and football stadium' and this was vital to challenging the existing social, religious and political divisions and enabling Liverpool's long transition from a bastion of working-class Conservatism to the Tory desert it is today. He writes that leading Liverpool politicians of the 1960s such as Bessie Braddock and Eric Heffer used the emergence of the Beatles and other Merseybeat bands to recast traditional socialist attitudes towards popular culture, and in particular towards popular music.[30]

Hipsters and Hegel: the Sounds of the Hobbyists

When it comes to music, the identity Left tends to one of two extremes. Often they have no taste at all, perhaps assuming that popular music is a bourgeois distraction from the primacy of the struggle; I remember thinking during the 2015 Labour leadership election that while I agreed with much of Corbyn's domestic policies, I couldn't trust someone who claimed 'Imagine' was his favourite song. On the other hand, hobbyists who do care about music tend to project their own political views on acts that often want nothing to do with them, and claim ownership of music and groups that are not political in the way they think they are. Hence, artists with complicated and sometimes reactionary politics are seized on as flag bearers for the Left; and musical tastes owing to personal preference are held to be representative of class or racial signifiers.

One of the ways in which political hobbyism relates to music is the notion that great music is not only written by left-wingers, but is somehow inherently radical. Yet an examination of musical history reveals that that is certainly not the case. For example, in the Beatles' song 'Paperback Writer', the aspiring novelist is working for the *Daily Mail*. It was through a January 1967 edition of the same newspaper that John Lennon learned about the 4000 [pot]holes in Blackburn, Lancashire featured in 'A Day in the Life'. A month later, the same paper carried the story that provoked Paul McCartney to write 'She's Leaving Home'. All of which begs the question: why did the most revolutionary and influential group of the 1960s – the paradigmatic radical decade – spend so much time reading the *Daily* bloody *Mail*?

In fairness, the *Daily Mail* of the 1960s had a different editorial line to the 'Hurrah for the Blackshirts!' *Mail* of the 1930s and the soft-porn-and-xenophobia *Mail* of today. But it was still a middle-brow tabloid, with fairly conservative views, and the Beatles' readership of the paper serves as a reminder that great music often comes from conservative inspiration.

Apparently the *Mail* was Lennon's favourite paper, something I can easily believe – if Lennon were alive today I have no doubt that he would have become an embittered reactionary; for proof of this see the political transformation of Morrissey. Traditionally assumed to be on the Left, the former Smiths frontman has become increasingly right-wing in recent years, supporting Brexit and wailing against immigration. He is also resident in Ireland for tax purposes, thus denying the UK welfare state much-needed funds, and – perhaps most unforgivably for many Smiths fans – is a full-throated supporter of Israel.

Compare Morrissey's behaviour with that of the late George Michael, never as cool as his fellow 1980s warbler, but a secret philanthropist, who in addition to giving millions to charity also helped countless individuals with smaller sums. This is similar to the respective fates of Hall and Oats and Queen – back in the 1980s, the former refused to tour apartheid South Africa, while the latter did so willingly. Nonetheless, today it is Queen that are (relatively) critically respected, while Hall and Oats are often the punchline of a joke.

Nearly all supposedly radical musical heroes turn out to be not quite what they seem, or, if they live long enough, to have feet of clay. Joe Strummer and Shane MacGowan were privately educated; John Lydon became a butter salesman and reality TV contestant; Neil Young supported Reagan in the 1980s and Bob Dylan became a born-again Christian. In contemporary music, Frank Turner – lauded by some, presumably deaf people with no sense of irony, as the 'Billy Bragg of his generation' – was a contemporary of princes William and Harry at Eton.

Even when music and politics combined effectively, as with Rock against Racism in the 1970s, there were still divisions. Paul Gilroy recalls a RAR gig in Brighton, headlined by Misty in Roots, featuring support from the Fabulous Poodles, with their song 'Tit Photographer Blues'. This tune 'wasn't appreciated by feminists in the audience', who 'stormed the stage and tried to get the band off. It was a horrible event, and in my mind it did expose the cracks in RAR. You were trying to hold this combination of things that in some ways didn't belong together.'[31]

The hobbyist conception of pop and politics perhaps found its apogee with punk. Yet punk itself has been massively overhyped both in terms of its appeal to young Britons at the time, and in terms of its anti-establishment credentials. According to Gildart, glam rock 'was arguably more politically and socially transgressive and generated a much broader popular appeal' than the punk rock that followed.[32]

Writing at the time of punk, Dick Hebdige noted at the Clash's performance at the Rainbow, although seats were ripped out and thrown at the stage, the last two rows were entirely occupied by record company executives and talent scouts, and CBS, the Clash's label, paid for the damage without complaint. For Hebdige, 'there could be no clearer demonstration of the fact that symbolic assaults leave real institutions intact'. Dave Haslam has one grizzled old rocker claiming that punk was 'championed by the music press who needed a new gimmick. I think the Clash were the only ones with any talent.' Another early punk told writer Jon Savage that the Sex Pistols' appearance on the Bill Grundy show 'was the end of it for me really...From something artistic and almost intellectual in weird clothes, suddenly there were fools in dog collars and 'punk' written on their shirts in biro.'[33]

Nor was punk appreciated by the broad Left at the time. Sixteen women in the Transport and General Workers Union at an EMI Records factory in north west London refused to handle any material produced by the Sex Pistols after witnessing the Grundy interview. Their actions won public support from members of the Electrical, Electronic, Telecommunication and Plumbing Union. For Keith Gildart this incident is a reminder that working-class female trade unionists in the mid-1970s used industrial militancy not only to gain wage equality but also to preserve a particular notion of femininity and working-class respectability.[34]

In his analysis of the broader reaction to the Sex Pistols' 1976 tour, Gildart draws historical parallels between sections of the working class reacting to 'alien incursions into its community', specifically between working-class attempts to prevent the Sex

Pistols performing in their town and the resistance to soldiers and police during the industrial unrest of the early decades of the twentieth century.[35] The local Labour parties in places such as Derby and Newcastle also criticised the decision by venue-owners to allow the band to perform. According to Gildart, this criticism was couched in terms of a lament for a 'working-class world we have lost'. Yet at the same time, to the chagrin of Labour leaders, 'a particular section of working-class youth was rescinding its traditional loyalties. The rhetoric of the Sex Pistols and the basis of their appeal were indicative of such a process.'[36]

Significantly, one of the few left-wing musical heroes never to sell out or abandon his principles is Bruce Springsteen. He is also considerably less cool than the likes of Dylan or Young; famously, he never used drugs, and hardly drinks; his mammoth 3-hour sets appear to be powered entirely by cheese. But this is surely no coincidence. Springsteen, much more so than the likes of John Lennon or Bob Dylan, is intimately connected to his working-class routes, and has never abandoned them. As David Hepworth notes in his book *Uncommon People*, Bob Dylan 'wore work clothes even though it was clear that he had never done any hard work. This was something he shared with Bruce Springsteen, who was to sing about the working life despite never having done a hand's turn of it himself.'[37] Yet despite this inauthenticity, Springsteen's family were solidly working-class, and his politics came from experience and community, rather than philosophy and theory. In this, at least, he has never wavered. He has shown no interest in psychedelics, holistic medicine, Eastern philosophy; nor in Christian fundamentalism or free market economics. And as with high-profile musicians, so with politicians, academics and journalists: those who learned radical politics through books, theory and student activism are more likely to move to the Right or the centre than those who were born and brought up with certain values, or those who have been moulded by the rigours of their own experience.

The wilful misremembering of certain musicians is less objectionable than the claiming of different artists for specific political causes. A common feature of performative radicalism is the assumption that the people responsible for critically-acclaimed music were political radicals, and the projection of a political significance onto their personality and music. This is best exemplified by the response to the 2016 death of David Bowie. In an article published at the time Laurie Penny wrote:

He saw that the people of this angry little blue planet lacked glitter in their lives. He saw that this world was full of strange, lost children who needed, more than anything, a story to hang on to, a legend to dance to. So he decided to become an idol...And there was once a kid who felt like an alien, a kid who was lost and ashamed and wondering if it was worth the effort to grow up, to make art, to live in a world that seemed so grey. This kid heard the music, the first brazen chords of it, and realised that it was OK to be an alien. That it was OK to be strange...And this kid, who might have been a boy or a girl or something else altogether...was me, of course, but that kid was probably you, too.[38]

Responding to the coverage of Bowie's death, journalist Thomas Jones spoke of how he 'couldn't bear to watch or listen to or read most of it', as 'like every star's every fan, I think I'm special; I know I'm not'. Despite his acknowledgement that he was just one Bowie fan out of millions, with no special connection to the man, Jones continues with an attempt to claim him, if not for himself, then at least for his politics:

Fifteen minutes on the *News at Ten* and a memorial pull-out in every paper was all it took for Bowie, not two days dead, to be resurrected as a national treasure. Never mind that he had turned down a knighthood, and refused to take part in the 2012 Olympic closing ceremony ('Heroes' echoed around the stadium as the British athletes paraded before the games, everyone apparently as oblivious as ever to the song's far from subtle irony), and had lived in New York since 1992. Never mind that his most famous personas were a polymorphously perverse Martian and a cocaine-addled anorexic satanist. Or that when he wrapped himself in the union flag in 1997, it had been slashed and burned and soiled and made into a frock coat by Alexander McQueen, as patriotic as the Sex Pistols' version of 'God Save the Queen'.

This labelling of Bowie as a political radical conveniently ignores much of his political history, from his endorsement of fascism to his imploration – via Kate Moss at the 2014 Brit Awards – that Scotland should vote against leaving the United Kingdom. Jones is also guilty of solipsistic snobbery, assuming not merely that the people in charge of the Olympic ceremony track-listing were oblivious to the deeper significance of 'Heroes' (unlike a true Bowie fan such as himself), but that millions of people around the world were also unaware. Surely the point about great music is that it takes on a special significance for each individual, and cannot be dragooned by miserable journalists who would dictate what it means and how it should be understood.

In fact, Bowie's adoption as a totem of the Left is relatively recent; he used to be seen by many as the face of nihilistic consumerism. Writing in the 1970s, the sociologists Ian Taylor and Dave Wall claimed that Bowie:

Colluded in consumer capitalism's attempt to re-create a dependent adolescent class, involved as passive teenage consumers in the purchase of leisure prior to the assumption of 'adulthood' rather than being a youth culture of persons who question...the value and meaning of adolescence and the transition to the adult world of work.[39]

Of course, there are more blots on Bowie's copy sheet than encouraging consumerism: his fascistic ramblings served as one of the inspirations for the creation of Rock against Racism in 1976. Yet Bowie's endorsement of fascism, unlike Eric Clapton's Enoch Powell moment, is largely forgotten and forgiven; something that further suggests someone's perceived 'coolness' matters more to the hobbyist Left than what they actually say or do. Bowie may have thrown a Hitler salute and called for a fascist dictatorship; but he was bisexual and gender fluid and had great music, so he can be forgiven, whereas Eric 'Enoch was Right' Clapton is massively naff and mostly enjoyed by Jeremy Clarkson types, and so is beyond redemption. Proof, if it were needed, that while justice may not be blind, it certainly isn't deaf.

This claiming of artists for the radical Left despite evidence to the contrary is by no means limited to Bowie. Speaking to Canada's *Maclean* magazine, Kate Bush – beloved of left-wing hobbyists such as Caitlin Moran and Lauren Laverne – said of Theresa May:

> I actually really like her and think she's wonderful. I think it's the best thing that's happened to us in a long time. She's a very intelligent woman but I don't see much to fear. I will say it is great to have a woman in charge of the country. She's very sensible and I think that's a good thing at this point in time.[40]

This process – of assuming that artists you like share your politics - is in keeping with the simplistic binary of the identity Left: on the one hand, straight, uncool, middle-class white men; on the other: gays, women, people of colour and critically-acclaimed musicians.

It is not just hobbyist music fans who project their politics onto their favourite artists; in some cases, bands make the same assumptions about their audience. For example, at Barcelona's Primavera Festival in 2016, Scottish group Belle and Sebastian lectured the crowd on Catalan independence, perhaps oblivious to or unconcerned by the fact that Catalans made up only a fraction of the crowd. During one of their numbers at that year's Glastonbury festival, the band invited dozens of people from the crowd to join them on stage. Many of these people began taking photographs and selfies of themselves and their friends on stage, which prompted singer Stuart Murdoch to interrupt the song and berate them for not appreciating the moment. I think this nicely encapsulates the difference between people as they are and people as they are seen by the hobbyist Left: Murdoch assumed that most people were like him; they would be caught up in the moment and would not dream of sullying it by doing anything as gauche as whipping out their mass-produced smart phone to take a picture. The reality, of course, is quite different.

The truth is that most people in the UK do not really care about music; they listen to whatever is played on Radio 1 and the main commercial stations. And that is absolutely fine: there is nothing virtuous about having a good taste in music, and you certainly don't need an electorate to be really into its music to elect a radical socialist government (fortunately). Even people who think they are into their music are often putting on a façade: a 2012 poll by 6music to find their listeners' favourite tune since the station launched had a song by Coldplay in the number one slot.

Writing in *Vice* – the house bible of post-ironic hipster arseholes – Josh Hall notes that the inaugural 6Music festival was rather white. Of more than 70 musicians, fewer than ten were people of colour, and American singer Kelis was the only black artist to appear live on the main stage on either of the 2 days. According to James Stirling, 6Music's Head of Programmes, 'the diversity always comes through the music, like Gilles Peterson'. Yet Hall notes that 'it is telling that 6 Music's vision of a diverse line-up is one in which that music is played by predominantly white DJs'. Further, Hall finds that 'at the time of writing just three of the acts on the station's 31-strong playlist include people of colour. Their albums of the year lists for both 2012 and 2013 are almost exclusively white, so too is its roster of 20-plus featured presenters' with the notable exceptions of Craig Charles and Don Letts. 'But they remain flourishing outposts of an otherwise monocultural station – and their influence is certainly nowhere to be seen on 6 Music's main playlists.'[41] As a long-time 6music listener, I initially took umbrage at this blogpost, but it is undeniable that there is an absence, not of 'black' music, but of a certain *type* of 'black' music on that station.

If you listen through from Shaun Keaveny to Gideon Coe, you'll hear plenty of reggae and 1960s soul, but very little hip hop, particularly contemporary hip hop, from either the US or UK (although this has changed somewhat since the *Vice* article). I suspect this is because of the age, taste and politics of the shows' presenters. As Paul Gilroy argues, in recent decades there has been a sharp turn away from the Caribbean and towards America as the major source of inspiration for black British culture.[42] Hence the decline of British soul and reggae and the rise of grime. It is not the amount of black music 6music plays, or the quantity of black music that middle-class whites like, but rather the *type* of black music. This is not to say that Skepta and Stormzy are more political than Steel Pulse or Sly and the Family Stone, but their targets are slightly different. It is easy for a white, middle-aged and middle-class British man to enjoy the easy skanking of Toots and the Maytals; perhaps less so for him to enjoy more contemporary urban music.

This is certainly not the case for young white middle-class men, such as Josh Hall himself. In fact, the preoccupation of a certain type of white middle-class man with black music – the more urban and 'authentic' the better – is a key feature of hobbyist leftism. I was first alerted to the existence of Lady Lesshur – queen of UK grime – by a very white, very middle-class historian who personifies the seamless fusing of Hegel and hispterism that defines the hobbyist Left and music. At every gig I've been to featuring black artists, the audience has been predominantly white. Doubtless this owes something to demographics – black people only constitute around 3 per cent of the UK population – but it is difficult to argue that middle-class white people have some sort of issue with black music; on the contrary, they are often its biggest supporters.

This is related to the contested understandings of 'middle class'. There is a tremendous website, RAM Album Club, which asks various 'celebrities' to listen to classic albums for the first time, and write a review. In his review of Half Man Half Biscuit's *Voyage to the Bottom of the Road*, the football writer Iain Macintosh describes the final song on the album, 'Paintball's Coming Home', as an 'amazing...brutal takedown of the middle class'. This reveals the contested understanding of exactly what 'middle class' means. For Macintosh, being middle class is about knowing 'where things are in B&Q' and having 'nothing but total respect for Annie Lennox'. For others it is about vegetarianism, cycling and Palestinian liberation.

Similar to the contested understanding of 'middle class', is the use of Glastonbury festival as some sort of shorthand for a gathering of radical working-class kids. Describing the prospect of appearing as the support act to Paloma Faith, Owen Jones writes that he:

> Comforted myself with the positive response I received when I took to the stage at Glastonbury to rail against injustice and nuclear weapons in 2013. This audience would be rather different, it was pointed out. [But] the blue-collar hero Bruce Springsteen was radicalised by Ronald Reagan, and – rather like Paloma Faith – railed against the demonisation of immigrants.

Ignoring that Jones compared Bruce Springsteen to Paloma Faith, this reveals an inaccurate understanding of the kind of audience Glastonbury draws. I remember Jones' appearance at Glastonbury that year, and I remember how, as with Caroline Lucas' appearance a previous year, the main reaction from the audience was bored, sceptical indifference.[43] Most attendees at music festivals, just like most university students, simply do not care for radical politics.

In contrast, I remember the exhilaration of my first Durham Miners' Gala. What with all the bands, the drinking and the pervasive festival atmosphere, I remember thinking that it was a sort of left-wing Glastonbury. I then remembered that Glastonbury *was* pretty left-wing, and a more fitting description would be a *working-class* Glastonbury. The crowds mainly consisted of ordinary men, women and kids from the North East, many of whom no doubt didn't care about the labour movement but were there for a good time. The red and white of Sunderland shirts mixing with Barcodes; well-built lads with skinheads and short-back-and-sides; girls with towering heels and layers of fake tan; you could have been in Liverpool city centre on a Saturday night as much as a field in Durham. It was as far away from the aesthetics and values of the hobbyist Left as you can get, in the best possible sense.

Oxfam Casual: Of Clothes and Cranks

In April 2017, Twitter flew into a rage over Owen Jones wearing a swanky jacket for an interview with GQ magazine. There was a degree of hypocrisy here: Jones himself has bragged on Twitter that he buys most of his clothes from charity shops. But this prolier-than-thou approach to clothes and fashion is misguided, whoever it comes from. Not only does this (possibly literally if there was an Angora jumper in a Sheffield Oxfam shop) hair-shirted approach fail to win over young (or older) working-class or poorer voters; it is offensive and patronising to assume that it might. In a similar vein, Jeremy Corbyn's previous scruffy appearance mattered, and he has done well to sharpen up his image over the course of his leadership.

The biggest scruffs on university campuses are often those from relatively privileged backgrounds: flip-flops, pyjamas and the obligatory hoodie with their former school chums' names on the back. Attend many hard-Left demonstrations and, along with the whiteness of the skin and the roundness of the vowels, a common factor is the scruffy clobber and ill-assorted garb. This is not a recent phenomenon. As far back as the 1970s, John Denham remembers that he and his student friends would attend Labour meetings, deliberately dressing down to enhance their proletarian credentials. Yet all the older men, mostly current or former manual workers, would be immaculately turned out.[44] Since the locus of the Left has shifted, however, from people who really needed to improve their own situation towards people who wanted to improve the lives of others, there has been a decline in well-dressed working-class activists and a rise in middle-class scruffs.

There is a long and proud history of well-dressed Labour leaders, and this was of a piece with the style-consciousness of working-class Britons. Ramsay MacDonald – although famously of uncertain parentage – was a renowned sharp-dresser. Geordie steelworker Arthur Henderson, East End activist George Lansbury and the Haileybury and Oxford-educated Clement Attlee were always impeccably attired. Harold Wilson substituted a pipe for cigars in order to burnish a 'man of the people' image, yet he did not consider dressing down: to do so would have been insulting and ridiculous.

A glance at footage of football terraces from the period after the Second World War reveals crowds dressed uniformly in suits and ties. Off the terraces, in the dancehalls and coffee shops of the post-war period, fashion remained tremendously important for the working class. Keith Gildart, after noting that the 'wearing of a suit for weekends in the pub remained a feature of working-class dress' well into the 1960s, quotes a *Sunday Times* feature from the 1950s about a 17-year-old from the Potteries, who said that if he won money on the football pools, the first thing he would do is 'buy about two-dozen shirts, all different colours and about a dozen pairs of jeans'.[45] A decade later, the American writer Tom Wolfe described one attendee at a Mod club in London as a 'working-class boy...left school at 15 [and] has been having his suits custom-made since he was 12'.[46]

In the 1970s, as football fans embraced European labels encountered while following their teams on the Continent, terrace fashion shifted to expensive leisure wear brands such as Adidas and Lacoste, and the suits and ties were left behind. Nonetheless, fashion continued to matter to the working class, as it does today. Millions of ordinary Britons care a great deal about their appearance and spend a great deal of time, effort and money to this effect. Vilifying someone – prominent left-winger or otherwise – for wearing a fancy coat implies a patronising assumption about the spending habits and concerns of ordinary people and is a sure sign of a hobbyist.

'...And the Tories Should be Worried'

It is undeniable that Labour performs well among younger voters. According to Lord Ashcroft Polls, in 2010 Labour was around 3 per cent ahead among 30-45s; by 2015 it was nearer 14 per cent; and by 2017 they were 36 per cent ahead of the Tories in this age group. Part of this, no doubt, is down to the personal appeal of Jeremy Corbyn, combined with youth-friendly policies in the 2017 manifesto. Despite a YouGov poll in September 2016 revealing that 18-25-year-olds preferred May to Corbyn by 25 points, Labour's 2017 campaign energised young people in a way more cynical types thought impossible. However, the reasons for this may not be as straightforward as they appear, and we should be wary of assuming that the young have been captured by the Left for good.

The writer Owen Jones has little more in common with young people than the frequency with which his driver's licence traverses the route from wallet to hand of sceptical bouncer or off-licence cashier. As such, he is always looking for ways to connect with 'the youth'. Before the 2015 election, he championed Russell Brand, claiming that 'just 28% of young people think Brand "doesn't know what he's talking about"', while another 40 per cent "wish more people like Russell Brand got involved in politics". Leave aside for one moment that – even among young people – almost one-third are aware that Russell Brand doesn't know what he's talking about; the phrase 'people like' is so vague as to be almost meaningless. This didn't stop Jones from seeing Brand as a great white hope with the potential to put Ed Miliband in Downing Street. Under the now infamous headline 'Russell Brand has endorsed Labour – and the Tories should be Worried', Jones declared that 'however much bluff and bluster the Tories now pull', Brand's endorsement of Labour 'will worry them'.[47] Three days later, the Conservative Party won its first Parliamentary majority in 23 years.

Even if Brand's potential to win support for the Left was self-evidently tosh, this is a man who rode into his wedding on the back of an elephant, who appeared on Russian state propaganda channel Russia Today, and, in the words of blogger Tom Owolade, has the 'nauseating audacity to inaugurate "the next Orwell" as if he were a notable expert on Orwell'. As Nick Cohen points out, Brand 'is a creature of a malign culture, which is turning public debate into celebrity babble. When the *New Statesman* needs a circulation lift or the BBC needs a ratings boost, they turn to Brand'.[48] He is from the same stable as George Galloway or Nigel Farage, but with less erudition.

In an earlier column, Jones noted that 'when tens of thousands protested against tuition fees, the official response was police kettling and batons' and that young people 'have been at the forefront of campaigns over tax justice and the housing crisis, helping to shift the terms of debate in the process'.[49] But crucially this is only true of *some* young people. Only one-third of school leavers go to university, and only a small minority of them are involved in protests or any kind of student politics. Likewise, as we have seen from Anthony Heath's study into political activism, the small percentage of people who do get involved with petitions, protests and marches tend to be whiter and better-off than the general population, and to be less affected by the issues involved.

Aside from involvement in politics, which has about as much appeal to young people as it does to the rest of the population, it would be an error to assume that young people are particularly radical. For example, one study on people in their mid-teens questioned more than 2000 14 and 15-year-olds on a range of issues and asked them to rate their opinions on same-sex marriage, transgender rights and marijuana legalisation, on a scale of one to five, from very liberal to quite conservative. Fully 59 per cent of these 'Generation Z' respondents said that they were on the conservative end of the spectrum, compared with 83 per cent of Millennials and 85 per cent of Generation X respondents who said they were either 'quite' or 'very liberal'. One in seven of Generation Z took a 'quite conservative' stance on these issues, compared with only 2 per cent of Millennials and 1 per cent of Generation X. Only those born before 1945 had a higher rating of 'quite conservative', at 34 per cent.[50] Perhaps most surprisingly, young people also have the highest levels of trust in politicians: a 2018 poll by Ipsos MORI found that those born after 1995 are more trusting of government ministers than any other generation.

Post-modernism is the Opium of the Left

Politics in the UK and many other comparable economies is becoming ever more divided along lines of education. For example, back in the early stages of Jeremy Corbyn's leadership, with the party struggling in the polls, a survey in Wales found approval of Corbyn was -55 among those who left education at 15; -37 with those who took GCSEs or their equivalent; -11 for people who started A Levels; and a whopping +41 for those with university degrees. At the 2017 election itself, 55 per cent of those with GCSEs as their highest qualification voted Conservative, with only 33 per cent voting Labour. For those with A Levels the split was more even: 45 per cent for the Tories and 40 per cent for Labour; however, for those with undergraduate degrees and above, fully 49 per cent voted Labour, and only 32 per cent plumped for the Tories.[51]

It is a similar story with newspaper readership. As might be expected, 79 per cent of the *Daily Telegraph*'s readers voted Tory, but *The Times* was the only other broadsheet whose readership substantially backed the Conservatives (58 per cent to Labour's 24 per cent). Most bizarrely, the readership of the *Financial Times* was evenly split, with 40 per cent voting Tory and 39 per cent Labour, although this may be explained by *FT* readers backing Labour as the anti-Brexit party. In contrast, all of the tabloids except the *Mirror*, from the *Daily Express* (77 per cent) to *The Sun* (59 per cent) had a readership with a majority in support of the Conservatives.[52]

In an increasingly well-educated society, this need not be an electoral problem for Labour. But what does it mean when the left-wing party in a democracy is sustained more and more by the best-educated, while its traditional working-class base drifts further to the Right? The increasing intellectualism and prominence of academic discourse on the broader Left, and the influence of post-modernist and post-structuralist theory within academia, is both a cause and a symptom of this new kind of politics. Unfortunately, it is alienating many of those with lower educational levels from the party that was their traditional champion, and at the same time, causing many on the Left to isolate themselves from their fellow citizens.

Take the realm of student politics. While the path from student radical to middle-aged reactionary is a well-trodden cliché, the drastic rise in the proportion of school leavers going on to university in recent years has affected the significance of this. Because, irrespective of the effect on the career prospects and indebtedness of young people and the impact to the UK's economy, one notable result of this rapid expansion in higher education access is increasing inter-generational strife among two core Labour voting blocs. This is not merely about the discrepancy between those who received free education and were able to get onto the housing ladder on the one hand and younger generations on the other. Rather it is between those from traditional working-class backgrounds who did not have the opportunity to go to university no matter how gifted, and their children and grandchildren, who often do. Charles Clarke recalls that council leaders in Hackney in the 1980s had usually not been to university and as a result 'were very much against' political hobbyism. Their children, however, did, and imbibed all manner of incidental causes, 'and this alienated them from their parents'.[53]

Likewise, while John Denham concedes that he 'almost fell' into politics through becoming the secretary of the athletic union in 1975, he is quick to point out that by that time his 'value system was in place already' from his home environment and community.[54] It could be an electoral problem for Labour if its policies and general image serve as a wedge issue among its supporters, especially if the radicalism of young Labour activists fades with time, as it usually does. One of the main indicators that student radicalism does not survive into middle age is the vast number of right-wing and centrist politicians and journalists who were on the hard-Left at university. Recalling his days as a student Communist, *The Times'* David Aaronovitch writes that:

There were always people even further to the left than us who...genuinely believed that if only students properly understood their manifesto...then the majority would be theirs. All this moderate stuff, they thought, got in the way of the mass struggle. Others didn't care: for them the NUS was just a vehicle to help 'radicalise' a minority and if it expired in the process, then it was no great loss.

Although most of those former student radicals will today have little or no interest in politics, there are always exceptions. Speaking of new members who joined his Constituency Labour Party after 2015, Aaronovitch notes that 'one of the most aggressive and persistent of these new members is someone who used to shout at me in NUS meetings all those years ago'.[55]

Another reason why Labour shouldn't bet on the youth is that despite most university lectures being left-wing, especially in the arts and humanities, the great surge in university attendance over the past 20 years or so has not resulted in a consistently radical generation, even if they do largely vote Labour for now. Ahead of the inauguration of Donald Trump in 2017, which given Trump's incomprehensible ignorance and proud philistinism was an even bleaker moment for academics than for the rest of the world, one historian enquired on Twitter what scholars could do to resist the Trumps of this world. But I think that, unfortunately, is beside the point: for generations, left-wing professors have taught left-wing students who have become left-wing academics and teachers and social workers and civil servants, but none of it has been able to prevent majorities and pluralities voting for reactionary nationalists.

Journalist Rod Liddle may 'marvel at the way in which [the Left] has achieved total cultural hegemony', but clearly, it hasn't really, at least not where it matters: the highest levels of government, business and the civil service. Instead they have to content themselves with the BBC, academia, social work and so on.[56] The Right may moan about the near-monopoly of the Left in academia, but I would much rather have universities full of Tories and boardrooms and green benches packed with socialists. The current status quo suits international capital all too well: 20 years ago Richard Rorty warned that 'what goes on in Anglophone philosophy departments has become largely invisible to the rest of the academy, and thus to the culture as a whole'. He realised that 'the Foucaldian academic Left in contemporary America is exactly the sort of Left that the oligarchy dreams of'.[57]

The frustrating thing is, people may trust academics, but they don't listen to them. Just before the EU referendum, the pollsters Ipsos MORI asked people which sources of information they trusted most. 73 per cent plumped for friends and family; other high scorers included work colleagues and the ordinary man or woman in the street, both on 46 per cent. In contrast, journalists scored only 16 per cent and politicians a measly 12 per cent. Interestingly, academics came second on 66 per cent. However, given that so many scholars – from economists to gender theorists and everyone in between – supported Remain, this suggests that while people might trust academics, they don't feel as though their advice matters.[58]

In response to the evident gulf between academics and the wider society and issues such as nationalism and immigration, academia, having had its values apparently rejected by society, has decided to turn its back on the world. A good example of this isolation of academics from their wider community was a tweet by a distinguished American historian about the 'take a knee' protests in US sports. The original tweeter wondered why the hashtag was #TakeaKnee, rather than the simpler #Kneel. Another (American) interjected that maybe it had something to do with agency, and that 'take a knee' was more active than the passive 'kneel'. Many of those who, like me, don't know the first thing about American football, will nonetheless be aware that 'take a knee' is a common instruction from US sports coaches to their players. That two American academics – who presumably attended high school and university in the US – not only had never heard this phrase before, but imputed some abstract meaning accordingly, is sadly revealing.

It is surely no coincidence that in countries where chauvinism and philistinism are an even bigger part of the national psyche than in the UK – such as Israel, Australia and the United States – academia is even more radical. According to a Jenkins Group study, 42 per cent of US college graduates never read a book after graduation. Eighty per cent of American families do not buy a book in a given year. In France, the spiritual home of turn-your-back-on-the-world academic theorising, one-third of the country recently voted for a fascist to be President.

There will be many reasons for this, but I postulate that one of them is the increasingly insular and abstract focus of much academic research. This is compounded by the way in which post-structural or post-modernism frameworks can themselves act as a balm for academics frustrated by the politics of the time, which allows them to avoid engaging with reality, or even denying itself existence. In some ways, post-modernism can be understood as the opium of the academic Left: the people consistently fail to vote as they should, indeed appear to favour pig ignorant nationalists? Well, throw on a turtle neck and spark up a Galois, here's Foucault to tell you that there's no such thing as objective reality. One of the very few moments of respite during the dreadful events of the past few years has been to see so many of the same people who have been assuring students that 'there's no such thing as truth' now complaining about alternative facts and fake news.

The journalist Giles Coren, discussing his failed attempt to make it as a novelist, consoled himself by noting: 'I look around at the biggest names in British fiction – Barnes, McEwan, Mantel, Amis – and I think, "Does anyone in the wider world give a f*** what they think about anything?"' I am not sure of the proximity of Coren's tongue to his cheek in this instance, but exactly the same can be said for most of those working in academia, or in the arts and humanities anyway. The sociologist Manuel Castells claimed that when people are unable to control the world they shrink the world to the size of their community. He was talking about disadvantaged groups, but cannot the same be said about academia?[59]

Responding to a jokey poll by the *New Statesman* writer Helen Lewis as to what the term "neoliberal" meant, one Twitter user and aspiring historian claimed 'you obviously think, or want to pretend to think, that Paul Mason and Jeremy Corbyn made it up just to be obscure, but that simply isn't the case. You're supposed to be a serious journalist at a top political magazine, for God's sake.' To which Lewis offered her apologies 'that like many men on the internet, you didn't get a woman's joke and defaulted to thinking she must be thick'. Unchastened, the historian continued by advising Lewis that there were plenty of people on Twitter who would tell her 'how thick you are but you've already blocked them all'. At this point another would-be academic weighed in: 'If it's a joke, what is the joke's object? The impenetrability of the concept "neoliberalism"? Because locking down the money supply & privatising public assets doesn't strike me as conceptually impenetrable.'

Given the almost non-existent state of the academic job market, with full-time, permanent job openings increasingly rare at the same time as ever more PhDs are churned out, we have a whole phalanx of well-educated young people with poor career prospects and, perhaps more importantly, no one listening to their vast array of expertise. Studies have found that when aspiring intellectuals face highly restricted employment opportunities, they often take refuge in extreme politics. In a 1996 study, the sociologist Jerome Karabel wrote: 'Especially conducive to the growth of political radicalism are societies in which the higher levels of the educational system produce far more graduates than can be absorbed by the marketplace.'[60]

The American professor Josh Shepperd noted, apparently without any irony or self-awareness, that he had 'so many smart & politically astute people in my Twitter feed that it's become a respite from how the world actually thinks and works'. The journalist Martin Robbins goes further. Writing on Facebook he conceded that:

> This is going to sound *awful*' before asking whether anyone else get[s] sick of being in the top percentiles for intelligence...I'm sure I can or could do 80% of things better than 80% of people. That means I go through life surrounded by and relying on people who are less capable than I would be...plumbers, shop workers, managers, voters, you name it. I read things I could write better, watch things I could make better, eat food in restaurants I could cook better.

This transition has been a long time coming. As noted by Richard Rorty of the United States, at the same time as the relationship between intellectuals and trade unionists dissolved, 'the study of philosophy – mostly apocalyptic French and German philosophy – replaced that of political economy as an essential preparation for participation in leftist initiatives'. Rorty warned that for the academic Left 'it is almost impossible to clamber back down from their books to a level of abstraction on which one might discuss the merits of a law, a treaty, a candidate, or a political strategy'. Ultimately he advised the American Left to 'put a moratorium on theory', and to 'try to kick its philosophy habit'.[61]

Terry Eagleton claimed that post-structuralism was a product of the 'euphoria and disillusionment, liberation and dissipation, carnival and catastrophe' of 1968: 'Unable to break the structures of state power, post-structuralism found it possible instead to subvert the structures of language. Nobody, at least, was likely to beat you over the head for doing so. The student movement was flushed off the streets and driven underground into discourse.'[62]

There is even an argument that the stultifying conformity among academia may contribute to the nationalistic and misogynist backlash of recent years. Angela Nagel writes in *The Atlantic* of how:

At a moment in history when the right seemed to have died of terminal uncoolness, this strategy of making the left seem puritanical and humourless represented no small cultural revolution...the earnestness and fervor of contemporary progressives, particularly on college campuses, opened the left up to mockery.[63]

In his well-received 2001 book *The Intellectual Lives of the British Working Classes*, Jonathan Rose argues that 'at any given point, the reading tastes of the British working classes consistently lagged a generation behind those of the educated middle classes', but that this 'cultural conservatism...often coexisted with political radicalism'. Rose also recounted how Richard Hoggart – founder of Birmingham University's Centre for Contemporary Cultural Studies – 'within a few years...began to wonder what he had created...There was the spreading plague of jargon and abstractions used as "props or crutches, substitutes for thought, ways of showing others and assuring themselves that they belong to an inner group".'[64]

There is also a tendency among some to say that casting aspersions on the intellectualism of the general population is dreadful class snobbery. Yet working-class intellectuals were usually isolated by their activities from the communities that nurtured them. Rose notes that Ellen Johnson, the so-called Factory Girl Poet, attracted abuse from her contemporaries. Margaret Thomson Davis claimed her parents said 'writers were a different breed from us' and maligned her literary aspirations; her father was the local branch secretary of his trade union. Jane

Mitchell, from a working-class background in Glasgow, enjoyed classic literature, but struggled at Oxford initially as they read nothing of the sort. Her mother took pride in her adoption of socialism as for her it was 'a symbol of my having entered a society of intellectuals'. Ultimately, Rose noted that 'loneliness of the self-educated worker...they felt alienated from their class and pressured to conform to philistine values'.[65]

Furthermore, the organic intellectuals who became Labour politicians and trade unionists – at least those highlighted by Rose in his study – almost always represented culturally conservative traditions in the labour movement. These included the militarist and patriot Robert Blatchford; John Ward, who led a volunteer army of British labourers to fight against the Bolsheviks in the Russian civil war; John Clynes and Stephen Walsh.[66]

There is an important but now largely forgotten incident that demonstrates the intersections of developments in academia with identity leftism. Back in the summer or 1981, the so-called MacCabe affair bitterly divided the University of Cambridge English Faculty, and was so acrimonious it even garnered coverage in the mainstream national press. Colin MacCabe was an English scholar who applied for a position as a full lecturer in the Faculty, only for his appointment to be blocked by senior academics who disapproved of the post-structuralist angle of MacCabe's work. After the resulting intra-Faculty dispute, he left Cambridge to take up a professorship at Strathclyde University.

Speaking of the MacCabe affair 25 years later, one of the chief antagonists, Sir Christopher Ricks, makes the interesting recollection that at the time there was 'all this stuff about me being very right-wing', despite him being a 'life-long Labour voter'.[67] For Ricks, his lifelong loyalty to the Labour Party matters less than his erroneous stance on a niche, esoteric, academic dispute; because he took the wrong stance against the modernisers, it was assumed that he was right-wing. This is perhaps one of the first instances of the now common phenomenon whereby the litmus test of someone's politics is not necessarily their actual political allegiance, but rather their stance on a particular theory or abstract concern. This is a problem faced today by academics such as the military historian Gary Sheffield, whose work praises the evolution of the British military during the First World War and supports commanders such as Douglas Haig. Sheffield complains on Twitter that people often assume he is a Tory, merely based on his area of specialisation or the thrust of his scholarly arguments.

Naturally, academics should be properly funded, able to study whatever they want, and reach whatever conclusions they see fit, without any influence from government or fear of tabloid headlines. But the language and thought processes of academia are not appropriate for the cut-throat world of politics. Parties in office who need to make and implement policy will need academic expertise; but parties on the outside looking to obtain office have little need of this, and we need to build a firewall between academia and the public discourse and policies of the Labour Party.

Conclusion

Back in 2001, Jon O'Neill identified a convergence of post-modern leftism with the neoliberal ideas of the market, and warned that there was a real danger of winning cultural battles but losing the class war.[68] Today, this danger seems more apparent than ever, but it has been a long time coming. Historically, elements of the British Left have been ill-at-ease with mass culture, but this trend was counteracted by the ballast provided by the weight of numbers of ordinary workers. Today, as the composition of the Left shifts, there is an increasing dissonance between the culture of the hobbyists and the mass culture.

Most people are not avid readers. Most people have terrible taste in music and enjoy 'comedy' barely deserving of the name. Any illusions hobbyists have about the electorate would be swiftly dispelled if they switched on a daytime quiz show – and I should know, I've been on enough of them – or watched a few minutes of the highest-rated TV shows. All of this is perfectly fine – there is nothing particularly virtuous about being well-read or having a refined taste in music.

More importantly, there is absolutely no need to have a cultured electorate in order to effect radical change. The problem is when left-wing hobbyists insist that the mass of the electorate are actually just like them, and that it is indicative of class hatred to say otherwise. The hobbyist Left has an idealised vision of the electorate. But not only does this fantasy electorate not exist, it does not need to exist to have a genuinely transformative socialist government.

Conclusion

The seven chapters of this book have highlighted various characteristics and practices indicative of identity leftism. Prominent among them is a concern with semantics and a tendency to police language. Intertwined with this is a habit of prominently broadcasting their politics, both in general and in relation to specific issues, via social media and other forms. This involves staying up to date with the evolving language of identity leftism and prominently using these terms. The total inefficacy of this is distinguishing today's left-wing hobbyists from their antecedents. There have always been people who allied with disadvantaged groups and sought to help them, but historically they actually did some good, or at least intended to.

When people use words and phrases such as global south (which most people think is the successor to the Housemartins), intersectional, ableist, cis, people of colour and even misogynist (instead of the more accessible sexist) the effect is not to make anyone's life any better, but rather to position the speaker within a particular group of people. Perhaps the best example of this is the word 'problematic'. This is a word so vague as to be almost meaningless, so imprecise that it has no argumentative value; instead the purpose of this word is to signal the erudition and righteousness of the speaker, and the general undesirability of whatever it is that has just been critiqued. It is the most weasely of all the words in the vocabulary of identity leftism: it allows the speaker to identify something as undesirable, something 'people like them' ought not to approve of, without identifying the precise fault.

Very often, the intention of this use of language, as with hobbyism leftism more broadly, is merely to be transgressive. For some people, saying 'did you know Churchill was a racist?' gives them a subversive rush. When idiots on Twitter claim that whiteness is evil or men are trash, or wear a Hezbollah t-shirt to a family dinner, they are not trying to make serious political points, but rather looking for their fix of transgression. In this they are no different to previous generations, but crucially flappers, teddy boys and punks weren't held to be representatives of a radical political movement, nor were they offered *Guardian* op eds and book deals.

For hobbyists, their left-wing politics are their identity, their *raison d'etre* and the source of much of their sense of self-worth. But unlike earlier radicals, they are not at the vanguard of a movement, but are instead largely removed from the groups they seek to represent. Groups as varied as the early twentieth-century labour leaders, the Southall Black Sisters and gay rights activists could all take heart that there was a broad phalanx of workers, ethnic minorities and gays and lesbians who supported their cause and profited from their victories. In contrast, another defining characteristic of the identity Left is that they talk about specific groups of people, but they do not speak for them. They largely do not represent ethnic minorities, gays or transgendered people. They are usually both economically and demographically distinct from the people they seek to represent, and the groups they claim to support often reject their values.

One of the unfortunate paradoxes the Left has to contend with is that some of the most structurally disadvantaged people are among the least likely to appreciate the significance of structural disadvantage. Very often those most sensitive to such issues are people with a higher level of education and relatively privileged finances; contrastingly people from historically disadvantaged groups – such as the working class and recent immigrants – tend to emphasise personal responsibility and self-reliance. In many ways the crucial future battles for the Left will be fought in the space between reality and how different groups perceive reality to be.

There are two reasons for the phenomena of Jeremy Corbyn and Bernie Sanders. On the one hand, you have scandalous inequality, a prolonged squeeze on living standards, insecure jobs and a drastic shortage of housing. At the same time, you have class-political realignment and a glut of highly-educated, underemployed young people. The former was a primary reason for Corbyn's landslide leadership wins and Labour securing 40 per cent of the vote in 2017, and for Sanders' showing in the Democratic primaries. The latter, however, is a primary driver of identity leftism. It is a cruel irony that it coincides with this unfortunate time in history, and helps to blunt the appeal of the Left when radical ideas are most needed.

Even though they suffer from the same economic ill-winds as most other people, identity leftists are relatively privileged compared to those who are really suffering: unable to acquire jobs commensurate with their qualifications and trapped in private renting, yes, but usually not surviving on foodbanks, living in hostels or being beaten up or killed because of who they are. They are well-educated, usually technologically adept, have time on their hands and a righteous and entirely justified anger at the state of the world. However, their attempts to remedy injustice are self-defeating, overshadowed by the primary concerns of ideological consistency, identity and belonging, and their primary focus on language, aesthetics and theory. This is one of the reasons the global Left is in the mess it's in and why the Corbyn project may yet fall short: the state of the world requires confident, pragmatic, practical politics; we've ended up with a Left dominated by identity, for whom politics is more of a pastime. While the Right is filled with passionate intensity, the Left is crippled by handwringing cranks, as Yeats might have said.

Their focus on language, semantics and aesthetics is a tacit recognition that things will never really change. Hence, we have a group on the Left who have largely accepted the status quo, and instead divide their time between carefully demonstrating their own group identity and attacking others similar to them who have transgressed slightly, all the while existing in a hermetically sealed bubble that bares no relation to the lives of the people they claim to speak for. That identity leftism has developed in step with neoliberalism is no coincidence. In a 2018 paper, French economist Thomas Piketty argues that the decline in the working-class base of left-wing parties in Britain, America and France has led to increasing inequality over the past 50 years, and a lack of political will to challenge this.[1] Meanwhile Len McCluskey, recalling the changes wreaked by Margaret Thatcher's governments, claims those 11 years witnessed not just socio-economic rupture, but also a vast cultural change: 'Greed was rewarded, not just entrepreneurship, or individuality, but actual greed...There was a development of an "I'm alright Jack" mentality, which did a tremendous amount of moral damage.' According to McCluskey, 'moral standards went out of the window. Now people were to be *rewarded* for scamming someone. Rewarded for being greedy.'

Yet the Left responded to the ravages of Thatcherism not with a resurgent, muscular collectivism, but rather by turning its back on collectivity. Or rather, by embracing moral and liberal individualism through focusing on LGBTQI+ rights, environmental campaigns and civil liberties. All important issues, to be sure, but the Left's successes in these fields has sometimes come at the expense of an ability to talk in terms of community and mutualism. When the modern Left does talk of collectivism, it is often in terms of religious or ethnic communalism: no longer are people to be organised according to neighbourhood or work; no longer should we think of Scousers or dockers, Geordies or miners; increasingly they are organised according to their own peccadilloes or religious beliefs.

In his 1996 book *Jihad vs. McWorld*, Brendan Barber argued that the future would be divided between those who struggle to muster an interest about anything apart from consumerism and the minutiae of their own lives, and those who obsess over a particular issue. In explaining the growth of these two phenomena, Barber wrote that 'the public faith of democracy sometimes seems to have been lost in the baggage thrown overboard when the public faith of socialism was jettisoned. By democracy, I understand not just government by, for, and of the people, but government by, for, and of citizens. Citizenship is power's political currency and is what gives democracy its civic solvency.'[2] He argued that governments and political movements have become less concerned about citizens and citizenship, with attempting to construct a national project, and creating a sense of community, and that this has led to a drift towards the twin threats of consumerist nihilism and ideological obsession.

Another one of the characteristic features of the identity Left is that it doesn't actually change anything. While I remain sceptical as to how much of a challenge identity leftism poses to the success of social democratic movements around the world, it is not too much of a stretch to say that left-wing hobbyism is not effective. Almost all identity leftists spend a great deal of time expending venom on social media – not at the far Right, or even the centre Right – but at fellow leftists with whom they have minor disagreements. Slavoj Zizek describes these 'tweet rejoinders [as] a mixture of self-righteousness, political correctness and brutal sarcasm'.[3] People who have divergent views are not treated as misunderstood comrades who might be persuaded, but instead as Blairites, Zionists, transphobes, white supremacists and so on. This public denouncing is a hallmark of the identity left for two reasons. Firstly, it is very easy, and achieves nothing: just denounce using the germane term relevant to the specific misdemeanour and move on. Secondly, because the denouncing itself serves to demarcate that person's left-wing identity, for the benefit of whoever might be watching.

Left-wing hobbyism has about as much effect on, say, poverty, homophobia and peace in the Middle East as online arguments by football fans have on their teams' performances on the pitch, or the punks of the 1970s had on abolishing the monarchy or bringing anarchy to the UK. One problem with this analogy is that, to be fair to online football fans and punks, having a tangible effect on something is not and was not the point. With identity leftists, on the other hand, they are supposed to be making a difference.

Another thing that all three groups have in common is that their activity results from their powerlessness. Supporters can't do much to affect the fortunes of their team outside of match day, so they spend the time in between with petty arguments online. With punk, the lack of jobs or ubiquity of shit jobs and the misery of everyday existence motivated the fans, and the same issues account for the groups themselves, allied with the inability to play three chords. When people can't really affect the world around them, so their symbolic attempts to do so become tribal and uncompromising.

All of this is important, because when conservatives say that 'feminism/anti-racism/LGBT rights have gone too far' they clearly aren't talking about the end of gender pay gaps, racist violence or LGBT teen suicides. What they are talking about is the language of online activists and the attention-seeking schemes of identity leftists. Therefore there is a strong case that the rise of the identity Left coinciding with the growth of reactionary nationalism around the world is no coincidence.

It is abominable that the hard-Right, whether Donald Trump or Ukip, is able to articulate the language of dispossession so effectively, while the Left is unable to channel these frustrations. In terms of moving beyond identity leftism, a crucial first step is to recognise that there is no binary division in society between good and bad, no easy dichotomy between rich, white Tory men on the one hand and women, gays, ethnic minorities and the working class on the other, much as some on the Left may wish and write and act as though there is. This recognition must be central to the philosophy and practice of the future Left.

Because ordinary people are so put off by fantastical schemes and abstract thinking, it is essential that we do not talk of the Left as though it is a religion or great moral crusade. (Or at least, if we have to treat it like a religion, we should frame it as a banal and performative type of religion, where symbolism and association is more important than rigid adherence to doctrine.) It should be deeply linked to people's cultural, environmental and everyday experience, rather than a theoretical set of principles.

At the same time, a future successful Left shouldn't have to rely on mass movements. Richard Rorty put it succinctly when he advised: 'We need to get rid of the Marxist idea that only bottom-up initiatives, conducted by workers and peasants who have somehow been so freed from resentment as to show no trade of prejudice, can achieve results.' Likewise Ta-Nehisi Coates notes that 'the fact of history is that black people have not – probably no people have ever – liberated themselves strictly through their own efforts'.[4]

Back in April 2010, in a survey on attitudes towards David Cameron's 'Big Society' proposals, Ipsos MORI asked voters if they wanted more involvement in the provision of local public services. Only one in 20 wanted 'involvement', whereas one in four wanted 'more of a say' and half of them only wanted 'more information'. An earlier MORI poll had asked voters to what extent, if at all, they would like to be involved in 'decision-making' in their local communities, and fully 50 per cent responded 'not very' or 'not at all'. Finally, when asked about being involved in the running of the country as a whole, 55 per cent of people said they were uninterested.[5] These figures gave little optimism for hopes of a Big Society (the very mention of which disappeared from Cameron's lips after forming the Coalition); what odds, then, on the formation of a great left-wing 'mass movement' to bring Britain to socialism?

On the same subject, the journalist Jackie Ashley writes that:

> My humble experience at local level has taught me two things: everyone wants a say in how an organisation is run. And very few people are prepared to give up their precious time to help. Have you ever tried recruiting volunteers to a PTA, to become a Brown Owl or to organise safety checks for a sports club...? It can be a depressing experience, and it's always those who complain the loudest who are least likely to step forward to help...Perhaps the biggest problem is that the politicians dreaming up these plans are different from the rest of us. After all, they are quite happy to spend 24 hours a day, seven days a week working at politics. The rest of the country have a life.[6]

People simply cannot be bothered. Ahead of the 2011 Labour Party Conference in Liverpool, *The Guardian*'s Zoe Williams toured that city, investigating the level of awareness that the famously left-wing area had of its Labour MPs. Williams reported that, 'I can put you out of your misery and say that nobody could recognise any of those MPs.'

Some people pointed to Stephen Twigg, MP for West Derby, and said: 'I know him.' One man knew that Steve Rotheram (then MP for Walton) was a former Lord Mayor of the city – not because he recognised him but because he was wearing his ceremonial chain in the photo. Another woman knew almost everything about Maria Eagle (MP for Garston and Halewood) – 'she's from over the water [the Wirral], she's got a sister, twins, lesbian...' – except what her name was. And yet this did not dent overall loyalty to Labour. 'Everybody here – even Carly, 23, who wouldn't even look at pictures of MPs, so sure was she that she wouldn't know who they were – says they voted Labour, and they'll vote Labour again.'[7]

This anecdotal evidence is supported by research. A poll in

Liverpool conducted by the Campaign Company found that, of those who had heard of the 'Big Society', Pioneers (well-educated liberals) were marginally in favour of the concept, Prospectors (the materially motivated) split 3:2 against, and Settlers (the traditional working class) split 4:1 against. According to Nick Pecorelli, who conducted the research: 'Settlers are often harder to reach, and their more fatalistic world view makes it more challenging to sell such a concept to them.'[8] That is to say the exact sort of people Labour need to win over are the least likely to be attracted by the chance of involvement in a 'mass movement'.

Even Owen Jones admits that 'having a vision that cannot inspire enough people to transform the country is an exercise in self-indulgent futility...mass membership does not automatically translate into a social movement...So far there is little evidence of a surge of activity on the ground.' He also notes that the Oxford Labour Party had seen its membership swell overall, yet in the city's solidly working-class Blackbird Leys ward, only a couple of dozen members have joined, while other constituency Labour parties 'have grown three-fold yet experienced little or no increase in door-knocking; some even report a decline'.[9]

Jones is right to argue that the great progressive changes of the past – democracy, workers' rights, the welfare state, women's rights, anti-racist movements – were not granted by the top but seized by the bottom, but these movements were led by vanguards of professional trade union organisers and politicians. As Laurie Penny conceded of the protest movements during the 5 years of the Coalition: 'There are career activists and romantic student adventurers leading the charge.'[10] The key difference between the protest movements of the past and those of today is that today the protestors do not represent the most disadvantaged groups. Resistance to austerity has by and large not been led by the working class and people of colour, but rather by students and white, middle-class radicals; people like Penny herself. These people are in it for the thrill, the excitement and the comradeship, and not motivated by anything as prosaic and tedious as affecting real political change. Ultimately, it is understandable why most hobbyists are relatively privileged white people: only they can afford to do this; it allows them to show off their advanced education and relatively privileged status without appearing gauche, or, worse, a Tory; it doesn't make any difference and hence won't challenge their own socio-economic position.

That is not to say that inefficacy is a necessary condition of left-wing hobbyism: very many people who do a great deal of valuable and exhausting work and activism that really does make a difference might still be considered as identity leftists. The crucial question is one of identity: how far does this person make their activism a central part of their personality? Is their politics less what they believe, and more what they are? The fact that plenty of people on the identity Left have dedicated years of struggle to the labour movement only serves to help legitimise the bulk of the performative radicals.

A final characteristic of the identity Left is a reinvention of radical tradition to make the history of the labour movement more palatable to their values. Yet there is absolutely no need to distort the history of the Left and the British working class in order to sustain radical politics. One can admit the truth about historical working-class nationalism and hostility to immigration today, and the increased incidence of VAW and/or homophobia in other communities, and *still* argue for an inclusive, anti-racist, tolerant society. Yet for the hobbyists this sort of honesty is difficult, if not impossible. Their concept of politics is built not on looking the world squarely in the face and doing the best you can, but rather on a fantastical, romantic, Manichean sense of good and evil.

This has resulted in a kind of *sola fide* leftism, a radical politics through faith alone; it doesn't matter what you do; only what you claim to believe. This may work for religious dominations, but it will not do for a political movement. The ultimate result will be that being 'left-wing' becomes one more of any number of identities available to people, along with their football team, favourite band or brand of footwear. This phenomenon is much more highly developed in the US and Israel, and the state of left-wing politics in those polities, especially the latter, is all the worse for it. Israel in particular acts as a sort of terrifying if still unlikely vision of a possible future UK: a highly-educated, privileged elite which recoils from nationalism and militarism outweighed and outvoted by a reactionary precariat mass beneath.

Ultimately, if you want to implement progressive policies to radically alter the world, the identity leftists are going the wrong way about it. The great liberal reforms of the 1960s were only introduced because a Labour government, focused on getting into power and improving people's lives, was able to grant Parliamentary time for the legislation to pass. Roy Jenkins and Harold Wilson did not position these cultural issues prominently in the party's appeal to the electorate – if they had done, there may not have been a Labour government between Attlee and Blair – and the many people affected by the liberalisations of the 1960s reaped the rewards. Today's identity leftists would do well to emulate them: subsume their niche interests and esoteric concerns for the greater good, the better to realise the type of world they desire.

Notes

Introduction

1 Henry Collins, 'The Marxism of the Social Democratic Federation', in Asa Briggs and John Saville (eds.), *Essays in Labour History 1886-1923*, 64.

2 Alan Bullock, *The Life and Times of Ernest Bevin* vol. 1, 1960, 532.

3 Daniel Bell, *The Coming of Post-Industrial Society*, Basic Books, 1999.

4 'The new electoral map of Britain: from the revenge of the Remainers to the upending of class politics', *The Guardian*, 11 June 2017.

5 YouGov survey of 52615 people, 9-13 June 2017.

6 ibid.

7 See Donald Green, Bradley Palmquist, Eric Schickler, *Partisan Hearts and Minds: Political Parties and the Social Identities of Voters*, New Haven: Yale University Press, 2002; Shanto Iyengar, G. Sood and Y. Lelkes, "Affect, Not Ideology: A Social Identity Perspective on Polarization." *Public Opinion Quarterly* 76 (2012): 405-31; Shanto Iyengar and Sean J. Westwood, 'Fear and Loathing across Party Lines: New Evidence on Group Polarization', *American Journal of Political Science*, 59 (2015): 690-707; Leonie Huddy, Lilliana Mason and Lene Aaroe. "Expressive Partisanship: Campaign Involvement, Political Emotion, and Partisan Identity." *American Political Science Review* 109, no. 1 (2015): 1-17.

8 Eitan Hersh, 'Political Hobbyism', 34.

9 A.F. Heath et al., *The Political Integration of Ethnic Minorities in Britain*, Oxford: OUP, 2013, 183.

10 E.P. Thompson, 'The Peculiarities of the English', *The Socialist Register* (1965): 353.

11 Interview with Len McCluskey, 28 May 2016.

12 Interview with Charles Clarke, 9 June 2016.

13 Interview with Len McCluskey.

14 Martin Pugh, *Speak for Britain! A New History of the Labour Party*, Vintage, 2011, 303-4 and 348.

15 Interview with Charles Clarke, 9 June 2016.

16 Richard Rorty, *Achieving our Country. Leftist Thought in Twentieth-Century America*, Cambridge: Harvard University Press, 1998, 35.

17 ibid., 36 and 79.

18 Thomas Frank, *Listen Liberal. Whatever Happened to the Party of the People?*, Melbourne: Scribe, 2016, 228.

19 Laurie Penny, 'What really happened in Trafalgar Square', *New Statesman*, 26 March 2011.

20 Laurie Penny, 'What the "transgender tipping point" really means', *New Statesman*, 24 June 2014.

21 Afua Hirsch, *Brit(ish). On Race, Identity and Belonging*, London: Jonathan Cape, 2018, 607.

Got Any ID?

1 Laurie Penny, 'No, identity politics is not to blame for the failures of the left', *New Statesman*, 30 November 2016.

2 Cited in Rebecca Solnit 'From Lying to Leering', *London Review of Books*, 19 January 2017.

3 Shanto Iyengar and Sean J. Westwood, 'Fear and Loathing across Party Lines: New Evidence on Group Polarization', *American Journal of Political Science* 59 (2015): 696.

4 Jasbir Puar, *Terrorist Assemblages*, Durham NC: Duke University Press, 2007, 133.

5 Fawzia Afzal-Khan, 'How my daughter's interracial relationship opened my eyes', *Salon*, 25 December 2017.

6 Tariq Modood, 'Political blackness and British Asians', *Sociology* 28 (1994): 859.

7   Quoted in Satnam Virdee and Keith Grint, 'Black self-organization in trade unions', *The Sociological Review* 42 (1994): 208-9.

8   Interview with Charles Clarke, 9 June 2016.

9   Jon Cruddas speech at Anglia Ruskin University, 11 March 2016.

10   Interview with John Denham, 12 April 2016.

11   Interview with Lord Larry Whitty, 24 April 2016.

12   Andrew Murray and Lindsey German, *Stop the War: The Story of Britain's Biggest Mass Movement*, London, Bookmarks, 2005, 62.

13   Peter Wilby, 'The Thin Controller', *New Statesman*, 16 April 2016.

14   Seumus Milne, 'It isn't Facebook that feeds terror. It's war and tyranny', *The Guardian*, 27 November 2014.

15   Richard Seymour and Ashok Kumar, 'The smear campaign against Lutfur Rahman is an insult to democracy', *The Guardian*, 30 May 2014.

16   Quoted in Aditya Chakrabortty, 'I'm Bengali and I'm black – in the same way that my parents were', *The Guardian*, 30 October 2014.

17   Quoted in Satnam Virdee, *Racism, Class and the Racialized Outsider*, London, Palgrave, 2014, 153-4.

18   Ambalavaner Sivanandan, *Communities of Resistance: Writings on Black Struggles for Socialism*, London, Verso, 1990, 124-6.

19   H.S. Mirza, 'Everyday Making and Civic Engagement among Muslim Women', in Waqar Ahmad and Ziauddin Sardar (eds), *Muslims in Britain: Making Social and Political Space*, Routledge, 2012, 148.

20   Andrew Gilligan, 'Labour "terrifies black women", says sacked councillor Amina Lone', *The Sunday Times*, 27 August 2017.

21   Afua Hirsch, *Brit(ish). On Race, Identity and Belonging,*

London: Jonathan Cape, 2018, 140-1 and 289.

22 Tariq Modood, *Multicultural Politics. Racism, Ethnicity and Muslims in Britain*, Edinburgh: Edinburgh University Press, 2005, 81-99.

23 Laurence Janta-Lipinski, 'I tried to prove the Canary wrong and you'll never guess what happened next', *LabourList*, 5 October 2016.[https://labourlist.org/2016/10/i-tried-to-prove-the-canary-wrong-and-youll-never-guess-what-happened-next/]

24 Shamit Saggar, *Race and Representation. Electoral politics and ethnic pluralism in Britain*, Manchester, Manchester University Press, 2000, 170-2.

25 Modood, *Multicultural Politics*, 194-5.

26 Giles Fraser, 'The world is getting more religious. Because the poor go for God', *The Guardian*, 26 May 2016.

27 Mehdi Hasan, 'The power of a dangerous idea: Mehdi Hasan on how faith can inspire', *New Statesman*, 13 December 2011.

28 Mehdi Hasan, 'What the jihadists who bought "Islam for Dummies" on Amazon tell us about radicalization', *New Statesman*, 14 August 2014.

29 Giles Fraser, 'How Ludwig Wittgenstein helped me get over my teenage angst', *The Guardian*, 19 August 2013.

30 Les Back et al, 'New Labour's White Heart: Politics, Multiculturalism and the Return of Assimilation', *Political Quarterly* (2002): 452.

31 See Dan Weinbren, 'Social Capital: London's Labour Parties, 1918-45', in Mathew Worley (ed.), *Labour's Grass Roots*, London: Ashgate, 2005, 209.

32 A point often made by Maurice Glasman. See Rowenna Davis, *Tangled Up in Blue*, London: Ruskin Publishing, 2011.

33 Zoe Williams, 'The Church has blown it. England's ticked that box', *The Guardian*, 12 December 2012.

34 Interview with Len McCluskey, 18 May 2016.

35 In the words of John Bohstedt, there is a need to rescue

people of different religious and ethnic groups 'from the enormous condescension of labour history'. See John Bohstedt, 'More than One Working Class: Protestant and Catholics Riots in Edwardian Liverpool', in John Belchem (ed.), *Popular Politics, Riot and Labour: Essays in Liverpool History*, Liverpool: Liverpool University Press, 1992, 176.

36 Sam Davies, *Liverpool Labour*, Keele: Keele University Press, 1996, 225.

37 ibid., 82.

38 Steven Fielding, *Class and Ethnicity: Irish Catholics in England, 1880-1939*, Buckingham: Open University Press, 1993, 105.

39 ibid., 113-15.

40 ibid., 107.

41 ibid., 108.

42 ibid., 126-30.

43 Camilla Schofield, 'A nation or no nation? Enoch Powell and Thatcherism', in Ben Jackson and Robert Saunders (eds), *Making Thatcher's Britain*, Cambridge: CUP, 2012, 106.

44 Afua Hirsch, *Brit(ish). On Race, Identity and Belonging*, London: Jonathan Cape, 2018, 7 and 24.

45 ibid., 119-20.

46 Ta-Nehisi Coates, 'This is How We Lost to the White Man', *The Atlantic*, May 2008.

47 Jerry Phillips, 'Richard Price and the Ordeal of the Postmodern City', in Ronald Strickland (ed), *Growing Up Postmodern*, Rowman & Littlefield Publishers, Lanham, MD, 2002, 54.

48 Paul Gilroy, *Aint No Black in the Union Jack*, London, Routledge, 2010, 60-1.

49 Gargi Bhattacharrya, 'Racial Neoliberal Britain?', in Nisha Kapoor, V.S. Kalra and James Rhodes (eds), *The State of Race*, Basingstoke: Palgrave Macmillan, 2013, 44-6.

50 Interview conducted 12 February 2018.

51 Interview with Gary Elden, 2 March 2018.

52 Thomas Frank, *What's the Matter with Kansas?*, New York, Picador, 2004, 241.

53 Paul Gilroy, *Small Acts. Thoughts on the Politics of Black Cultures*, London, Serpent's Tail, 230.

54 ibid., 179.

55 Lorraine Hansberry, *To Be Young, Gifted and Black: Lorraine Hansberry in Her Own Words*, New York: New American Library, 1969, 63.

56 Asad Haider, *Mistaken Identity: Race and Class in the Age of Trump*, London: Verso, 2018, 13.

57 Quoted in Haider, *Mistaken Identity*, 19-20.

58 Haider, *Mistaken Identity*, 40.

59 ibid., 32.

60 ibid., 34.

61 ibid., 67.

62 Wesley Yang, 'The Bari Weiss Pile-On', *Tablet*, 26 February 2018.

63 Quoted in Haider, *Mistaken Identity*, 48, 68-71, 74.

64 Stephen Bush, 'Marvel's Black Panther and the politics of diverse superheroes', *New Statesman*, 16 February 2018.

65 Kamel Daoud, 'Black in Algeria? Then You'd better Be Muslim', *New York Times*, 3 March 2016.

66 Haider, *Mistaken Identity*, 80-1.

67 Quoted in Haider, *Mistaken Identity*, 20.

68 Gilroy, *Small Acts*, 179.

69 Interview with Charles Clarke, 9 June 2016.

70 Chenchen Zhang, 'The curious rise of "the white left" as a Chinese internet insult', *OpenDemocracy.net*, 11 May 2017. [https://www.opendemocracy.net/digitaliberties/chenchen-zhang/curious-rise-of-white-left-as-chinese-internet-insult]

71 Bim Adewumni, 'There's An Elephant In Harvey Weinstein's Hotel Room', *BuzzFeed*, 19 October 2017 and Aditi Natasha Kini, 'I'm tired of watching brown men fall in love with white women', *Jezebel*, 7 June 2017.

'Those Fucking Mugs'

1   Jeremy Corbyn Interview, *The Andrew Marr Show*, BBC1, 19 June 2016.

2   Sunny Hundal, 'We failed to defeat the Tories because the left has stopped understanding the public', *LabourList*, 10 June 2015.

3   Bobby Duffy and Tom Free-Smith, 'Perceptions and Reality: Public Attitudes towards Immigration', *Ipsos MORI*, October 2014.

4   Vron Ware, *Who Cares About Britishness? A Global View of the National Identity Debate*, London: Arcadia Books, 2007, 15-16 and 39.

5   ibid., 15-16.

6   Reni Eddo-Lodge, *Why I'm No Longer Talking to White People about Race*, London: Bloomsbury, 2018, 190.

7   Ambalavaner Sivanandan, *A Different Hunger: Writings on Black Resistance*, London: Pluto Press, 1982, 104-5.

8   Les Back et al, 'New Labour's White Heart: Politics, Multiculturalism, and the Return of Assimilation', *The Political Quarterly* 73 (2002): 449.

9   Tom Peterkin, 'Majority of Scots want to end freedom of movement post-Brexit', *The Scotsman*, 10 January 2018.

10   Owen Jones, 'Farage flourished on TV – but then, so did Clegg once', *The Guardian*, 27 March 2014.

11   Zoe Williams, 'Why make paupers and foreigners fight over a crust?', *The Guardian*, 21 July 2011; Richard Seymour, 'Why is there so much hostility to immigrants in the UK?', *The Guardian*, 14 October 2014.

12   Giles Fraser, 'Labour is partly to blame for the racists' capture of the EU debate', *The Guardian*, 30 June 2016.

13   Afua Hirsch, *Brit(ish). On Race, Identity and Belonging*, London: Jonathan Cape, 2018, 263-4.

14   Jon Lawrence, 'Blue Labour, One Nation Labour, and the lessons of history', *Renewal*, 21 (2013): 6-13.

15 Nick Cohen, *Pretty Straight Guys*, London: Faber & Faber, 2003, 227-8.

16 Interview with John Denham, 12 April 2016.

17 Interview with Phil Woolas, 15 March 2016.

18 'Perceptions and Reality: Public Attitudes to Immigration', *Ipsos MORI*, January 2014.

19 Interview with Charles Clarke, 9 June 2016.

20 Selina Todd, *The People: The Rise and Fall of the Working Class*, London: John Murray, 2014, 188.

21 Fred Lindop, 'Racism and the working class: strikes in support of Enoch Powell in 1968', *Labour History Review* 66 (2001): 82.

22 Satnam Virdee, *Racism, Class and the Racialized Outsider*, London: Palgrave Macmillan, 2014, 48-9, 63 and 84.

23 E.P. Thompson, 'The Peculiarities of the English', *The Socialist Register* (1965): 337.

24 J. H. Grainger, *Patriotisms. Britain 1900-1939*, London: Routledge Kegan Paul, 1986, 30-2.

25 Thompson, 'The Peculiarities of the English', 338.

26 Quoted in Thompson, 'The Peculiarities of the English', 338.

27 Labour Party Archive and Study Centre, War Emergency: Workers' National Committee files, WNC.3/12/1 – letter to Arthur Henderson, 2 December 1916. Emphasis added.

28 Reni Eddo-Lodge, *Why I'm No Longer Talking to White People about Race*, London: Bloomsbury, 2018, 14.

29 Virdee, *Racism, Class and the Racialized Outsider*, 92.

30 Stephen Howe, *Anti-colonialism in British politics*, Oxford: Clarendon Press, 1993, 282 and 322.

31 Stephen Howe, 'Labour and international affairs' in Duncan Tanner, Pat Thane and Nick Tiratsoo, *Labour's First Century*, Cambridge: CUP, 2000, 123.

32 Stuart MacIntyre, 'Imperialism and the British Labour movement in the 1920s', *Our History* 64 (1975), 12.

33 Virdee, *Racism, Class and the Racialized Outsider*, 102.

34 Kathleen Paul, '"British Subjects" and "British Stock": Labour's Postwar Imperialism', *Journal of British Studies* 34 (1995): 233-76.

35 Paul Foot, *Immigration and Race in British Politics*, London: Mass Market Paperbacks, 1965, 191 and 177.

36 Shirley Joshi and Bob Carter, 'The role of Labour in the creation of a racist Britain'. *Race and Class* 25 (1984): 65.

37 Ken Lunn, 'Immigrants and British Labour's Response, 1870-1950', *History Today* 35 (1985): 51.

38 Joshi and Carter, 'Role of Labour', 56.

39 Ken Lunn (ed.), *Race and Labour in Twentieth Century Britain*, London: Cass, 1985, 158-9.

40 Foot, *Immigration and Race*, 73 and Todd, *The People*, 290.

41 Interview with Larry Whitty, 24 April 2016.

42 Sivanandan, *A Different Hunger*, 24.

43 Avtar Brah, 'The "Asian" in Britain', in *A Postcolonial People*, 47.

44 Randall Hansen, 'The Kenyan Asians, British Politics, and the Commonwealth Immigrants Act, 1968', *The Historical Journal* 42 (1999): 809.

45 ibid., 810-11.

46 Amy Whipple, 'Revisiting the "Rivers of Blood" Controversy. Letters to Enoch Powell', *The Journal of British Studies* 48 (2009): 726-8.

47 Dave Hill, *Out of His Skin: The John Barnes Story*, London: WSC Books, 2001, 30.

48 Owen Jones, 'No wonder Jeremy Corbyn's rivals for the Labour leadership are rattled', *The Guardian*, 8 July 2015.

49 Owen Jones, 'If Jeremy Corbyn's Labour is going to work, it has to communicate', *The Guardian*, 16 September 2015.

50 Owen Jones, 'Two rootless, soulless parties have cleared the way for Ukip', *The Guardian*, 12 October 2014.

51 Mehdi Hasan, 'Silent on immigration? Hardly', *The Guardian*, 18 April 2010.

52 Mehdi Hasan, 'So David Cameron wants to talk about immigration? Bring it on', *The Guardian*, 16 April 2011.

53 Mick Hume, *Revolting! How the Establishment are Undermining Democracy and What They're Afraid Of*, London: William Collins, 2017, 153.

54 Eddo-Lodge, *No Longer Talking*, 134.

55 Pnina Werbner, *Imagined Diasporas among Manchester Muslims*, Santa Fe: School of American Research Press, 2002, 149.

56 Andrew Hindmoor, *What's Left Now? The History and Future of Social Democracy*, Oxford: OUP, 2018, 61.

57 Ben Riley-Smith, Robert Mendick and Rory Mulholland, 'Revealed: The missed warnings over child refugees', *Daily Telegraph*, 24 October 2016.

58 Afua Hirsch, *Brit(ish). On Race, Identity and Belonging*, London: Jonathan Cape, 2018, 298.

The 'P' Word

1 Nick Cohen, *What's Left? How the Left Lost its Way*, London: Harper Perennial, 2007, 213.

2 Anatol Lieven, 'Why the Left Needs Nationalism', *Prospect*, 3 January 2017.

3 Richard Rorty, *Achieving our Country. Leftist Thought in Twentieth-Century America*, Cambridge: HUP, 1998, 3 and 85.

4 Vron Ware, *Who Cares About Britishness? A Global View of the National Identity Debate*, London: Arcadia Books, 2007.

5 Chris Gourlay, 'UK Muslims are Europe's most patriotic', *The Sunday Times*, 13 December 2009.

6 Paul Gilroy, *Small Acts: Thoughts on the Politics of Black Cultures*, London: Serpent's Tail,, 1993, 68.

7 Tariq Modood, *Multicultural Politics. Racism, Ethnicity of Muslims in Britain*, Edinburgh: EUP, 2005, 191-6.

8 Afua Hirsch, *Brit(ish). On Race, Identity and Belonging*, London: Jonathan Cape, 201, 267.

9   Jon Lawrence, 'Blue Labour, One Nation Labour, and the lessons of history', *Renewal*, 21 (2013).

10   Ellie May O'Hagan, 'The Olympic spirit?', *New Statesman*, 29 July 2012.

11   Seumus Milne, 'The London Olympics is a corporate lockdown – why not a Games for all?', *The Guardian*, 10 July 2012.

12   Zoe Williams, 'Less viable than his gran', *The Guardian*, 20 September 2005.

13   Laurie Penny, 'The case for disrupting the royal wedding', *New Statesman* 20 January 2011.

14   Laurie Penny, 'Buns, bunting and retro-imperialism', *New Statesman*, 27 April 2011.

15   Doug Sanders, 'Why foreign-born Brits love the Queen more than the natives', *The Globe and Mail*, 4 June 2012.

16   Seumus Milne, 'A "pause" in centuries of British wars is not enough', *The Guardian*, 12 February 2014.

17   Owen Jones, 'Jeremy Corbyn must become the soldiers' champion', *The Guardian*, 4 September 2015.

18   Jeremy Corbyn speaking at the Sky News Labour leadership debate, 3 September 2015.

19   Mehdi Hasan, 'David Cameron worships at the altar of the military', *New Statesman*, 11 June 2010.

20   Clement Attlee, 'Leader's speech at Scarborough', 1951 [http://www.britishpoliticalspeech.org/speech-archive. htm?speech=161] and Jon Lawrence, 'Blue Labour, One Nation Labour, and the lessons of history', *Renewal*, 21 (2013).

21   The prefix 'Great' is meant to signify the size of the conflict and is not celebratory. Similarly 'Great' Britain originally meant Greater Britain, as in Greater London or Greater Manchester.

22   Laurie Penny, 'Poppy Day is the opium of the people', *New Statesman*, 7 November 2010 and 'A century of royals looking

sad in expensive hats doesn't take away the horror', *New Statesman*, 14 August 2014.

23 Seumus Milne, 'First World War: the real lessons of this savage imperial bloodbath', *The Guardian*, 16 October 2012 and Seumus Milne, 'First World War: an imperial bloodbath that's a warning, not a noble cause', *The Guardian*, 8 January 2014.

24 Neal Blewett, 'The Franchise in the United Kingdom 1885-1918' *Past and Present* 32 (1965): 27-56.

25 Report of the Fifteenth Annual Conference of the Labour Party.

26 Clement Attlee, *Memoirs*, 2. Emphasis added.

27 Trevor Wilson, *The Myriad Faces of War*, London: Polity Press, 1986, 155.

28 Catriona Pennell, *A Kingdom United. Popular Responses to the Outbreak of the First World War in Britain and Ireland*, Oxford: OUP, 2012, 100.

29 Wilson, *The Myriad Faces of War*, 522.

30 Keith Laybourne and Jack Reynolds, *Liberalism and the Rise of Labour*, London: Croom Helm, 1984, 184-9.

31 Gervase Phillips, 'Dai bach Y Soldiwr: Welsh Soldiers in the British Army, 1914-1918', *Llafur* 6 (1993): 945.

32 Report of the Twenty-First Annual Conference of the Labour Party: National Agent's Report.

33 As opposed to 46 per cent of the Conservative candidates, 10 per cent for the Coalition Liberals and 6 per cent for the independent Liberals. See I.G.C. Hutchinson, 'The Impact of the First World War on Scottish Politics', in C.M.M. Macdonald and E.W. McFarland, *Scotland and the Great War*, East Linton: Tuckwell Press, 1999, 49.

34 David Weinbren, 'Social Capital: London's Labour Parties, 1918–45', in Mathew Worley (ed.), *Labour's Grass Roots*, London: I.B. Tauris, 2005, 201.

35 Quoted in Lucy Bland, 'White Women and Men of Colour:

Miscegenation Fears in Britain after the Great War', *Gender & History* 17 (2005): 29-61.

36　*Daily Herald*, 10 April 1920.

37　Conversation with Darren Treadwell, 21 April 2016.

38　Selina Todd, *The People: The Rise and Fall of the Working Class*, London: John Murray, 2014, 83.

39　Judith Cook, *Apprentices of Freedom*, London: Quartet Books, 1979, 17-24.

40　ibid., 52 and 75.

41　Seumus Milne, 'This isn't self-determination. It's a Ruritanian colonial relic', *The Guardian*, 12 March 2013.

42　C. Carman, R. Johns, J. Mitchell, *More Scottish than British. The 2011 Scottish Parliament Election*, London: Palgrave Macmillan, 2014, 88.

43　Laurie Penny, 'Ten years ago we marched against the Iraq war and I learned a lesson in betrayal', *New Statesman*, 14 February 2013.

44　Philip Cowley and Rob Ford, *Sex, Lies and the Ballot Box. 50 Things You Need to Know About British Elections*, London: Biteback, 2014.

45　Mehdi Hasan, 'Afghanistan silence is deafening', *The Guardian*, 22 April 2010.

46　A.F. Heath et al, *The Political Integration of Ethnic Minorities in Britain*, Oxford: OUP, 2013.

47　Richard Seymour, 'The anti-war movement's dilemma – and how to resolve it', *The Guardian*, 27 February 2011.

48　Nick Cohen, *What's Left: How Liberals Lost their Way*, London: HarperCollins, 2007, 307.

49　Robert Fisk, 'Charlie Hebdo: Paris attack brothers' campaign of terror can be traced back to Algeria in 1954', *The Independent*, 9 January 2015.

50　Dave Rich, *The Left's Jewish Problem. Jeremy Corbyn, Israel and Anti-Semitism*, London: Biteback, 2016, 235.

51　Jeremy Corbyn 'not happy' with shoot-to-kill policy, BBC

News, 16 November 2015. http://www.bbc.co.uk/news/uk-politics-34832023

52 Rachel Sylvester, 'Corbynistas won't protect us from terrorists', *The Times*, 17 November 2015.

53 Seumus Milne, 'They can't see why they are hated', *The Guardian*, 13 September 2001. Emphasis added.

54 Seumus Milne, 'Can the US be defeated?', The Guardian, 14 February 2002.

55 Seumus Milne, 'To blame the victims for this killing spree defies both morality and sense', *The Guardian*, 5 March 2008.

56 Seumus Milne, 'It's an insult to the dead to deny the link with Iraq', *The Guardian*, 13 July 2007.

57 Seumus Milne, 'There must be a reckoning for this day of infamy', *The Guardian*, 20 March 2008 and 'Terror is the price of support for despots and dictators', *The Guardian*, 7 January 2010.

58 Seumus Milne, 'Woolwich attack: If the whole world's a battlefield, that holds in Woolwich as well as Waziristan', *The Guardian*, 20 December 2013.

59 Seumus Milne, 'Paris is a warning: there is no insulation from our wars', *The Guardian*, 15 January 2015.

60 Seumus Milne, 'It isn't Facebook that feeds terror. It's war and tyranny', *The Guardian*, 27 November 2014.

61 Colin Brown and Sarah Schaefer, 'Anti-bombing MPs are appeasers, says Short', *The Independent*, 21 April 1999.

62 Seumus Milne, 'Can the US be defeated?', *The Guardian*, 14 February 2002.

63 George Monbiot, 'Brown's contempt for democracy has dragged Britain into a new cold war', *The Guardian*, 31 July 2007.

64 Owen Jones, 'Putin is a human rights abusing oligarch. The left must speak out', *The Guardian*, 26 January 2016.

65 Seumus Milne, 'Far from keeping the peace, Nato is a threat to it', *The Guardian*, 3 September 2014.

66 Mehdi Hasan, 'Book me a slot on Press TV', *New Statesmen*, 16 July 2009.

67 Mehdi Hasan, 'If you lived in Iran, wouldn't you want the nuclear bomb?', *The Guardian*, 17 November 2011. Emphasis added.

68 Simon Tisdall, 'Iran unrest: it's the economy, stupid, not a cry for freedom or foreign plotters', *The Guardian*, 5 January 2018.

69 Zoe Williams, 'The real dinosaurs? Those who are still lobbying to keep Trident', *The Guardian*, 28 February 2016.

70 David Torrance, 'Losing Trident too big a blow to 'prestige' obsessives', *The Herald*, 23 March 2015.

71 Clive Lewis and Emily Thornberry, 'This Trident vote is a contemptible trick. That's why we are abstaining', *The Guardian*, 17 July 2016.

72 George Monbiot, 'Only America can end Britain's Trident folly', *The Guardian*, 22 March 2010.

73 Giles Fraser, 'Theresa May is lying over Trident. Or at least I hope she is', *The Guardian*, 21 July 2016.

74 Owen Jones, 'Anti-Trident arguments need to be heard but they can't blow Labour apart', *The Guardian*, 19 July 2016.

75 Andrew Grice, 'Trident: Majority of Britons back keeping nuclear weapons programme, poll shows', *The Independent*, 24 January 2016.

76 John McTernan, 'Is Unite going to nuke Jeremy Corbyn's Trident-free utopia?', *The Telegraph*, 8 January 2016.

77 Owen Jones, 'Trident is too important an issue to be shouted down', *The Guardian*, 9 February 2016.

78 Slavoj Zizek, 'Why Donald Trump is wrong about American history and liberals are wrong about the West', *The Independent*, 5 September 2017.

79 Vron Ware, *Who Cares About Britishness? A Global View of the National Identity Debate*, London: Arcadia Books, 2007, 120-1.

The Anti-imperialism of Fools

1   Soldier E, Staff Sergeant, unit: Nahal, Hebron 2004, testimony catalogue number: 41727. http://www.breakingthesilence. org.il/testimonies/database/41727 [Accessed 2nd May 2017]. On the mapping procedure, see Michal Huss, 'Mapping the Occupation: Performativity and the Precarious Israeli Identity', *Geopolitics*, published online 8 November 2017.

2   Soldier K, Staff Sergeant, unit: Nahal Brigade, Hebron 2005, testimony catalogue number: 41727. http://www. breakingthesilence.org.il/testimonies/database/41727 [Accessed 2nd May 2017].

3   Soldier L, Major, Hebron 2005, testimony catalogue number: 504074. http://www. breakingthesilence.org.il/testimonies/ database/504074 [Accessed 2nd May 2017].

4   *Jewish Chronicle*, September 1983.

5   Jenni Frazer, 'Arabs Speech at Labour Rally', *Jewish Chronicle*, October 1986.

6   Seumus Milne, 'This slur of anti-semitism is used to defend repression', *The Guardian*, 9 May 2002.

7   Seumus Milne, 'Israel and the west will pay a price for Gaza's bloodbath', *The Guardian*, 8 January 2009.

8   Seumus Milne, 'The impunity of Israel and its allies will carry a price', *The Guardian*, 17 December 2009.

9   Mehdi Hasan, 'Does Israel "cause" anti-Semitism?', *New Statesman*, 24 July 2009.

10   Mehdi Hasan, 'The sorry truth is that the virus of anti-Semitism has infected the British Muslim community', *New Statesman*, 21 March 2013.

11   David Hirsh, C*ontemporary Left Antisemitism*, Abingdon: Routledge, 2018, 227.

12   Steve Cohen, *That's Funny You Don't Look Anti-Semitic: An Anti-Racist History of Left-anti-Semitism*, Beyond the Pale Collective, 1984.

13   ibid., 31.

14 Quoted in Satnam Virdee, *Racism, Class and the Racialized Outsider*, 51.

15 *Manchester Evening News*, 11 November 1895.

16 *Labour Leader*, 3 April 1904.

17 Ken Lunn, 'Introduction' in Ken Lunn (ed.), *Race and Labour in Twentieth Century Britain*, Frank Cass, 1985, 2-5.

18 Gareth Schaffer, *Racial Science and British Society, 1930-62*, Palgrave Macmillan, 2008, 112.

19 Robert Fine and Philip Spencer, *Antisemitism and the left. On the return of the Jewish Question*, Manchester: Manchester University Press, 2017, 48-9.

20 David Cesarani, *The Left and the Jews: The Jews and the Left*, London: Labour Friends of Israel, 2004.

21 Dave Renton, 'Docker and Garment Worker, Railwayman and Cabinet Maker: The Class Memory of Cable Street', in Tony Kushner and Nadia Valman (eds.), *Remembering Cable Street: Fascism and Anti-Fascism in British Society*, London: Vallentine Mitchell, 2000, 95.

22 Cesarani, *The Left and the Jews*.

23 Virdee, *Racism, Class and the Racialized Outsider*, 95.

24 Reported in *The Times*, 16 July 1938.

25 James Vaughan, '"Keep Left for Israel" Tribune, Zionism, and the Middle East, 1937-1967', *Contemporary British History* 27 (2013): 5.

26 ibid., 3-9.

27 ibid., 7.

28 ibid., 1-2.

29 ibid., 13.

30 Dave Rich, *The Left's Jewish Problem. Jeremy Corbyn, Israel and Anti-Semitism*, London: Biteback, 2016, 5.

31 June Edmunds, 'Evolution of the British Labour Party on Israel from 1967 to the Intifada,' *Twentieth Century British History* 11 (2000): 25-30.

32 Rich, *The Left's Jewish Problem*, 67.

33 James Vaughan, 'Mayhew's outcasts': anti-Zionism and the Arab lobby in Harold Wilson's Labour Party', *Israel Affairs* 21 (2015): 27.

34 ibid., 33.

35 Edmunds, 'Evolution of the British Labour Party', 25-30.

36 ibid., 33.

37 Fine and Spencer, *Antisemitism and the left*, 142.

38 Rich, *The Left and the Jews*, 14.

39 David Hirsh, *Contemporary Left Antisemitism*, Abingdon: Routledge, 2018, 3.

40 ibid., 227.

41 Fine and Spencer, *Antisemitism and the left*, 124.

42 ibid., 99-100.

43 ibid., 8.

44 Hirsh, *Contemporary Left Antisemitism*, 51, 60 and 250.

45 Spencer and Fine, *Antisemitism and the left*, 117.

46 Rich, *The Left's Jewish Problem*, 36.

47 Spencer and Fine, *Antisemitism and the left*, 124.

48 Hirsh, *Contemporary Left Antisemitism*, 116.

49 Slavoj Zizek, 'Junction 48: Sexual is Political', *The Huffington Post*, 26 April 2016.

50 Interview with Jon Denham.

51 Hirsh, *Contemporary Left Antisemitism*, 100-1.

52 ibid., 35.

Is This What a Feminist Looks Like?

1 Gail Braybon, *Women Workers in the First World War. The British Experience*, Croom Helm, 1981, 72 and 226.

2 Duncan Tanner, 'Gender, Civic Culture and Politics in South Wales: Explaining Labour Municipal Policy, 1918-1939', in Mathew Worley (ed.), *Labour's Grassroots*, London, 2005, 175-6.

3 Sam Blaxland, 'The Right-Wing Women of Wales: A Secret History', *History Matters* [http://www.historymatters.group.

shef.ac.uk/right-wing-women-wales-secret-history]

4   Interview with Larry Whitty.

5   Hadley Freeman, *Life Moves Pretty Fast. The Lessons we Learned from Eighties Movies*, New York: Simon & Schuster, 2016, 194.

6   Selina Todd, *The People*, 308.

7   Owen Jones, 'The British tradition that Thatcher could not destroy', *The Guardian*, 18 August 2014.

8   Todd, *The People*, 282.

9   ibid.

10 Ayesha Hazarika, 'Feminism should be for all women, not just those of us who tweet #MeToo to our mates', *Evening Standard*, 8 March 2018.

11 Ellie May O'Hagan, 'In 2014 feminists spoke up. This year we're taking to the streets', *The Guardian*, 29 January 2015.

12 Laurie Penny, 'Laurie Penny on Pussy Riot: "People fear us because we're feminists"', *New Statesman*, 22 June 2013.

13 Lucie White, 'Subordination, Rhetorical Survival Skills, and Sunday Shoes', *Buffalo Law Review* 38 (1990): 6.

14 Quoted in Nick Cohen, *What's Left*, 111.

15 Ellie May O'Hagan, 'Women of Britain, let's form our own feminist party', *The Guardian*, 15 September 2014.

16 Laura Silver, 'Yorkshire Feminists Feel "Betrayed" By The Women's Equality Party Leader's Bid To Become Their Local MP', *BuzzFeed*, 25 April 2017. [https://www.buzzfeed.com/amphtml/laurasilver/yorkshire-feminists-feel-betrayed-by-the-womens-equality]

17 b. hooks, *Aint I a Woman?* Pluto Press, 1982, 148.

18 K.E. Noss, 'Knowledge Is Made For Cutting: Genealogies Of Race and Gender in Female Circumcision Discourse', Unpublished MA Thesis, University of Toronto, 2010.

19 Jasbir Puar, *Terrorist Assemblages*, 88-9.

20 Holly Baxter, 'Qatar's accidental vagina stadium is most gratifying', *The Guardian*, 18 November 2013.

21 Ben Beaumont-Thomas, 'Taylor Swift's groping trial marks her long-awaited political awakening' *The Guardian*, 15 August 2017.

22 Chris Martin, 'Intersectionality Is a Political Football; Here's Why It Doesn't Have to Be', *Heterodox Academy*, 17 April 2017 [https://heterodoxacademy.org/2017/04/17/intersectionality-is-a-political-football-heres-why-it-doesnt-have-to-be]; Jessica D. Remedios, Alison L. Chasteen, Nicholas O. Rule, Jason E. Plaks, 'Impressions at the intersection of ambiguous and obvious social categories: Does gay+ Black=likable?', *Journal of Experimental Social Psychology* 47 (2011): 1312-15 and David S. Pedulla, 'The Positive Consequences of Negative Stereotypes: Race, Sexual Orientation, and the Job Application Process', *Social Psychology Quarterly* 77 (2014): 75-94.

23 Puar, *Terrorist Assemblages*, 206-12.

24 Zoe Williams, 'Does the hard-left have an "old-fashioned misogyny" problem?', *The Guardian*, 11 April 2016.

25 Helen Lewis, 'With Assange holed up, the left will want another hero with feet of clay', *The Times*, 16 August 2015.

26 Mat Whitehead, 'Joss Whedon's Ex-Wife Pens Scathing Letter Calling Him A "Hypocrite Preaching Feminist Ideals"', *Huffington Post*, 21 August 2017.

27 Emily Steel, 'At Vice, Cutting-Edge Media and Allegations of Old-School Sexual Harassment', *New York Times*, 23 December 2017.

28 Michael Sheridan and Rebecca Myers, 'Oxford professor Tariq Ramadan "sexually abused Swiss teens in his car"', *The Sunday Times*, 5 November 2017.

29 Noor Nanji, 'French official knew of Tariq Ramadan's 'violent' sexual encounters but failed to act', *The National*, 1 November 2017.

30 Zoe Williams, 'The market beyond porn', *The Guardian*, 25 July 2007.

31 Zoe Williams, 'Lapdancing's naked truths', *The Guardian*, 23 April 2008.

32 Cas Muddle, 'The Paternalistic Fallacy of the "Nordic Model" of Prostitution', *Huffington Post*, 8 April 2016.

33 Zoe Williams, 'Wake up. Feminism is more than just capitalism with tits', *The Guardian*, 4 July 2007.

34 Catherine Rottenberg 'The Rise of Neoliberal Feminism', *Cultural Studies*, 2013 1-20; Angela McRobbie 'Postfeminism and Popular Culture', *Feminist Media Studies*, 4, 2004, pp. 255-64 and *The Aftermath of Feminism: Gender, Culture and Social Change*, London, Sage, 2008.

35 David Swift, 'From "I'm not a feminist, but ... " to "call me an old-fashioned feminist ... ": conservative women in parliament and "feminism", 1979–2017', *Women's History Review* [forthcoming].

36 Zoe Williams, 'Wake up. Feminism is more than just capitalism with tits', *The Guardian*, 4 July 2007.

TERF Wars

1 Dave Haslam, *Not Abba: The Real Story of the 1970s*, London: Fourth Estate, 132-3.

2 Laurie Penny, 'Laurie Penny on trans rights: What the "transgender tipping point" really means', *New Statesman*, 24 June 2014.

3 Jackie Ashley, 'I want my university to debate ideas, not gag free speech', *The Guardian*, 20 January 2016.

4 Interview with John Denham.

5 Owen Jones, 'What Alan Carr taught me about gay men's homophobia', *The Guardian*, 20 April 2014.

6 Owen Jones, 'Sam Smith's Oscar faux pas shows LGBT people must learn their history', *The Guardian*, 1 March 2016.

7 Jasbir Puar, *Terrorist Assemblages*, 61.

8 Caspar Salmon, 'LGBT people need to rediscover their rage in this age of protest', *The Guardian*, 2 April 2018.

9   *The Guardian*, 19 February 2016.

10   Interview with Larry Whitty.

11   Lucy Robinson, *Gay Men and the Left in Post-War Britain* (Manchester: Manchester University Press, 2007), 38.

12   ibid., 21.

13   ibid., 38-9.

14   ibid., 43-5.

15   ibid., 83 and 100.

16   ibid., 171.

17   ibid., 69 and 78.

18   ibid., 146.

19   ibid., 165-9.

20   Daryl Leeworthy, 'For our common cause: Sexuality and left politics in South Wales, 1967–1985', *Contemporary British History* 30 (2016): 273.

21   Ruth Hunt, 'However You Identify We Must All Be Trans Allies', *HuffingtonPost*, 5 November 2017.

22   Janice Turner, 'Meet Alex Bertie, the transgender poster boy', *The Times*, 11 November 2017.

23   Sian Griffiths, 'Gender-fluid girls boards with boys', *The Times*, 1 October 2017.

24   Paris Lees, 'No one would listen to Stephen Fry if he was poor', *The Guardian*, 12 April 2016.

25   Zoe Williams, 'Are you too white, rich, able-bodied and straight to be a feminist?', *The Guardian*, 18 April 2013.

26   Zoe Williams, 'Silencing Germaine Greer will let prejudice against trans people flourish', *The Guardian*, 25 October 2015.

27   Peter Tatchell, 'The intolerant student Left has turned on even me – a lifelong civil rights campaigner', *The Daily Telegraph*, 15 February 2016.

28   Jack Monroe, 'The Brave Man video is a fair portrait of trans life – it does not deserve your rage', *The Guardian*, 20 October 2015.

29 Sarah Mirk, 'Laverne Cox and bell hooks had a Discussion about Gender and Pop Culture,' *Bitch Media*, 8 October 2014.

30 Slavoj Zizek, 'The secret to Corbyn's success was rejecting PC culture as much as he rejected rabble-rousing populism', *The Independent*.

The New Labour Aristocracy

1 Tariq Modood, 'Political blackness and British Asians', *Sociology* 28 (1994): 873.

2 Interview with Larry Whitty.

3 Laurie Penny, 'Why I Despise the World Cup', *New Statesman*, 11 June 2010 and Harriet Agerholm, 'Jeremy Corbyn claims drinks after work are unfair on mothers', *The Independent*, 2 September 2016.

4 George Monbiot, 'Only America can end Britain's Trident folly', *The Guardian*, 22 March 2010 and 'Why your favourite TV show is problematic', *The Guardian*, 3 August 2017.

5 Afua Hirsch, *Brit(ish). On Race, Identity and Belonging*, London: Jonathan Cape, 2018, 3-5.

6 Hannah Richardson, 'England "divided into readers and watchers"', *BBC News*, 11 March 2014. [https://www.bbc.co.uk/news/education-26515836]

7 Quoted in Martin Pugh, *Speak for Britain! A New History of the Labour Party*, London: Vintage, 2011, 170.

8 Richard Hoggart, *The Uses of Literacy: Aspects of Working-Class Life*, London: Chatto and Windus, 1957, 61.

9 Julia Swindells and Lisa Jardine, *What's Left? Women in culture and the Labour movement*, London: Routledge, 1990, 42.

10 Elizabeth Ross, '"Not the Sort that Would Sit on the Doorstep": Respectability in Pre-World War I London Neighbourhoods', *International Labor and Working-Class History* 27 (1985): 44.

11 Gareth Stedman Jones, 'Working-Class Culture and

Working-Class Politics in London, 1870-1900: Notes on the Remaking of a Working Class', *Journal of Social History* 7 (1974): 472 and 479.

12 John Greenway, *Drink and British Politics since 1830: a study in Policy-Making*, Basingstoke: Palgrave Macmillan, 2003, 48-9.

13 ibid., 8.

14 ibid., 116.

15 ibid., 149-51 and 157.

16 A. Davies, 'Leisure in the "Classic Slum"', in A. Davies and S. Fielding (eds.), *Workings' Worlds. Cultures and Communities in Manchester and Salford, 1880-1939*, Manchester: MUP, 1992, 108 and 111.

17 Stedman Jones, 'Working-Class Culture', 481.

18 *The Clarion*, 11 June 1915.

19 The *Clarion*, 15 October 1915.

20 *Plebs*, May 1917.

21 *Plebs*, August 1917. The *Cambridge Magazine* was a prominent Lib-Lab publication; its offices were attacked during the war by an unlikely combination of university undergraduates and ANZAC servicemen.

22 *The Clarion*, 31 March 1916.

23 *Railway Review*, 19 May 1916.

24 Gareth Stedman Jones, 'Working-Class Culture and Working-Class Politics in London, 1870-1900: Notes on the Remaking of a Working Class', *Journal of Social History* 7 (1974): 472.

25 *The Clarion*, 23 April 1915. 'Little Bethelism' was a strict, Puritanical movement popular in the late-Victorian period and lampooned by Charles Dickens in *The Old Curiosity Shop*.

26 Modern Records Centre (MRC), MSS.74/6/2/81-117 - Papers Relating to Ben Tillett, letter to Ian Mackay from E.A. Rogers, 22 January 1951.

27 MSS.74/6/2/81-117 - Papers Relating to Ben Tillett, letter to Mackay from Graham W. Thompson, 22 January 1951.

28 MSS.74/6/2/81-117 - Papers Relating to Ben Tillett, letter to Mackay from S.F. Whitlock, 22 January 1951.

29 Daryl Leeworthy, 'Partisan players: sport, working-class culture, and the labour movement in South Wales 1920–1939', *Labour History* 55 (2013): 582-4.

30 Keith Gildart, *Images of England through Popular Music: Class, Youth and Rock 'n' Roll 1955 – 1976*, Basingstoke: Palgrave Macmillan, 2013, 84.

31 Dave Haslam, *Not Abba: The Real Story of the 1970s*, London: Fourth Estate, 2005, 254.

32 Keith Gildart, *Images of England through Popular Music: Class, Youth and Rock 'n' Roll 1955 – 1976*, Basingstoke: Palgrave Macmillan, 2013, 155 and 134.

33 Dick Hebdige, *Subculture: the meaning of style*, London: Routledge, 1991, 160 and Haslam, *Not Abba*, 224.

34 Gildart, *Images of England*, 141.

35 ibid., 138.

36 Gildart, *Images of England*.

37 David Hepworth, *Uncommon People. The Rise and Fall of the Rock Stars*, London: Bantam Press, 2017, 56.

38 Laurie Penny, 'Let's give thanks to a man who made it OK to be weird', *New Statesman*, January 2016.

39 Ian Taylor and Dave Wall, 1976, cited in Hebdige, *Subculture*, 61.

40 Elio Iannacci, 'In conversation with Kate Bush', *Maclean's*, 28 November 2016.

41 Josh Hall, 'Does BBC Radio Still Have a Diversity Problem?', *Vice*, 29 January 2014.

42 Paul Gilroy, *Small Acts.*

43 Owen Jones, 'I was Paloma Faith's support act – but politics can't reach the parts music can', *The Guardian*, 1 April 2015.

44 Interview with John Denham.

45 Keith Gildart, *Images of England through Popular Music: Class, Youth and Rock 'n' Roll 1955 – 1976*, Basingstoke: Palgrave Macmillan, 2013, 32-3.

46 Keith Gildart, *Images of England through Popular Music: Class, Youth and Rock 'n' Roll 1955 – 1976*, Basingstoke: Palgrave Macmillan, 2013, 98.

47 Owen Jones, 'Russell Brand has endorsed Labour – and the Tories should be worried', *The Guardian*, 4 May 2015.

48 Nick Cohen, 'Overrated: Russell Brand', *Standpoint*, December 2014.

49 Owen Jones, 'Stop the sneering – Ed Miliband's best route to young voters is Russell Brand', *The Guardian*, 28 April 2015.

50 Andrew Ellson, 'Teenagers oppose gay marriage and shun tattoos', *The Times*, 15 September 2016.

51 YouGov survey of 52615, 9-13 June 2017.

52 YouGov survey of 52615 people, 9-13 June 2017.

53 Interview with Charles Clarke, 9 June 2016.

54 Interview with John Denham 12 April 2016.

55 David Aaronovitch, 'My commie days were mild compared to this', *The Times*, 26 May 2016.

56 Rod Liddle, *Selfish, Whining Monkeys. How we ended up greedy, narcissistic and unhappy*, London; Fourth Estate, 2014, 150.

57 Rorty, *Achieving Our Country*, 129 and 139.

58 Mick Hume, *Revolting! How the Establishment are Undermining Democracy and What They're Afraid Of*, London: William Collins, 2017, 26.

59 Giles Coren, 'I wanted to be rich and famous and powerful, and desired by women', *The Times*, 29 February 2016.

60 Neil Gross, 'Professors Behaving Badly', *New York Times*, 30 September 2017.

61 Richard Rorty, *Achieving Our Country. Leftist Thought in Twentieth-Century America*, Cambridge: HUP, 1998, 77 and 91-3.

62 Quoted in Astra Taylor, 'Post-'68: Theory is in the Streets', in

Strickland (ed), *Growing Up Postmodern*, 209.

63 Angela Nagel, 'The Lost Boys', *The Atlantic*, 14 November 2017.

64 Jonathan Rose, *The Intellectual Life of the British Working Classes*, New Haven: Yale University Press, 2001, 116 and 366.

65 Jonathan Rose, *The Intellectual Life of the British Working Classes*, New Haven: Yale UP, 2001, 20, 86, 144 and 278.

66 ibid., 48-9, 123, 241 and 305.

67 Marcus Morgan and Patrick Baert, *Conflict in the Academy: A Study in the Sociology of Intellectuals*, Palgrave Macmillan, 2015, 56.

68 Jon O'Neill, 'Oh! My others, there is no other', *Theory, Culture and Society* 18:2 (2001).

Conclusion

1 Thomas Piketty, 'Brahmin Left vs Merchant Right: Rising Inequality and the Changing Structure of Political Conflict', WID.world Working Paper 2018/7.

2 Brendan Barber, *Jihad vs. McWorld*, New York: Times Books, 1995, 226.

3 Slavoj Zizek, 'The secret to Corbyn's success was rejecting PC culture as much as he rejected rabble-rousing populism', *The Independent*, 12 June 2017.

4 Ta-Nehisi Coates, *Between the World and Me*, Melbourne: Text Publishing, 2015, 96.

5 Mehdi Hasan, 'The myth of the "big society"', *New Statesman*, 14 April 2010.

6 Jackie Ashley, 'Who's got time for the Big Society?', *The Guardian*, 13 April 2010.

7 Zoe Williams, 'Liverpool knows Labour but not its MPs', *The Guardian*, 23 September 2011.

8 Nick Pecorelli, 'How One Nation Labour can bridge the values divide', IPPR (2013): 43.

9   Owen Jones, 'Mass membership alone doesn't make a social movement', *The Guardian*, 27 July 2016.

10 Laurie Penny, 'Hey, Dave: our society's bigger than yours', *New Statesman*, 18 February 2011.

CULTURE, SOCIETY & POLITICS

Contemporary culture has eliminated the concept and public figure of the intellectual. A cretinous anti-intellectualism presides, cheer-led by hacks in the pay of multinational corporations who reassure their bored readers that there is no need to rouse themselves from their stupor. Zer0 Books knows that another kind of discourse – intellectual without being academic, popular without being populist – is not only possible: it is already flourishing. Zer0 is convinced that in the unthinking, blandly consensual culture in which we live, critical and engaged theoretical reflection is more important than ever before.
If you have enjoyed this book, why not tell other readers by posting a review on your preferred book site.

Recent bestsellers from Zero Books are:

In the Dust of This Planet
Horror of Philosophy vol. 1
Eugene Thacker
In the first of a series of three books on the Horror of Philosophy,
In the Dust of This Planet offers the genre of horror as a way of
thinking about the unthinkable.
Paperback: 978-1-84694-676-9 ebook: 978-1-78099-010-1

Capitalist Realism
Is there no alternative?
Mark Fisher
An analysis of the ways in which capitalism has presented itself
as the only realistic political-economic system.
Paperback: 978-1-84694-317-1 ebook: 978-1-78099-734-6

Rebel Rebel
Chris O'Leary
David Bowie: every single song. Everything you want to know,
everything you didn't know.
Paperback: 978-1-78099-244-0 ebook: 978-1-78099-713-1

Cartographies of the Absolute
Alberto Toscano, Jeff Kinkle
An aesthetics of the economy for the twenty-first century.
Paperback: 978-1-78099-275-4 ebook: 978-1-78279-973-3

Malign Velocities
Accelerationism and Capitalism
Benjamin Noys
Long listed for the Bread and Roses Prize 2015, *Malign Velocities* argues against the need for speed, tracking acceleration as the symptom of the ongoing crises of capitalism.
Paperback: 978-1-78279-300-7 ebook: 978-1-78279-299-4

Meat Market
Female Flesh under Capitalism
Laurie Penny
A feminist dissection of women's bodies as the fleshy fulcrum of capitalist cannibalism, whereby women are both consumers and consumed.
Paperback: 978-1-84694-521-2 ebook: 978-1-84694-782-7

Poor but Sexy
Culture Clashes in Europe East and West
Agata Pyzik
How the East stayed East and the West stayed West.
Paperback: 978-1-78099-394-2 ebook: 978-1-78099-395-9

Romeo and Juliet in Palestine
Teaching Under Occupation
Tom Sperlinger
Life in the West Bank, the nature of pedagogy and the role of a university under occupation.
Paperback: 978-1-78279-637-4 ebook: 978-1-78279-636-7

Sweetening the Pill
or How We Got Hooked on Hormonal Birth Control
Holly Grigg-Spall
Has contraception liberated or oppressed women? *Sweetening the Pill* breaks the silence on the dark side of hormonal contraception.
Paperback: 978-1-78099-607-3 ebook: 978-1-78099-608-0

Why Are We The Good Guys?
Reclaiming your Mind from the Delusions of Propaganda
David Cromwell
A provocative challenge to the standard ideology that Western power is a benevolent force in the world.
Paperback: 978-1-78099-365-2 ebook: 978-1-78099-366-9

Readers of ebooks can buy or view any of these bestsellers by clicking on the live link in the title. Most titles are published in paperback and as an ebook. Paperbacks are available in traditional bookshops. Both print and ebook formats are available online.

Find more titles and sign up to our readers' newsletter at http://www.johnhuntpublishing.com/culture-and-politics

Follow us on Facebook
at https://www.facebook.com/ZeroBooks

and Twitter at https://twitter.com/Zer0Books